Green Economics

Methodology
An Introduction

**Beitostølen, Norway 2012
Admiring the beauty of nature
(Photo: Tone Berg)**

"The age of plenty is over. If we want a future, it must be the age of green economics which teaches us firstly how to share with each other."
Miriam Kennet

Edited by

Tone Hedvig Berg, Aase Seeberg and Miriam Kennet

The Green Economics Institute (GEI)

Green Economics: Methodology an introduction ©November 2012 Published by The Green Economics Institute

Registered Office: 6 Strachey Close, Tidmarsh, Reading RG8 8EP greeneconomicsinstitute@yahoo.com

Selection and editorial matter Tone Hedvig Berg, Aase Seeberg and Miriam Kennet

Typeset by Tone Hedvig Berg and Aase Seeberg

Printed on FSC approved stock by Marston Book Services Ltd.

www.greeneconomics.org.uk
greeneconomicsinstitute@yahoo.com

A catalogue record for this book is available from the British Library

ISBN: 978-1-907543-35-7

The Green Economics Institute

Photo: The Green Economics Institute's *Introduction to Green Economics Course* at Oxford University. (Photo by Bogusia Igielska)

The Green Economics Institute has worked to create a discipline or school of Economics called "Green Economics" and also to reform mainstream economics itself into a well-defined goals-based discipline which provides practical answers to existing and future problems by incorporating all relevant aspects, knowledge and complex interactions into a truly holistic understanding of the relevant issues. It uses complexity, holism, pluralism and interdisciplinary working in order to widen the scope of economics, adding the science from the green aspects, and the social ideas from economics discourses. This new scope for the first time avoids partial explanations or solutions and also biased and partial perspectives of power elites. According to economics professor, Jack Reardon from the USA (2007) The Institute has been very successful in creating a robust academic basis for this new idea.

The Institute has begun to influence the methodology of mainstream economics, according to Professor Tony Lawson of Cambridge University's Economics Department (2007). It uses trans-disciplinary and interdisciplinary methods so that it can factor in the complexity of nature into economics. It seeks to provide all people everywhere, non human species, the planet and earth systems with a decent level of well-being based on practical and theoretical approaches targeting both methodology and knowledge and based a comprehensive reform of the current economic mainstream. It can, for example, comfortably incorporate glacial issues, climate change and volcanic, seismic and earth sciences into its explanations and thus in this, and many other ways, it is far more complete and reflects reality much more closely than its predecessors on which it builds. The current narrow conventional economic approach using purposely designed methods, is challenged to bring areas and concepts into its scope which have been until now neglected. Existing outdated or inappropriate propositions and solutions are examined and revised to provide a realistic and more comprehensive understanding of the subject.

The Green Economics Institute argues for economic development based on economic access and decision making for all, including respect for cultural diversity and normative freedom. It does this by bringing together all the interested parties, who want to help in developing this progressive discipline, by inviting them to its events, and conferences and by means of such activities as writing books and publications and using its research, its campaigns and its lobbying and its speeches and lecturing all over the world.

The Green Economics Institute created the first green academic journal *International Journal of Green Economics* with publishers Inderscience and the first green book series *Green Growth, Green Economics and Sustainable Development* with its publishers Gower Management Publishers and Ashgate Academic Press.

The Green Economics Institute has its own delegation to the Kyoto Protocol, and is a recommended UK government reviewer on the Intergovernmental Panel on Climate Change (IPCC). Members of the Green Economics Institute have lectured or worked in governments and Universities around the world, for example Surrey University, the Schumacher College, The University of Bolzano, the Tyrollean Cabinet, via Skype in Thessaloniki, FYRO Macedonia, Turkey, the National Government School in the UK with top Cabinet Officials, at University in Cambridge and Oxford, Transition Towns, Oslo, Norway, Liverpool University, Lancaster University, Abuja, Nigeria and Gondar, Ethiopia and attended conferences in many places including Cancun, Mexico and Riga, Latvia and appeared on TV and radio in Italy and Tallin in Estonia and the UK and Bangladesh amongst many others and received invitations the President of Russia and from the governments and several universities in China and from several governments and Princes in several Gulf States as well as several parts of the United Nations and the International Labour Organisation!

This book is the first to bring the innovations in methodology to broader group of readers, students, policy makers, academics and campaigners in this ground breaking volume.

Directors
Miriam Kennet, UK,
Volker Heinemann UK, Germany
Michelle S. Galle d' Oliveiria UK, USA, Brazil

The Green Economics Institute Publications

Leading thinkers in the world of economics and environmental change and scientific theory and philosophy are beginning to publish with The Green Economics Institute.

Titles available from The Green Economics Institute include:

Books:

Green Economics Institute Reader Book Series :
The Green Economics Reader © 2012 Edited by Miriam Kennet

Green Economics and Citizen's Income © 2012 Clive Lord

Green Economics Institute Handbook Series
Handbook of Green Economics: A practitioner's guide ©2012 Miriam Kennet, Eleni Courea, Alan Bouquet, Ieva Pepinyte

Green Built Environment: A Handbook © 2012 Miriam Kennet and Judith Felton

Green Economics Voices of Africa © 2012 Miriam Kennet, Amana Winchester, Mahelet Mekonnen, Chidi Magnus Onahue

Green Economics: Womens Unequal Pay and Poverty © 2012 Miriam Kennet, Michelle S Gale de Oliviera, Judith Felton and Amana Winchester

Green Economics and Climate Change © 2012 Miriam Kennet and Winston Ka Ming Mak

The Greening of China and Asia © 2012 Edited by Miriam Kennet (UK), Winston Ka Ming Mak (UK and Hong Kong), Norfayanti Kamaruddin (Malaysia)

Green Economics and Young People © 2012 Edited by Miriam Kennet (UK) and Juliane Goeke (Germany)

Green Economics The Greening of Energy Policies © 2012 Edited by Ryota Koike and Miriam Kennet.

The Green Economist Magazine ©2006, 2007, 2008, 2009, 2010, 2011,2012
Series edited by Miriam Kennet, Volker Heinemann, Eleni Courea (Cyprus),
Kristina Jociute (Lithuania)
Published by The Green Economics Institute

Journal:

Inderscience Academic Journal:

The International Journal of Green Economics 2006, 2007 vol 1, 2008 Vol 2, 2009 Vol 3, 2010 Vol 4, 2011 Vol 5, 2012 Vol 6
2012 Vol 6 Issue 1 Edited by Miriam Kennet, Juliane Goeke and Kristina Jociute
Founded and Edited by Miriam Kennet

Proceedings:

The Green Economics Institute Oxford University Conference Proceedings Series
© Edited by Volker Heinemann, Miriam Kennet and Kristina Jocuite, Published 2006, 2007, 2008, 2009, 2010, 2011,2012

Green Economics Institute Philosophy Conference Proceedings 2008
© Edited by Miriam Kennet and Volker Heinemann, Lancaster

Green Economics Methodology Conference Proceedings 2011 & 2012
© Oxford University November 2011 & 2012
Edited by Kristina Jociute and Miriam Kennet

Gower Management and Management Press Books Series: Green Economics
Series Editor: Miriam Kennet
Ashgate Academic Publishers: 20th and 21st Century Thought
Editors Professor Marie Louise Seeberg and Miriam Kennet and Ryota Koike

The Economics of Abundance 2010 Wolfgang Hoerschele

Plan For the Planet 2011 Ian Chambers and John Humble

Oekonomie Der Zukunft 2001 Volker Heinemann Books on Demand

Contents

Part 7: How to avoid further catastrophic runaway climate change

List of Contributors

Tone Hedvig Berg is a Norwegian economist qualified from Norwegian University of science and Technology (NTNU). She has a specialization in Business from Trondheim Business School (TØH). Her main field of interest are development economics, public and political economics. She is a member of the book team at the Green Economics Institute. (GEI).

Sophie Billington is an economist and econometrician at Bristol University. Her main areas of interest are developmental economics and econometrics. Sophie is interested in applied econometrics, econometric theory and the wide ranging and changing approaches to modelling economic problems. She has been instrumental in methodology debates in Green Economics.

Davide Bottos is an Italian Master student of Economics at the Università degli Studi di Udine in Italy. After high school he enrolled in the faculty of economics in Udine, where he obtained his first degree in January 2008 with a presentation of a thesis on the classical theory of price discrimination. In 2009 he studied for six months at the "Skarbek Graduate School of Business Economics" in Warsaw (Poland) as an Erasmus student. He became interested in the Green Economy by reading news that concerned the environment, mobility, energy and climate change. His opinion is that we must act so that governments implement all the policies that drive economic activity to a lower waste of resources and greater sustainability.

Alan Bouquet has an MSc in Climate Change from the University of East Anglia. He has always been interested in how humanity interacts with the world around us; how we perceive nature and the impacts we have on it. He has written for the All Parliamentary Group for Aid, Debt and Trade and blogged on various environmental issues. He is now working for the Green Economics Institute.

Rosita Bujokaite is at Vytautas Magnus University in Kaunas, Lithuania. She specialises macroeconomic analysis and economic politics. Her main topics of interest are related to economic crisis phenomenon and crisis management as well as the economic anti-crisis politics. She is participating in the activity of Lithuanian NGO Kaunas Club "TheEconomists" and is a member of Lithuanian economic association (LEA). She is a member and economics advisor to the Green Economics Institute.

Juliane Göke is a member of the editorial board for the International Journal of Green Economics and has studied International Business Management and Governance at Paderborn, Hagen and Sheffield Universities. She worked in Germany and Indonesia in the Consultancy sector. Her research interests are sustainable business solutions and renewable energies in developing countries. For the latter she recently participated in a renewable energy project in Sub-Saharan Africa.

Edward Goldsmith was an Anglo-French environmentalist, writer and philosopher. A deep ecologist and systems theorist, Goldsmith was an early proponent of the Gaia hypothesis, having previously developed a similar cybernetic concept of a self-regulating biosphere. He was the founder and editor of the Ecologist Magazine. He co-authored the influential *Blueprint for Survival* with Robert Prescott-Allen, becoming a founding member of the political party "People" (later renamed the Green Party), itself largely inspired by the *Blueprint.*

Volker Heinemann is an economist who studied at the Universities of Goettingen, Kiel and Nottingham. He is a specialist in international and developing economics, monetary economics and macroeconomic theory and policy. He is author of the book "Die Oekonomie der Zukunft," "The Economy of the Future," a book outlining a green structure for a contemporary economy that accepts the pressing changes that are needed to outdated current economic thinking. He is co-founder and Director and CFO of the Green Economics Institute, a member of the Institute of Chartered Accountants in England and Wales, trained at PWC and other major Institutions and is a Deputy Editor of the International Journal of Green Economics. He is a popular radio and TV speaker in Europe and a former Die Gruenen Councillor.

Kristina Jociute is an Economist interested in analysis and policy of macroeconomics and is at at Vytautas Magnus University in Lithuania. She is a member of both the Association of Lithuanian Economists (LEA) and the NGO's Kaunas club "Economists" (Lithuania), and is an associated member of The Green Economics Institute (UK). Her interests include human welfare and well-being, poverty issues, behavioural economics, sustainable development and macroeconomics. She is executive editor of the International Journal of Green Economics and a manager of the Green Economics Institute.

Miriam Kennet is a specialist in Green Economics, she is the Co-Founder and is CEO of the Green Economics Institute. She also founded and edits the first Green Economics academic journal in the world, the *International Journal of Green Economics,* and she has been credited with creating the academic discipline of Green Economics. Green Economics has been recently described by the Bank of England as one of the most vibrant and healthy areas of economics at the moment.

Having researched at Oxford University, Oxford Brookes and South Bank University, she is a member of Mansfield College, Oxford University and the Environmental Change Institute. She has taught, lectured and spoken at Universities and events all over Europe, from Alicante to Oxford and Bolzano, and to government officials from Montenegro and Kosovo to The UK Cabinet Office, Transport Department, National Government School and Treasury and spoken in Parliaments from Scotland to Austria and The French Senat and Estonia. She is also a regular and frequently speaks at public events of all kinds, and after dinner speaker, this week advising in the Uk Parliament and the Bank of England and in Brussels on the Eurozone crisis, the high speed rail and the general economics situation.

She is also very active in spreading Green Economics in Asia, China, and all round Africa where people find it may be one of the beacons of hope at the moment in an age of Austerity and Cuts as it provides a completely new way of looking at the world. Her work is very practical and she worked in factories and engineering for many years in the past. Sje is on the Assembly of the

Green European Foundation and also on the steering group of the European Network of Political Foundations. She studied Chinese and Japanese history at University and put in the ditigal telecoms backbone into the Chinese network and watched it evolve!

She has a delegation to the UNFCC COP Kyoto Climate Change Conferences and and headed up a delegation to *RIO + 20 Earth Summit: Greening the Economy* in RIO Brazil where she is very active. She regularly speaks on TV around Europe, most recently in Belgium, and Estonia and this year the BBC has made a special programme about her life and work. She runs regular conferences at Oxford University about Green Economics and this year has run 8 events from Youth in Action for Young People from Egypt involved in the revolution, People from FYRO Macedonia, Italy and other countries, as well as the Green Built Environment, The Greening of China as the Chinese government is very interested in her work, Womens Unequal Pay and poverty, Green Economics and Methodology, truth,fact and reality with critical realism and several other events.

Publishing regularly and having over 100 articles, papers and other publications, as well 4 book series, one with Ashgate Academic Press, one with Gower Management Publishers, as well as a *Handbook series* and a *Green Economics Reader Series*. This years edited volumes include *Green Economics:Voices of Africa, The Green Economics Reader, Handbook of Green Economics: A Practitioners Guide, The Green Built Environment, Women's Unequal Pay and Poverty, Green Economics and Climate Change, as well as a new chapter on the green built environment and climate change for Wileys publishers in Lamond, Hammond and Proverbs*. She also publishes in scientific papers, this year including the Latvian National Scientific Papers and Journals for example and book chapters including this year the University of Syracuse in the USA and she has been featured in the *Harvard Economics Review* and *Wall Street Journal* as a leader. Recently she was named one of 100 most powerful unseen global women by the Charity One World action for her global work on increasing women's economics power.

Shuhan Liu is President of Tianjin University of Commerce, P.R.China and Professor, Ph.D in Economics of Osaka City University. His academic research fields are Industrial economics and economic development, Service economy, and International economy and trade.

Clive Lord was a founder member of the English and Welsh Greens in 1973, He served as a Probation officer for 30 years, retiring in 1994. Clive's book, 'A Citizens' Income - a Foundation for a Sustainable World' was published in 2003 and Green Economics and Citizens Income in 2012. He maintains that his cohtrbution to the debate on sustainability is fundamental to those from others able to take matters forward.

Igor A. Makarov is a Lecturer of Environmental Economics and Politics at the National Research University – Higher School of Economics (Moscow, Russia) and a researcher at the Center for Comprehensive European and International Studies at the same university. The areas of his professional interest include international climate change economics and policy, international economics of water and food scarcity. He is the author of various articles on the economic aspects of climate change, food and water scarcity and their impacts on Russian economy in leading Russian academic journals.

Mizoxolo Elliot Mbiko was a Ford Foundation Scholar, and studied with the Green Economics Institute and works for the South African Government. An economist from South Africa, Eliot is interested in Development Economics.

Michelle S. Gale de Oliveira is a Director of the Green Economics Institute, UK. Qualified in International Relations at Richmond, the American International University in London (RAIUL), and at SOAS, London University and lives in the remote rainforest in Brazil. She has edited the Green Economics Institute's members' magazine, *The Green Economist,* and was a deputy editor for the International Journal of Green Economics. Her writing has been featured in *Europe's World*, one of the foremost European policy magazines. She lectures and speaks on Environmental and Social Justice, Gender Equity, and International Development from a Green Economics perspective. She is founder/ chair of the Gender Equity Forum and has just founded Gender Progress an NGO in Brazil. She organised a Green Economics conference on women's unequal pay and poverty in Reading, UK, and lectured on Green Economics in Berlin, Germany, at retreats in Glastonbury, UK, and and the American University in FYRO Macedeonia. She is a regular speaker at international conferences, and was on the Green Economics Institute's Delegation to Copenhagen COP15 Kyoto Conference and headed up its delegation to Cancun Mexico COP16 Kyoto Conference.

Chidi Magnus Onuoha is a Development Economist/Research Fellow with the African Institute for Applied Economics, Enugu, Nigeria. He served as a National Expert in the United Nations Industrial Organization UNIDO)/ Institute of African Studies, Oxford University, UK, survey of the manufacturing sector in Nigeria in 2004. Member, Climate Change Roundtable, Nigeria's Federal Ministry of Environment. He is the Executive Director, Green Economics Nigeria.

Sandra Ries edits and writes some of our publications and coordinated our Youth in Action Project and our stalls. She was an award winning representative of her country of Denmark at the International Young Climate talks in Poland. She has a special interest in Development and International Relations and has spent her life equally in Denmark and New Zealand giving her unusual insight into two cultures on different sides of the world.

Maria Delfini Rossi is a young academic and green activist. She has an honours degree in Economics from the Autonomous University of Barcelona and a Masters of Research in Economics in the European University Institute. Delfina works in the European Parliament for a Green MEP and was also the co-spokesperson of the Federation of Young European Greens.

Aase Seeberg is a Norwegian economist qualified from the University of Oslo (UiO) and University of Bergen (UiB). Her main field of interest are monetary policies, developing economics and fiscal policies. After high school she enrolled at the university of Bergen (UiB), where she obtained her first degree in August 2012 with presentation of a thesis on how the debt crises in the Euro Zone affects the Norwegian Monetary policies. She is a member of the bookteam at the Green Eonomics Institute (GEI).

Jigme Tashi Tsering is currently working as a Senior Analyst in the Department of Investment, Druk Holding and Investment, the commercial arm of the Royal Government of Bhutan. Jigme has a Bachelors in Civil Engineer from the Indian Institute of Technology (ITT) Delhi, and a Masters in Environmental Engineering from the University of Melbourne. He has over eleven years of working experience and has worked in various capacities in the Government (engineer, technical auditor, and environmentalist). He enjoys travelling, which goes hand in hand with his passion – photography.

Dr. Natalie West Kharkongor, currently an Assistant Professor of Economics at IIM Shillong, received the Broad Outlook Learner Teacher Award from the Prime Minister, Dr. Manmohan Singh in 2004. She also received the Rashtriya Gaurav Award with Certificate of Excellence in 2011 in New Delhi. She has presented and published a number of papers. She was the Joint Secretary of North Eastern Economic Association and the Vice President of Meghalaya Economic Association.

Peter Yang was an Associate Research Professor in international economics in China, who wrote on its economic reform policies and strategies in the early reform years. He is currently an Associate Professor and teaches at the Case Western Reserve University, USA, the Chinese and German economies and sustainable policies, among other courses. His research focuses on China's public finance and its relationship with China's environmental and energy issues, as well as the potentials of using public finance as green economic tools.

Introduction

Tone Hedvig Berg, Aase Seeberg and Miriam Kennet

Were you aware that due to dangerous and runaway climate-change, much of humanity may be forced to migrate, towards the Polar Regions and to live together at a density previously unimaginable, as many of the other areas of the planet may become uninhabitable or unable to sustain our crops or our food? Scientists predict this is a realistic scenario if we do not change the way we treat our planet. HurricaneSandy is just the latest episode in this process. The cost of Sandy has been estimated up to US $60 billion, and this is, according to many scientists, only just the beginning of what they have predicted! We,human beings and our economy, are entirely dependent on benevolent climatic conditions, in which we can thrive and on which our entire " civilisation" has developed up to now. We don't really know what will happen under very different conditions! The New York Stock Exchange for example had to be shut down for the first time in years, because of the hurricane.

Are you concerned about environmental problems, but always wondered how, for example, climate change will affect you and your society, and wondered what can be done? This book will introduce you to what Green Economics is, and how you can take a critical look at the mainstream economic modelswhich are used in today's economy.

The book is an edited volume and a compilation of essays, views, speeches about Green Economics its the methodology. It includes a wide range of the background discourse of Green Economics and how it already has affected politics in different societies and challenges main stream assumptions.

You will find discussions on how Green Economics questions and replaces basic economic ideas such asgrowth, mass consumption and savings, and also how Green Economics gives the reader knowledge ofhow we can meet the challenges of climate change and the degradation of biodiversity. Some articles discuss other environmental approaches for example sustainable development and the Stern Review.

In the last few years, there has been a dramatic increase in interest in environmental problems and the transformation towards Green Jobs and a Green Economy. Inequalities between people, within and between nations, and between present and future generations as well as social and environmental destruction is threatening the human species, but today's global mainstream economy does not seem to take these risks into account (Kennet 2012).

So, an important question is to ask is, what is Green economics? According to Jociute and Turk (2011) the world has changed, and Green Economics, as a discipline which inherently takes account of the long term effects of widespread population inequality, climate change and biodiversity loss, has been waiting to take the mantle. Its time has now arrived.

Green economics looks at the current dualism between ecology and the economy, and argues that these two must go hand in hand together, because mass consumption in today's world leads to the exhaustion of natural resources and it risks even causing the extinction of the human species. Today's markets are correctly reflecting and indicating that traditional economic instruments and tools are no longer are working (Jociute and Turk 2011). Therefore new methods of creating a more natural "economics of abundance, " a truly green economics need to be urgently developed and implemented and this book tells its story so far and how to use it in your work and your activities and also how to nuture this small seed of hope which is doing the rounds of governments all over the planet. Green Economics is at once a beacon of hope for a more equitable planet and also one of the most exciting drivers of contemporary world economics innovation!

Part 1: Introducing Green Economics

Kathmandu , Nepal 2012
Green Economics- Valuing the biodiversity which lives all around us ?
Photo By Maren Hovhaugholen Gimnes

"The fate of the living planet is the most important issue facing mankind"
Gaylord Nelson

1.1 Green Economics and what it means

By Miriam Kennet

We need to recalibrate what our terms mean in economics. The very word economics is from the word "oikia" or household and estate management. (Kennet and Heinemann 2006). The integrity of the household today is the last thing considered in economics and the realm of women is not included in "homoeconomicus", the basic unit in which economics modelling occurs. Green Economics moves beyond this and can be considered "post homoeconomicus" and part of a new era where economics is practised by all people everywhere, and is not "done to" or advised by one group on another group. Each person on the planet forms an equally valid economics unit. It is no longer led by white middle class western educated men trained on Wall Street or at Harvard (Kennet 2009).

Green Economics is about access for everyone and provisioning for everything on the planet. The needs of the plankton regulating our climate are as important, if not more so, in the consideration of a new construction project as the men in suits. In reality this has a two fold aspect, firstly intrinsically – their own existence value, their own right to "just simply be" part of life on earth and secondly their use to us and our survival value, or need to continue as a species, as we need them there instrumentally in order for us to survive in a non-hostile climate. This instrumental approach is often called the Ecosystem Services Approach, where the value of the ecosystem in providing human services is measured as a "use value" to us.

Similarly, one objection to the whole modelling and homo economicus approach is that most of the planet is not homo economicus. At least half is gyny oikonomika. One fifth of people are poor and hungry, and have no ability to achieve their personal buying preferences as rational economic men. Indeed their decisions are based simply on meeting their needs from day to day. In fact the very word civilisation means living in towns. We have now become "civilised" we have tamed nature and we have achieved economic superiority to other species in harnessing much of the ecosystem at the moment to provide for our own purposes. However as soon as we reached this position, it became clear that this is not an hospitable position to be in and neither is it sustainable or achievable for most people.So women, for so long excluded from economics considerations, are now starting to run banks and whole economies in a more holistic way, redressing some of the worst imbalances, for example women have started an important trading floor in Ethiopia, are running the banks in Iceland and have taken over as heads of state in several countries. A green economy is characterised as a diverse and inclusive economy with special needs and all abilities recognised and valued. Learning is regarded as a lifelong activity, rather then something done just once at school. The key to getting out of poverty and recognising the Millennium Development Goals is regarded as ending maternal mortality and educating girls and women. This is one green way of reducing population and regarded by the head of the European Environment Agency Jacqueline McGlade (2009) as the single most important aspect of creating a green economy.

One of the biggest questions currently is – what is the right solution to climate change, and what is the green solution? Is there a quick fix solution to stop the runaway climate change predicted in most reports? Are we really going to get to 6 degrees of warming - as warm as the dinosaur period? (Lynas 2007) Can humans really survive into such an era? As we bask in a huge heatwave again in the northern hemisphere with a major drought, what is the right approach?

Strategic choices in a green economy

There are at least 4 strategic choices we can make.

a) Market Mechanisms

These involve continuing to use the market to sort out the climate. In particular, the main well known method is the Kyoto Protocol, where carbon is priced and then traded using the Clean Development Mechanism in less developed countries to trade and to allow money to be exchanged towards poorer countries and those countries that have traditionally had higher carbon emissions to trade and pay for their right to pollute. This method was invented by Chichilnisky (2009) and is currently in discussion within the United Nations Framework committee to extend it to a second phase. The latest idea is to provide geo-engineering and giant scrubbers into Africa to allow Africa to go carbon negative, in other words in return for money income, they will clean up the carbon richer countries use. However although in theory-theoretical economics – this should work – in practice the Stern Review (2006) showed that "climate change is the single biggest market failure the world has ever seen". In fact more people are talking about the crisis of capitalism as a result and mainstream economics is facing some of its harshest criticism. Markets are undoubtedly part of the current mix.

b) Geo-engineering

However another method which is being developed is geo-engineering, where new technologies are being attempted in a rush to halt the rising tide. As has been mentioned some of these include creating artificial volcanoes, or carbon capture and storage where carbon is collected at source of a fossil fuel power station and stored under ground for many years to remove it from the atmosphere. The problem is that few of these projects have been tested and no one knows if they work, by the time we find out it could be too late as the climate would have altered significantly and dangerously.

c) Regulation

There are many things we can do to halt the use of fossil fuels and methane production which are causing melting of permafrost and tundra, releasing very potent greenhouse causing climate agents. It is known that the average person in the United States of America is consumes 25 tonnes per year of carbon dioxide equivalent (Kennet et al 2009, Cologna 2010). The average African uses less than 1 tonne, the average European about 10 tonnes and the average Chinese person now about 5 tonnes of carbon.

The first thing that could be done which would solve many of the issues is to educate women, as they tend to educate their children (Kennet 2008, New Scientist 2008). Secondly to create a huge push towards "contraction and convergence" (Kennet et al 2009). This would mean that the world's larger economies would contract so they would not consume as much and the world's poorest economies would be allowed and managed to increase. So there would be a convergence of levels both of economy and also of climate inducing carbon footprint eventually for equality. This was considered a radical idea when first proposed by Greens. However today, the Stern team (Stern 2009) is arguing that we need the "fastest period of growth the world has ever seen in order to pay for the technical developments we need to meet the climate change imperative." In fact they argue that such growth will peak in around 2030. This greatly enhanced growth looks increasingly unlikely to occur given the current economic downturn. And as with the last 50 years of "high mass consumption of goods" (Rostow 1960) and the artificially created demand through advertising, what has happened is an exhaustion of the world's resources and still one fifth of humanity is poor and hungry. A recipe of more of the same – and greater and accelerated growth and even more resource consumption and use – has led us to the state of massive debt which could take a generation to fix. Stern's (2009) high market growth solution does not look attractive or viable and this time we don't have time to experiment.

On the other hand, the strategy of government regulation, so that people can only use initially 2 tonnes of carbon and then negative carbon, looks more promising as if people know that they have to make changes and that everyone is doing the same they are far more likely to do it. This is effectively rationing but it does provide for everyone equally and so removes the incentive for cheating. As climate change and polar ice melting become visible realities, the acceptability of such a scheme becomes much more likely and more desirable as a preferred option, a bit like a war time adoption; everyone shares in it together equally and with pride.

d) Lifestyle changes

The preferred green solution is lifestyle changes. By making life style changes we argue that we are creating a new future for humanity and that it can be an exciting and high tech future. We can choose to do things differently. For example we can all cut down our carbon foot print, measuring it with a carbon calculator and cut it by 10 % every 10 weeks. We can use slow travel when moving around and switch from plane to train even for business trips, I tend to try to use the train, in one year alone having been to Montenegro, Italy and Norway and Spain using the overnight trains. The slow movement for food and for slow cities, the Citislow (Hoerschele 2010) movement is also starting to gather interest. We can choose to source locally from our community to remove embedded carbon and to recreate viable local communities and take an interest in planning in order to ensure that it meets the criteria outlined above for a longer term perspective. We can choose to cycle more and walk more.

However, conversely, we will have to severely adjust our economy and with it our built environment to live within the earth's carrying capacity and within the realms and limits that nature imposes upon us. These will be technological constraints and also economic constraints. They have been termed "The Limits to Growth", (1972) where resources and population support has reached a limit and growth must now equate to flourishing and growth as in nature. No longer can rainforest destruction, where trees are cut down for firewood be counted as growth, even if it leads to an increase in GDP, but now must be measured as destruction of natural assets or natural capital (Kennet 2007). A country clearly is less well off with a renewable resource such as a forest being depleted. It is not better off, no matter what the balance sheet or graphs are telling us.

1.2 Green Economics: its recent development and background

By Miriam Kennet and Michelle S. Gale de Oliveira

1. Introduction

a) Increasing interest in Green Economics and the Green Economy

Ban Ki Moon General Secretary of the United Nations, said that "We are living in an age of Global Transformation, an Age of Green Economics."

There has been a dramatic increase in interest in environmental and green economics and the transformation towards Green Jobs and a Green Economy.

Partly in response to concerns about unprecedented and rapidly accelerating anthropogenic climate change there are worries that "the very survival of the human species is at risk." We are also living in the 6th ever mass extinction of other species that the earth has ever experienced, (IUCN) with many mammals, fish and birds under threat. A growing population predicted at 9 billion, means the poor are more directly dependent than ever directly on the ecosystem, and geo political instability is becoming more common.

Inequalities between people, within and between nations, and between present and future generations as well as social and environmental injustices are now significantly affecting the world economy. The bundle of natural capital resources, (forests, productive seas, agricultural land, healthy soil, air and water, food resources, rainforests) we can leave to future generations may actually be smaller than those of today. Climate change and sea level rise mean that current and future generations may inherit a world in which there will be less land available for cultivation or habitation, as well as depletion of forests, bleaching of coral reefs, protective mangrove swamps and other resources of all kinds including viable fish stocks or productive oceans. Massive dead zones are appearing in the sea and increasing desertification and soil erosion and declining forests and whole Ecosystems services are declining and the economy will be under threat.

b) People and institutions are looking for alternative solutions and innovation in economics

The current economic crisis has exposed deficiencies of mainstream economic concepts and the creation of new ones. These include for example by Paul Krugman in the USA and Stigilz and Sen and Green National Accounting from President Sarkozy in France and McGlade at the European Environment Agency and more fundamental changes in economic thinking.

Ecological   economics (Daly) introduces absolute limits on "more is better than less." The mainstream regarded ecology related decision-making as having infinite natural boundaries, and simply aggregated human behaviour and "optimal" solutions from it.

If the air or sea is so polluted that they can't sustain life, or the soil removed, or we have passed certain thresh holds or tipping points from which the natural systems can't recover, green economists propose doing different things, rather than substitution of one raw material with another. Standard neo-liberal economics models are insufficient for today's issues and are in urgent need of not only a major overhaul and has become "unfit for purpose," but also need replacing.

c) The broadening of scope and the arrival of "Inclusion" in economics

According to traditional market explanations *"the invisible hand"* (Adam Smith) mechanism ensures that everyone benefits from the investment and activities of homo economicus or "rational economic man" and his spending preferences and choices. In spite of arising from selfish aims, they are presumed to benefit the whole of society. Most people on the planet are not white western educated wealthy men and cannot choose how to earn a living or how or become wealthy.

So the absolute hegemony of markets is being fundamentally questioned in all its aspects: from the need to separate investment from savings banking, to its ability to solve climate change and its ability to solve the problem of poverty for which absolute as well as relative evels continue to rise. Similarly the role of "homo economicus" in the collapse of for example Icelandic banks, has led to laws to increasing the number of women at the helm or are brought into corporate board rooms and to correct long standing imbalances of power, representation and wealth between men and women.

d) Mainstream economics solutions have reached a crossroads

Human economic development has always relied on technological advancement to address challenges in the past. So the switch from fossil fuels to biofuels to allow for the continuation of current transport modes, as business as usual, was a logical step which was fully embraced by large companies and large trading blocks such as the European Union. However, this competition over land uses and pushed up the price of fuel, caused a scarcity of land for dwellings, and food riots all over the world, creating more poverty and land price spikes. This increasing investment and speculation culminated in the bursting of the "bubble economy" and a complete collapse of land prices in several countries leading to a serious economic downturn. It has ended the economic period called the "Great Moderation" and we are now in a period called "The Great Contraction."

e) Vulnerability of the economy to Global environmental change: the example of Italy

In common with many other places today, the OECD has warned that the economy of Italy in common with several other countries is particularly vulnerable to the economics effects of global environmental change. There are changes in the climate, leading to health effects of encroaching tropical vegetation, "Alien Species" invasion, malaria and dengue fever reappearing. The warming world is causing sea level rise and affecting specific environments such as the city of Venice and its lagoon and many other coastal towns and in other countries whole small island states may disappear.

The increase in temperature is causing micro climate environments, leading to more warming in certain Alpine Regions, upsetting watersheds and the available Hydroelectric Power which drive the economy and industry. In particular the warming has led to melting of the glaciers, leading to the re-emergence of "Oetzee the Ice Man" for the first time in 5000 years. These changes are affectng tourism as the mountain tops are no longer snow covered. The rich agricultural traditions such as wine, apples and meat may be damaged in South Tyrol. Slope instability, caused by changes in water courses and other global environmental changes, has meant more train derailments in mountain areas too such as occurred this year in Bolzano.

A transformation in the role of the car has led to large scale shut downs of car factories in the south and bans on using cars on certain days in larger Italian cities. Agriculture has to cope with advancing climate change and in general species moving northwards in the northern hemisphere according to some studies by up to an observed 5 metres per year. Plankton in the sea are moving significantly northwards affected by increasing acidification in the sea. In Italy tourism, a significant part of the economy, is threatened by the encroachment of a warmer tropical world, replacing it as a reliable and comfortable Mediterranean attraction and as a ski and winter walking holiday destination.

The rapidly expanding Green Economy is particularly useful in offering the hope of Green Jobs and the creation of 1000s of new ones to create a more sustainable economy.

f) Mainstreaming Environmental and Green Economics

The climate and biodiversity crisis solutions evolve into a blueprint for leading the world in the Green Economy

Solving the complex mesh of social and environmental justice is included in all aspects of Green Economics thinking, as are the costs and effects of climate change on the world economy. For example, the Stern Review of the Economics of Climate Change (2007) showed that spending up to 1% of GDP (recently corrected to 2%) would actually be a cheaper option than allowing runaway climate change to persist.

The TEEB Report in 2010 by Sukhdev has done similar work in highlighting the even higher costs of biodiversity loss as we are now causing the 6th ever mass species extinction. For example, bee colonies are disappearing due to microwave disturbance to their navigation systems from mobile phones, and the cost of hand pollination (already happening in China) of crops would be catastrophic in the west. Einstein said that once the bees disappear humans will only have another 4 years to survive on the planet.

Green Economics is an interdisciplinary science; on the one hand it is concerned with the theory and practical management of Global Environmental Change in all its aspects and on the other with the development Economics providing provisioning, sharing and distribution of the wealth of nature and human and naturally occurring resources.

It is a developing progressive holistic approach which cannot be explained by simplistic, typically linear mathematics and fixed preferences of individuals.

It extends beyond ecological issues to wider considerations of ideology, history of thought, evolution of society, the level of objectivity and the time specificity of solutions in a social science environment to be taken into account. These provide a much stronger basis to criticize and replace current reductionist mainstream economics. It embraces a wider set of values, including but not exclusively ecological values.

2. The arrival of Green Economics

a) Green Economics Strategies for addressing current crises

The Green Economy Initiative of the United Nations (2008) describes the crises as "Fs", Food, Fuel and Finance" and advocates a more growthist solution and the Lisbon 2020 Agenda also suggests Smart, Green, Growth is possible and desirable.

A Green Economics perspective instead regards the crisis as a mixture of the current economics downturn, a crisis of poverty, climate change and biodiversity loss and proposes a composite set of solutions. These consist of a mixture of market instruments, such as carbon trading under the Kyoto Protocol, regulation, carbon quotas or even rationing of carbon use,as well as technological innovations and green developments. It advocates, most of all, a change in public attitudes and reduction in unnecessary consumption of the earth's resources and individual carbon footprints and for *life style changes*. A progressive holistic approach extends beyond ecological issues to wider considerations of ideology, history of thought, evolution of society, the level of objectivity and the time specificity of solutions.

The European Greens propose that the economy must adapt to what the natural environment can tolerate, aiming for ecological sustainability, equity and social justice as well as self-reliance of local and regional economies, encouraging a true sense of community, based on democracy, transparency, gender equality and the right of all people to express themselves and participate fully in decision-making.

b) Environmental Economics

Environmental economics aims to factor in the costs of activities and impacts external, to a particular economics transaction. Market failure, its central concept, means that markets fail to allocate resources efficiently and this occurs when the market does not allocate scarce resources to generate the greatest social welfare. The best and most famous example is that of climate change in the Stern review. Biodiversity loss is also as serious, if not even more costly. The previous discipline of Environmental Economics has quite a main stream framework and does not specifically change activities or prevent impacts and only aims to simply find out how much things cost. Although useful information, it will not change what is done. It so omits the point that other options are available, or reassessing what is actually required.

Similarly surveys are used to establish "Willingness To Pay," for its existence of a species, or its conservation or to visit a natural amenity for an environmental benefit popu;larised by David Pearce are often used for example in deciding on the fate of a natural amenity such as whether to conserve a species.

The Stern Review proposes introducing a price for carbon, REDDS -debt for nature swaps and Carbon Storage and Sequestration and Discounting the future.

Common Property Rights are another concern first identified in this context by Coase and Hardin. When it is too costly to exclude people from accessing a contested environmental resource, market allocation is likely to be inefficient. Hardin's (1968) The Tragedy of the Commons popularized the challenges involved in non-exclusion and common property. "commons" refers to the environmental asset itself. Hardin theorizes that in the absence of restrictions, users of an open-access resource will use it more than if they had to pay for it and had exclusive rights and thus will often cause environmental degradation. Ostrom (1990) won the Nobel Prize this year for work on how people using real common property resources do establish self-governing rules to reduce this risk.

c) Ecological Economics

Ecological economics moves towards the primary role of energy and the laws of thermodynamics and energy flows and democratic decision making as subsets of the natural environment in its discourse.

Ecological economics includes the study of the flows of energy, and materials and material flows and ecosystem services that enter and exit the economic system. For the first time we have a change to the core concepts and a move towards the human economy as a subset of the natural world. Ecological Economics now is being used in global institutions. Use and non use value for measuring costs of Ecosystems services degradation are being used for example by the United Nations.

d) The Renaissance of Economics; the Green Economy rediscovers the roots of economics

Green Economics works in what it terms the four pillars of scope or activity, namely-1. Political and policy making, 2. academia especially science and economics, 3. business and 4. civil society including NGOs and most recently adding in a fifth, the general public and consumers.

Everyone and everything on the planet is acknowedged to have economics or provisioning requirements to achieve desired optimal conditions. Green Economics describes itself as

"Reclaiming Economics, for all people everywhere, nature, other species, the planet and its systems. " As a result even the volcanic activity which cost European Economies dearly this year, was able to be incorporated. For example it has been discovered that allowing the glaciers and ice caps to melt will increase seismic activity. The earth has a self regulatory mechanism, Gaia Theory by James Lovelock) which controls the temperature at 14 degrees centigrade. Too much warming and the volcanoes erupt cooling down the planet. Too much cooling and the ice sheets form pressing down the magma and preventing earth quakes!

Green Economics a participatory approach is a development which   includes natural science data and works with it, as many of its teams are physicists and natural scientists who also have economics qualifications, so it is able to weld both natural and social science together.

It is at core multi- disciplinary, and inter – disciplinary and pluralist and its decisions are based on the twin imperatives of human and natural science futures. It fully accepts that we all inhabit the earth and there is no economy outside of it. It reflects the current knowledge about the complexity of reality,. It is characterised by a holistic perspective, the involvement of nature, and is very inclusive.

It has evolved from a complete and fundamental philosophical renaissance of the origins of economics from the Greek Word oikia- meaning household or estate management, now evolved to   meaning the *earth*. The "oikonomia" -of Xenophon is now the economics and provisioning for the needs of all people everywhere, nature other species, the planet and its systems and also of the "Good life" of Aristotle.

3. The Cultural, Institutional, Academic Umbrella and Positioning of the Green Economy and its Chronology

a) The Transformation of Economics Disciplines and Schools of Thought

Under   the   Heterodox   Economics   Umbrella,   are   found   alternative,   holistic interdisciplinary,pluralistic set of methodologies and contributions. Pigou (1920) working on external effects and Coase examining the role of property rights. The USA and the UK struggle to decide who is liable for BP 's huge oil spill in American waters.

The debate is evolving into a robust economics school or discipline and widening the scope of an alternative economic framework further, into Environmental economics by authors such as Hartwick and Solow, Ciracy Wantrup, Daly, Tietenberg, Markandya, Pearce, Boulding, Jacob, Hillman, Ekins, Chichilnisky) and Ecological Economics (Soderbaum, Daly, Martinez- Alier).

Green Economics is influencing the economic debate and transforming existing policies and decision-making. 'Green' and Writers include Kennet, Heinemann, Hillman, Ekins, Reardon, Porrit, Gale D'Oliveira, Dobson, Anderson ,Barry, Reardon, Rao and Turk and Jociute..

A rapidly growing branch of economics, Green Economics is spreading into policy development in governments for example the Korean Government   and also in Global Institutions such as the

United Nations and the International Labour Organisations and the OECD. Each of these has a Green Economy Initiative or a Green Jobs Programme. Green Economics is being taught in Universities around the world and is also featured by the Dow Jones and Wall Street. The Green Economics Institute was founded in 2003 and its academic journal, *The International Journal of Green Economics* founded in 2005. Its background is in the "Green movement " hence a strong policy orientation combined with Economics Heterodoxy, as well as Environmental Science and Global Environmental Change and Management.

The discipline builds on enlightenment ideas of reason and rights, post-modern ideas of different and power struggles and elites, and Malthusian limits to growth and the search for sustainability, and on eco-feminism. The Enlightenment brought a major impact on modern understandings of economics and the role of humanity in the natural world. However it tended to look for logic and reason rather than wisdom in nature, as Bacon explains : "The human mind which overcomes superstition is to hold sway over a disenchanted nature. What men want to learn from nature is how to use it in order to wholly dominate it and other men. That is the only aim." The backlash against 10 000 years of the domestication of animals, plants and women and the colonies is in full swing within Green Economics. So it is the acknowledgement that the quest for domination is over.

Green Economics argues that nature has its own intrinsic and existence value and extends this value to all life forms, (Deep Ecology Arnae Naess) and thus seeks toreform economics to "provision for all people everywhere, all other species, the biosphere, systems, and planet."

It is sometimes part of a broader ideology, sometimes part of Bhuddist economics (Welford, Guenter Wagner 2006) advocating de-centralist, non materialist, and co-operative values and the concept of "enoughness" or sufficiency is important, as well as leaving enough resources for future generations.

One key development was the book "Silent Spring" by Rachel Carson which exposed the effects of DDT and the practices of the chemical industry and the relationship between the economy, industry , the environment and our over all well being.

b) Sustainable Development Economics

Another important key development was the Sustainable Development Economics, devloped by Professor Graciela Chichilnisky, and our Common Future which addressed this area of futurity In 1987. the United Nations World Commission on Environment and Development (UNCED) issued the Brundtland Report, defining sustainable development as meeting "the needs of the present without compromising the ability of the future to meet its needs."

Sustainable Development economics gives equal weight to economics, environment and social aspects.

c) Green Economics as Practice

The Green Economy has been called the Economics of Sharing the earth and its economy amongst ourselves but also with other species and systems of the planet in addition but not exclusively also to ensure it remains hospitable for us and our way of life.

It is also the economics of doing and is intensely practical. For example this means that there is much focus on green supply chains and the greening of procurement with the aim of creating social and environmental justice. It also advocates greener transport methods and slower local smaller scale production, even with slow travel and more train travel, slow food and degrowth to keep within the earth's Carrying Capacity. It advocates *"Reduce, Reuse, Recycle, Repair, Restore, Relax, Recover"*

Green IT

The role of IT, once hailed as the ultimate saviour, is now regarded as a significant cause of climate change and so there is a move to decouple the big monopolies such as Microsoft and move towards more community owned human style, open source IT – and to limiting the carbon usage of server farms, saving carbon by virtualisation, using recylced and also recycling materials and managing and limiting the power usage much more.

Environmental and social dumping and checking for green and transparent supply chains

Large outsourcing of environmental and social standards to where they can't be seen (called dumping) is coming to an end. Equity, social and environmental justice are acknowledged as providing attractive competitive advantage in a modern economy.

Green Jobs

Increasing numbers of jobs are being created in this vast and innovative transformation- this green economy. The Green Jobs Initiative of the United Nations and the International Labour Organisation and the International Federation of Trades Union describes a green job as *"work in agricultural, manufacturing, research and development (R&D), administrative, and service activities that contribute(s) substantially to preserving or restoring environmental quality. Specifically, but not exclusively, this includes jobs that help to protect ecosystems and biodiversity; reduce energy, materials, and water consumption through high efficiency strategies; de-carbonize the economy; and minimize or altogether avoid generation of all forms of waste and pollution."* A Green Economics perspective of a Green Job is anything that is sustainable and contributes to social and environmental justice.

4. Instruments and Tools in Green and Environmental Economics

a) Geo engineering and Green Technologies

The use of technological solutions (also called Eco technology or Geo engineering or Technical Fixes). These include, solar radiation management, iron fertilisation of the sea, stratospheric aerosols, sucking carbon using giant artificial tree scrubbers, albedo management, air capture, urban albedo and algal-based CO_2 capture schemes,   Carbon Storage, Sequestration or Capture.

There is increasing concern with the idea that "Unintended Consequences" could occur if for example we seed the clouds as the Chinese Government has done this year to create rain or we use Sulphur Aerosol Particles to mimic the action of volcanoes in cooling the global climate.

The "Precautionary Principle" is a major feature of a green economy which advises against trying untested technology. This would for example be used to prevent the kind of the oil spill or engineering at great depth without a clear strategy for clean up by BP.

The change to green technologies involves the use of Rare Earth Materials, which are nearly all mined in China. Significantly this year, China ceased exporting them in order to supply its own home market and so made the production of green technologies more expensive and more difficult.

"Local Production for Local Needs" will mean that the private car will be slowly replaced by modern and attractive lower carbon public transport, including car clubs, car-sharing, more cycling, and train travel. Governments introduced a   green Car Scrapage scheme to encourage purchases of new cars.

Greener alternatives such as slow travel are taking off, and train-travel is once again fashionable. Slow travel, slow cities, and the Italian idea of slow food are gaining in popularity.

Lower carbon economies are now actively being created, to combat the current average of 10 tonnes carbon equivalent usage in Europe, 25 tonnes in the USA, 5 in China, and 1 in Africa. Policies include "Contraction and Convergence" firstly to limit each person's carbon to 2 tonnes of carbon equivalent per year, secondly to equalise global economies.

Additionally, the acceleration of melting permafrost and the release of catastrophic amounts of methane would set in motion rapid climate change and sea level rise. Mainstream fossil fuel dependence has unacceptable costs, including pollution damage to fisheries and geopolitical struggles over supply chains from Russia to the Middle East. Fossil fuels are being replaced by microgeneration, Renewables and SMART grids, (linking areas of high wind to areas of high solar availability) more self sufficiency. Local and micro generation of energy is possible with Feed in Tariffs introduced in Germany and the UK.

b) Changes in attitudes to energy production and use: Lower carbon economies

British Petrol (BP)'s Deepwater Horizon oil drilling leak in the USA is an example of how the role of oil and fossil fuels in the economy is starting to be acknowledged as a limiting factor and is being questioned. Roughly 10 per cent of UK pension funds are linked up with BP and so the cancellation of the dividend from BP has deeply affected the UK economy but the oil spill has affected the economy of the US ruining for example fisheries but also coastal tourism and wildlife. The cost of oil is also a feature of the much criticised Iraq war too which reduced public acceptability of the costs of our current life style and how the idea of freedom, liberty and nonviolence fits with the idea of safe energy supplies from hostile, undemocratic or unstable regimes. Additionally there have been concerns about the effect of CO2 use on climate and the acceptance that the 20th century economy was characterised by mass-production and economies of scale, ending the century with huge outsourced supply chains in human conditions for workers.

c) Carbon trading and market solutions Climate crisis : Kyoto Protocol and the Copenhagen Conference COP15

The Kyoto Protocol, (a market-based attempt to trade carbon to solve climate change), held its regular Conference of the Parties Conference in Copenhagen COP15 in December 2009. It received unprecedented interest, and over 40 000 people and most of the world's Heads of State flocked there. Small island states would disappear unless climate change is stabilised at an agreed at 1.5 degrees of warming. Other more powerful countries decided to ask for   costs of stabilisation of the climate at 2 degrees of warming. The huge response led to an actual failure of the Conference as the organisers UNFCC were completely overwhelmed with the level of interest people showed in limiting climate change.

Lord Stern said that "Climate Change was the biggest market failure the world had ever seen." Although he continues to remain within the market mechanisms promoting ever more growth as a solution, green economics tries to solve the climate problems by looking beyond only market mechanisms. Main stream Economics methods have to some extent relied on   Cost Benefit Analysis and Discounting The Future but in a world where future resources may be depleted, and a weaker economy we should be doing the reverse. What is needed is to do different things differently.

d) Environmental Taxes and Regulations

An external effect was defined by Arrow as a "a situation in which a private economy lacks sufficient incentives to create a potential market in some good, and the nonexistence of this market results in the loss of efficiency." Externalities are examples of Market Failures in which the unfettered market does not lead to an efficient outcome, such as the costs of clean up of an oil spill, or the raising of the climate by fossil fuel use, or wastes collected and treated and can include energy products, transport equipment and transport services, as well as measured or estimated emissions to air and water, ozone depleting substances, certain non-point sources of water pollution, waste management and noise, in addition to the management of water, land, soil, forests, biodiversity, wildlife and fish stocks and on unleaded petrol and the fuels efficiency and climate change impacts of vehicles, the CO2 emissions per km driven.

e) Regulations

The current economic crisis was caused in part by deregulation of the banking system which had separated casino banking or speculation in investment banking from that of the savings of the small investor. Regulation is a cornerstone of a green economy. Some of which include: REACH Directive on Hazardous Chemicals and the WEEE Directive on recycling of components for electronic equipment when purchasing electrical or electronic equipment, batteries and accumulators.

f) The Green New Deal – Keynsian Investment

Very popular with UNEP and with the Greens and with governments, implemented by the UN and by the Korean Government and many others using a Keynsian stimulus package to pump money into the economy and targeting it towards green innovations and sustainable projects. The age of stimulus projects is now over as the big clean up starts and frugality and living within our contemporary means is the order of the day.

5. The Broader Background of the Green Economy – Changes in Focus in Economics Today

a) The Limits to Growth

There is an increasing realization that we may have reached what has been termed the "limits to growth." We are brushing up against the finite limits to the earth's adaptability and its "carrying capacity" in the face of our human and continual onslaught on sustainable the climatic conditions, and use of resource assets have "overshot" beneficial levels. A green economics perspective argues that empowered and educated female citizens decrease population size faster while increasing a country's GDP. Some even suggest that overall "equity is the price of survival."

b) Prosperity without Growth

Currently gaining popularity, Prosperity Without Growth dialogues are spreading around Europe, and a fashionable Degrowth Movement has originated in France, promotes the kind of Steady State Economy envisaged by John Stuart Mill. Rather than being seen as a failed attempt at growth, Growth by Design is gaining in interest, if not in acceptance.

This is partly a result of growth actually stalling in many Western Countries and the realisation that growth above 2 tonnes of carbon equivalent per person is no longer a good long term proposition. The European Environment Agency and many other institutions are working on this and other aspects of Green Accounting and Indicators. In particular important benchmarks are progress towards the Millennium Development Goals, and the Millennium Ecosystems Services Assessment Goals, The GRI for measuring Corporate Social Responsibility, (O' Carrol) the GINI Co- efficient index,The HDI Human Development Index, the Happiness Index from the State of Bhutan and many other sustainability and social indicators as well as measurements of unemployment, trade deficit and sovereign debt. Since WW2 there has been an economics policy of encouraging high mass consumption but this has begun to be questioned. Conspicuous consumption is going out of fashion and we are moving into an age of more austerity and rebalancing. Commodity prices are fluctuating and there is a global economic downturn, large sovereign debt and rising unemployment all over Europe. Many countries and national institutions are exploring a green economy as the one ray of hope in this rather bleak landscape. The European Commission believes that this green technology will drive competitive advantage, and encourages green venture capital and Smart, Inclusive, Green, Growth as part of the Lisbon Agenda.

Conclusion

The Transformation into the Age of Green Economics is a very exciting period of economics innovation, offering choices of strategies from right across the spectrum. Much has happened in terms both of the evolution of Green Economics, Green Jobs and a much more effective economics system. It has spread as an important driver from Korea to the EU and as an important aspect of decision making such as in the successor to the deep sea oil spill. Environmental, ecological and green economics are all playing their part in this process as we move towards the development of an economics for the 21st century- an Age of global transformation- An age of the widely predicted 4th Industrial revolution, decarbonising our economies and working to enhance the future not to discount it!

A previous version of this chapter was first published in Encyclopedia Trecanni (in Italian), in 2010.

1.3 The Ten key values of Green Economics

By Miriam Kennet, Jeff Turk and Michelle S. Gale de Oliveira

The ten key values of the Green Economics Institute have been defined as follows:

1. Green Economics aims to provision for the needs of all people everywhere, other species, nature, the planet and its systems, all as beneficiaries of economics transactions, not as throw away inputs.

2. This is all underpinned by social and environmental justice, tolerance, no prejudice and creating quality of life for everyone including future generations and all the current generations, including older and younger people.

3. Ensuring and respecting other species and their rights. Ending the current mass extinction of species. Ensuring biodiversity.

4. Non violence and inclusion of all people everywhere, including people with special needs and special abilities. Ensuring all nations have equal access to power and resources. Local people having control over their own destiny and resources. Increasing life expectancy, human welfare and per capita GDP in the least developed countries.

5. Ensuring gender equity in all activities. Educating, respecting, empowering women and minorities.

6. Ending current high mass consumption and overshoot of the planet's resources and returning to live within the comfortable bounds of nature in the climatic conditions under which humans built their civilisation. Choosing lifestyle changes over techno fixes and eco technology. Lowering our own carbon usage and living lightly on the earth. Changing how economics is done: from being an abstract mathematical exercise to embracing realism and the real world we all live in and share and in which we are all concerned stakeholders.

7. Valuing and respecting all people equally.

8. Poverty prevention. Climate change and instability prevention, adaptation, mitigation. Protecting the most vulnerable from risk. Ensuring the future of small island states.

9. Quickly reducing carbon per capita globally to 2 tonnes in the next 5 years and zero soon after. Limiting and reversing climate change. Moving to renewable energy sources.

10. Building a future-proofed economics to solve the current economic uncertainty and downturn which is suitable for the 21st century. Creating and nurturing an economy based on

sharing, rather than greed and profit. Completely reshaping and reforming current economics to do all the above.

Picture; The Economics of Peace and Reconciliation, government officials from the Balkan Countries at one of our Training sessions at Venice International University.

Part 2: Green economics empirical

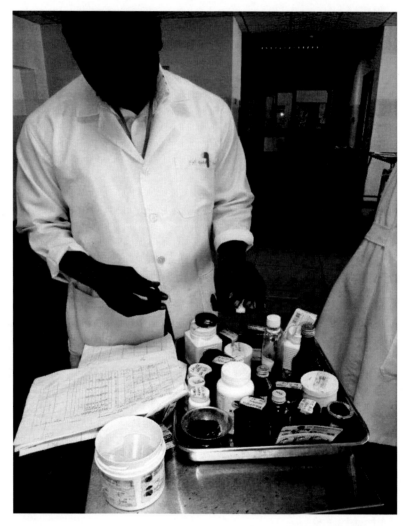

A doctor working at a hospital in Zambia, 2012. Photo by Elise Oedegaard

"I feel more confident than ever that the power to save the planet rests with the individual. "

Denis Hayes

2.1 How China Greens Its Economy: Steps and Accomplishments in Growing Renewables and Other Green Markets

By Professor Peter Yang

1. Introduction

The environmental and ecological consequences of burning coal and surging urban private car ownership have become a major concern on China's sustainability in consideration of the current rate of increase and the future needs in its energy consumption (Owen et al. 2010). This concern and the related domestic and international outcry, combined with the energy security concerns associated with country's limited domestic reserves of oil, and natural gas and the soaring energy prices on international oil markets forced China to seek actively to increase its renewable energy capabilities (Howell, 2010; Li, 2010).

Accordingly, the Chinese government added to its traditional reliance on fossil fuel solutions to meet its growing energy needs a new focus on developing "green" or renewable energy sources, an area, in which China is discovered to have a significant potential and is believed by many to have achieved a leading position (Li, 2010; Shah, 2011; Morales, 2011).

But China still faces significant challenges in its greening efforts. Most obviously, it has to overcome a gaping technological gap. According to a recent UNDP report, China currently only has 19 of the 62 core technologies (around 30 percent) that it needs to achieve a low carbon future, which emphasizes the need for China to advance R&D and master these technologies (UNDP, 2010). It is, therefore, a realistic call for avoiding the premature declaration of China as a green leader (Watson, 2011).

At the same time, China has presented some advantages in pursuing its greening goals. Although China has substantially transitioned from a centrally planned command economy to a largely market-driven one, most large industries, such as power generation, steel, and petrochemicals, are still owned or controlled by the national government. While the directives and commands under Mao's centrally planned economy proved to be notoriously inefficient, the country has been able to take advantage of a reformed centrally planning approach to, and have a direct impact on, the development and adoption of clean energy technologies in the largely market-driven economy since 1979. (Campbell, 2010).

Renewable energy incentives in China were granted in various forms depending on development stages of the individual RE projects. Generally speaking, direct subsidies were made available to projects in the early stage of research and development (R&D), while tax incentives are granted to manufacturing projects adopting the technologies or to consumers to help build demand for the RE products (Gnansounou, 2004).

This chapter will explore the legislative, administrative green economic instruments China has been using to grow renewable energy generation and promote other sustainable activities in order to green its rapidly growing economy and make it sustainable. It will also examine the challenges China faces in its greening efforts and evaluate the greening results it has achieved through the greening tools. The main purpose of this paper is to provide international scholars and policy makers involved in sustainable development with up to date insights into China's experience with greening its economy and its transition to a more sustainable economic development.

The remainder of the chapter will be organized as follows. Section 2 will review China's legislation promoting renewables development and generation. Section 3 will examine its green research and development programs. Section 4 will discuss the country's renewables incentives and subsidies. Section 5 will evaluate China's achievements in developing renewables markets. Section 6 will analyze the free public bike rental programs in some major Chinese cities. Section 7 will focus on remaining challenges to China's renewables industry. The concluding Section 8 will summarize the findings in this paper and discuss the implications of these findings for China's future economic transformation and development.

2. Laws Promoting Renewables

Legislative provisions promoting RE can be found in a number of early laws in China although they were not designed to achieve a strategic goal for its national energy structure, but rather as a rural development policy in distributed power generation schemes. In contrast to the German legislation promoting RE with clear mandates for RE development, the Chinese laws governing RE generally state goals to be achieved or what has to be accomplished. They lay out a framework, but do not lay out in detail how the RE goals will be achieved. The details on the implementation will be determined after the framework has been laid out (REN21, 2009; Campell, 2010).

The Electricity Law of 1995 for instance was China's first law to regulate the electric industry designed to promote its safe development by consolidating the control of existing regulatory agencies and restructuring state-owned electricity companies. As the main law regulating China's power generation sector, it identified RE as a means to develop electric power, especially in rural areas (EPL, 1996; Austin, 2005).

The Law for Prevention and Control of Air Pollution, adopted in 1995 and amended in 2000, considered RE as a solution to preventing and controlling air pollution and promoted the support and development of clean energy from RE sources such as "solar energy, wind energy and water energy" (Air Pollution Law, 2000).

The Energy Efficiency Law of 1997 was enacted to ensure sustainable growth of China's economy by promoting energy efficiency as a long-term strategy for economic development, supporting energy-saving technologies, and protecting the environment. While energy efficiency investment projects are given priority over energy development projects, the national government and local governments are authorized to allocate energy efficiency funds to support the development and use of renewable and clean energy sources. Governments at various levels, especially in rural areas, are required to use RE resources. Energy efficiency measures are seen as ways to lower the financial and environmental costs of funding China's growing economy (China.org, 1997).

The Renewable Energy Law of 2005 was the major law for China's RE deployment, which was intended to promote the development and use of renewable energy, improve the energy structure, diversify energy supplies, safeguard energy security, protect the environment, and realize the sustainable development of the economy and society. It authorized the government to set medium-term and long-term national targets for RE deployment (NREL and CREIA, 2005).

China's 11th Five Year Plan (2006–2010) mandated the country to reduce energy intensity by 20 percent by 2010 from the 2005 level. Meeting this goal may prove to be a huge challenge. According to a recent report, China almost achieved its GDP energy intensity reduction target; its energy consumption by unit GDP was reduced by 19.1 percent. In addition, China reduced its sulfur dioxide emissions by 14.29 percent, and its emissions of chemical oxygen demand by 12.45 percent from 2005 to 2010 (Xie, 2011).

The National Climate Change Program of 2007, the country's first global warming   initiative, recognized China's economic growth's climate change impact and aimed to reduce this impact by

reducing the economy's energy intensity through various energy efficiency programs (NDRC, 2007). This document represents the country's official position toward the ecological impact of country's fast growing economy and the conceptual foundation for key policy instruments that were developed later to address the impact.

In summary, China has been developing its legislative provisions promoting RE since 1995 in response to the growing environmental and ecological impacts of its fast growing economy. These RE promoting laws and regulations played a key role in laying the legislative foundation for the country's strategic transition from a quantity-based economic growth to a quality-based sustainable development and were therefore instrumental to China's transition from coal-fired generation that has accelerated its pace in recent years.

3. RE Research and Development Programs

In response to increasing air pollution concerns, China recently made large-scale investment in the development of clean energy technologies. More recently, China paid closer attention to mitigating its economic growth's impacts on global climate change. Accordingly, the national government played a pivotal role in pushing for policies and regulations for promoting RE deployment in China through five-year plans and more dedicated national, provincial, and local government programs (NREL and CREIA, 2005).

China's RE development has been on the one hand driven by the gap of its growing economy's unsatisfied demand for energy and the insufficient coal-dominant energy supply, on the other by urgent needs to reduce environmentally-harmful pollutants, such as sulfur dioxide, nitrous dioxide, methane, and climate impacting CO_2 emissions (Chow, 2007).

Over the last 30 years, China has developed a number of programs supporting the research and development of RE technologies through the Ministry of Science and Technology, including the following:

China's first national program aiming to address major science and technology issues in its economic and social development was the Key Technology Research and Development Program. It was initiated in 1982 and implemented through four five-year plans (MOST, 2006a). Part of the program's focus was to strengthen engineering research in application technologies, develop technologies and equipment for clean energy, and promote R&D for environmental pollution control and efficient use of energy and water resources.

The National High-Tech Program was created in March 1986 (therefore also called "863 Program") to boost innovation in strategic high technology sectors, make China independent of financial obligations for foreign technologies, and diversify research efforts away from purely military themes to civilian and dual-use technologies. The 863 Program has been carried out through several consecutive Five-Year Plans for National Economic and Social Development (or Five-Year Plans), which are, more than mere statements of political intent, action plans to carry out objectives set in various strategic programs, including environmental protection and RE deployment.

In 2001, with a strategy extended to enhance the international competitiveness of the Chinese economy, 863 Program became one of the 10th five-year (2001 to 2005) plan's focuses to "achieve breakthroughs in key technologies for environmental protection, resources and energy development to serve the sustainable development of our society" (MOST, 2006b). In this period, the program received $3 billion in research, and another $585 million was approved in 2008 jointly for the 863 and 973 programs. Energy technologies were identified as a focus beneficiary of the 863 Program, and hydrogen and fuel cells, energy efficiency, clean coal, and RE as targeted beneficiaries of some $172 million in funding for the period from 2006–2010 (CAP, 2010).

The National Basic Research Program was created in March 1997 (therefore also called "973 Program") focuses on more fundamental, basic research. It complements the more commercialization oriented 863 Program. Energy and sustainable development have been key features of the program since its founding. The program funded 382 projects between 1998 and 2008, with a total investment of $1.3 billion, of which one third was invested in energy and resource protection projects (CAP, 2010).

Of the 12 "mega-projects" based on the 863 and National Key Technologies Programs to achieve significant technological breakthroughs for China's industries implemented by the 10th Five Year Plan (2001–2005) with a total budget of $2.4 billion, four were energy efficiency and environmental protection related, including electric car, high speed train, water saving, and water pollution control technologies (MOST, 2006c).

The 11th Five-Year Plan (2006–2010) was the first to put the green agenda on the table. It introduced the country's environmental and sustainability targets, including a 20 percent energy intensity target (by 2010) and a 15 percent RE target (by 2020). It identified energy technologies as a focus of the 863 Program, with funds of $172 million for hydrogen, fuel cells, energy efficiency, clean coal and RE technologies, and made utility-scale RE and new energy development the 973 Program's main focus.

The plan promoted production and consumption of renewable energy, including wind, solar energy, biomass, geothermal energy, and ocean energy, and the increase of its share in primary energy consumption by promotional tax rates and investment policies and market share mandates. In particular, it set the goal of building 30 large wind power projects with an installed capacity of 100 MW each, GW level wind farms in Inner Mongolia, Hebei, Jiangsu and Gansu provinces, as well as 5 GW installed capacity of wind power connected to grid and 5.5 GW installed capacity of biomass power (gov.cn, 2006; Kwok, 2009; TABLE 1).

More recently, the Chinese government aimed to raise the country's original target of wind power capacity 30 GW to 150 GW by 2020, an unofficial target was even 150–200 GW. In addition, solar power target may be raised from 1.8GW to 20GW or more by 2020, according to a recent plan (Martinot and Li, 2010). With abundant wind resources in the Northwest China, some scholars in the West found that with its current pace of wind energy deployment, China could replace coal to meet the projected total energy demand from wind power alone by 2030 (Fairley, 2009; Howell 2010).

Energy Source	Estimated Potentials (GW)	2010 (GW)	2020 (GW)	
			2007 Plan	
Hydropower	540	190	300	
Biomass Power	75	5.5	30	
Wind Energy	1000	5	30	
Solar Power	220,000	0.3	1.8	
TOTAL	221,615	201	362	

Table 1: China's RE Targets, Capacities by Year (Sources: NDRC, 2007; Martinot and Li, 2010; Li et al., 2001; CREIA, 2011)

The current 12th Five-Year Plan (2011–2015) represents a dramatic change in China's approach to sustainability from administrative instruments to market-based and innovative instruments. In this plan period, China's economy is expected to grow by 40 percent to $8.5 trillion. It places low carbon growth and clean energy industries at the heart of the country's economic development strategy. The plan continues the previous five-year plan's strategic shift from a focus on the quantity-based growth to the quality-based development. Accordingly, it calls for achieving the following goals concerning environmental protection, ecological sustainability, and energy security by 2015 (IOSC, 2011):

- Reducing the energy consumption per unit of GDP by 16 percent the and the CO_2 emissions per unit of GDP by 17 percent;

- Reducing water consumption per unit of industrial added value by 30 percent;

- Increasing effective use coefficient of agricultural irrigation water to 0.53;

- Increasing the share of non-fossil fuels in primary energy consumption to 11.4 percent;

- Reducing the chemical oxygen demand and sulfur dioxide emissions by 8 percent, reducing ammonia nitrogen, nitrogen oxides emissions by 10 percent, and significantly reducing the total discharge of other major pollutants;

- Increasing the forest coverage to 21.66 percent, and the forest stock by 600 million cubic meters;

- Maintaining cultivated land at 1.818 billion mu (versus 1.826 billion mu in 2008).

There are also local programs such as Low Carbon City Initiative (LCCI), which strives to explore low carbon development models in various Chinese cities, improve energy efficiency in industry, construction and transportation sectors, and help develop RE to serve role models for other cities in China (WWF-China, 2009). LCCI supports the research and the implementation of policies which contribute to low carbon development, promotes capacity building on energy efficiency and renewable energy, and support demonstration projects, assists with energy efficient technology transfer and cooperation between China and developed countries, explores new finance and investment instruments and sustainable trade opportunities for energy efficiency and RE industry, promotes public awareness on climate change in order to enable and encourages Chinese citizens to save energy and the environment (SDT and NDRC-ERI, 2010).

4. Market-Oriented Green Instruments

To achieve the sustainability goals put forward in its 11th and 12th Five-Year Plans as discussed above, the Chinese government employed various market-oriented green instruments, including fiscal ones such as RE incentives (green subsidies) for RE investments and non-fiscal ones such as carbon credit and carbon trade.

1. Feed-in tariffs and energy (FITs)

The Chinese government's policy options promoting the RE sector include fiscal tools, such as subsidies on investments and tax incentives for production, and feed-in tariffs (FITs) for wind power and solar energy. At the height of the financial crisis in 2008, China announced a $46 billion "green" stimulus package. By the end of 2010, 70 percent of the funds had been spent. With $5.9 billion in new investment in renewables, China also led in public RE investments, compared with the global total of $49 billion (REN21, 2011). With an investment of $39.1 billion in 2009 and $54.4 billion in 2010, China led in new-build clean energy, making it the largest country in resuming utility-scale asset finance growth in last two years (see FIGURE 1).

China's leadership in large-scale public investments in clean energy and infrastructure is also reflected in approximately $1.54 trillion investment in clean energy projects over the next 15 years, with government investments through various financial institutions, such as state-owned investment corporations, financial institutions, and financial and tax policy agencies. Foreign investments are also expected to be involved in and benefit from the growing green energy sector, through mergers and acquisitions, especially between foreign businesses and Chinese companies as the former aspire to expand in China and the latter need to leverage on advanced foreign technology and expertise (Shi and Zhao, 2011).

2. Feed-in tariffs (FITs)

Feed-in tariffs (FITs), a successful policy instrument in growing RE markets in Germany, have also been introduced in China. In 2009, China set a fixed FIT for new onshore wind power plants in a move that will help struggling project operators to realize profits. Four categories of onshore wind projects were identified for the wind power tariffs at 0.51 yuan ($0.075), 0.54 yuan, 0.58 yuan and 0.61 yuan for wind power per kWh depending on wind locations. Areas with better wind resources will have lower FITs, while those with lower outputs will be able to access more generous tariffs. These wind power FITs represented a significant premium on the average rate of 0.34 yuan per kWh paid to coal-fired electricity generators (Chan, 2009).

In August 2011, China set national FITs at 1.15 yuan ($0.18) per kWh electricity generated from solar projects approved before July 1, and 1.00 yuan per kWh electricity from solar projects approved after July 1, 2011. This solar FIT policy was designed to help Chinese solar panel manufacturers keep making profits in a time of slowing global demand as big international markets such as Germany and Italy reduce subsidies for solar panels. At the same time, this Chinese national solar FIT is expected to propel the world's largeq1st maker of solar panels to become one of the world's biggest markets of solar panels (Rhein, 2010; Hook, 2011; Montgomery, 2011).

Before this move, China had promotional FITs for some special RE projects. For example, a "Golden Roofs" program released in March 2009 provided a subsidy of $2.93 kWh for roof-mounted PV systems over 50 kilowatts (kW), which could cover over half of a system's installation cost (Solangi et al., 2011). The national government appropriated 10.9 billion yuan to implement the so-called "Golden Sun" program, announced by NDRC in July 2009, to provide solar energy operators subsidies of up to 50 percent of solar power investments and up to 70 percent of such investments in more remote areas, such as the Western Region (MoF, 2010). The subsidies apply to solar power projects with a) a minimum capacity of 300 kW, b) a construction period within one year, and c) more than 20 years for planned operations. The Golden Sun Project targeted 500 MW to a maximum of 680 MW of solar projects to be deployed through 2011 (Finamore, 2009a).

The national government approved special feed-in prices for a small number of solar power stations. The government approved several solar feed-in rates for different solar power projects: a) a feed-in price for two pilot projects at 4 yuan per kWh in 2008, and another feed-in rate at 1.15 yuan/kWh in 2010 for four solar power stations, which is sharply lower than the one approved two years ago. This solar feed-in rate is slightly higher than the rate for Guangdong Nuclear Power Corp in the country's first major open tender project in northwestern Gansu province in 2009 and much higher than China's average grid FIT for coal-fired power stations at 0.354 yuan per kWh in 2008. The difference between the solar feed-in rate and the FIT for coal-fired power stations will be covered by a surge-charge on electricity users (China Daily, 2010). In addition, there were also provincial incentives for solar development, for example, a FIT from the Jiangsu provincial government for solar power from ground-based solar farms, rooftop, or building integrated PV systems installed in 2009 with respective rates of $0.31, $0.54, and $0.63 per kWh of electricity generated (Ariel, 2009).

3.   Carbon Credits

Carbon credits are another growing source of project finance for China's RE markets. Through the UN's Clean Development Mechanism, China received about $1.3 billion carbon credits in 2009 alone, according to the China Beijing Environmental Exchange, a major platform that facilitates CDM transactions in China. The carbon credits have helped Chinese businesses upgrade technologies to save energy and reduce carbon emissions (Liu, 2011). In 2009, the country started several utility-scale RE projects, including the world's largest wind farm, a 10 GW "Three Gorges of Wind Power" project in Gansu Province, and a 2 GW solar power plant in Northern China using Arizona-based First Solar's thin-film solar PV panels (Finamore, 2010). At the same time, electricity generated from biomass projects can receive a national FIT at $0.11 per kWh (Tong and Warren, 2010).

4.   Environmental and Carbon Taxes

In an effort to implement its ambitious goal of reducing its carbon intensity by 40 to 45 percent by 2020, China has become receptive to measures that more directly tackle CO_2 emissions, which include imposing environmental tax on pollution (Watts, 2011) and carbon tax on fossil fuels (Cohen-Tanugi, 2010; Hu, 2011), and experimenting domestic carbon cap and trade (Li, 2010).

5.   Carbon Trade

China even ventured in implementing domestic carbon cap and trade. The first carbon trade was sealed on a voluntary basis in August 2009, in which a Shanghai-based car insurance company purchased more than 8,000 tons of carbon credits generated through a green commuting campaign during the Beijing Olympics. Now the country is experimenting domestic carbon trading programs as a 12th Five Year Plan (2011–2015) project to help meet its ambitious carbon intensity reduction target. China sees carbon trading a market-based solution to help achieve the 2020 carbon reduction intensity target in a cost-effective manner (Li, 2010).

The NDRC has recently announced that China will pilot carbon trading in five provinces and eight large cities in the coming years. The selected five provinces are Guangdong, Liaoning, Hubei, Shaanxi and Yunnan, and the chosen cities are Tianjin, Chongqing, Shenzhen, Xiamen, Hangzhou, Nanchang, Guiyang and Baoding. These provinces and cities are expected to have their carbon emissions reduced considerably in the future (Liu, 2011).

The proposed domestic carbon trading was preceded by a careful study of the related experience in Europe. The recommendations of the research team include carrying out "carbon-source-and-carbon-sink" trading between the carbon-source provinces and the carbon-sink provinces in China (see TABLE 2 below) and using carbon as a rigid target for the monitoring, identification and control of economic activity. The main idea behind this carbon trading system is to incentivize carbon-source provinces or industries to invest in carbon-sink provinces and industries. The Chinese government realized that a high carbon development model will significantly impede the country's future growth, and a green, low-carbon economy will provide major opportunities for China to build an ecological society (Liu, 2011).

City/Province	Carbon Source	Carbon Sinks	City / Province	Carbon Source	Order	City / Province	Carbon Sinks	Order
Beijing	7694	93	Shandong	51773	1	Inner Mongolia	15212	1
Tianjin	7445	17	Shanxi	43358	2	Yunnan	14417	2
Hebei	35058	1146	Hebei	35058	3	Qinghai	6559	3
Shanxi	43358	1368	Henan	34596	4	Tibet	6074	4
Inner Mongolia	26591	15212	JiangSu	33046	5	Sichuan	4478	5
Liaoning	25409	2230	Guangdong	29907	6	Heilongjiang	3781	6
Jilin	13118	3554	Inner Mongolia	26591	7	Xinjiang	3664	7
Heilongjiang	16642	3781	Liaoning	25409	8	Jilin	3554	8
Shanghai	13467	19	Zhejiang	22969	9	Jiangxi	3298	9
JiangSu	33045	524	Hubei	18299	10	Guangxi	3172	10
Zhejiang	22969	152	Sichuan	17667	11	Guangdong	2819	11
Anhui	14771	809	Heilongjiang	16642	12	Fujian	2565	12
Fujian	10853	2565	Hunan	16606	13	Liaoning	2230	13
Jiangxi	8632	3298	Guizhou	15788	14	Hunan	2208	14
Shandong	51773	1220	Anhui	14771	15	Guizhou	2056	15
Henan	34596	1945	Shanghai	13467	16	Henan	1945	16
Hubei	18299	803	Shaanxi	13215	17	Chongqing	1899	17
Hunan	16606	2208	Jilin	13118	18	Gansu	1436	18
Guangdong	29907	2819	Yunnan	13085	19	Shanxi	1368	19
Guangxi	8311	3172	Fujian	10853	20	Shaanxi	1364	20
Hainan	1588	272	Xinjiang	9609	21	Shandong	1220	21
Chongqing	7591	1899	Jiangxi	8632	22	Hebei	1146	22
Sichuan	17667	4478	Guangxi	8311	23	Anhui	809	23
Guizhou	15788	2056	Beijing	7694	24	Hubei	803	24
Yunnan	13085	14417	Chongqing	7591	25	Jiang Su	524	25
Tibet	725	6074	Tianjin	7445	26	Ningxia	299	26
Shaanxi	13215	1364	Gansu	6945	27	Hainan	272	27
Gansu	6945	1436	Ningxia	5699	28	Zhejiang	152	28
Qinghai	2005	6559	Qinghai	2005	29	Beijing	93	29
Ningxia	5699	299	Hainan	1588	30	Shanghai	19	30
Xinjiang	9609	3664	Tibet	725	31	Tianjin	17	31

TABLE 2: China City / Provincial Carbon Sources and Sinks (in ton) (Source: CECPA and CIDSS, 2008)

6. RE Technologies

China's low carbon plan went hand in hand with the new focuses of a new "Strategic Emerging Industries Development Plan" on promoting seven innovations-based "strategic emerging industries," of which the following six industries directly address China's urgent needs for energy conservation, environmental protection, ecological sustainability, and energy security (Qiang, 2011):

- Energy saving and environmental protection

- New energy, e.g., renewables, nuclear, and carbon capture

- New materials e.g., building materials and LED lighting

- High-end equipment manufacturing, e.g., high-speed railway

- New-energy vehicles, vehicles running on alternative fuels, EV, PHEV, energy-efficient vehicles, batteries

- Next generation IT, e.g., smart grid.

China's 2009 green investment plan included $1.5 billion in subsidies over the next three years to develop alternative-energy vehicles. China is investing $9 billion a month on clean energy and its investment in clean energy R&D under its 863 Program is soaring at over 20 percent per year. Renewable energy jobs in China reached 1.12 million in 2008 and are climbing by 100,000 a year (Bradsher, 2010).

China invested $7.3 billion in its smart grid in 2010, just slightly more than the United States. The government planned to raise the seven industries' share in China's GDP from the current 3 percent to 8 percent by 2015 and 15 percent by 2020, which would represent a significant moving up of the value chain for China's manufacturing industries. Its new strategic sectors will be supported by increased annual public innovation spending accounting for 2.2 percent of GDP by 2015, up from 1.8 percent in 2011.

Although the country's absolute CO_2 emissions will continue to rise in the foreseeable future, its increased energy and carbon intensity targets as well as other green economic targets could save around 1 Giga ton of CO_2 emissions by 2015 and create strong market opportunities for low carbon industries (Buckley, 2012).

Recently, there have been some reductions of the earlier pledges to strategic emerging industries, such as the reduced national investments of RMB 600 billion in high-speed railway infrastructure construction for this year as versus RMB 600 billion for last year and in wind power because of a relative "overcapacity" of wind power due to the lag of power grid construction, which is needed to transfer most of China's wind power and solar energy plants located in the west and inland areas to the east coast (CIIPP, 2011). However, China's announced program promoting emerging industries could yield significant results in RE such as solar and wind power; energy- efficiency and environmental conversation such as waste recycling and clean coal technologies (IEA CCC, 2011); and new energy vehicles such as battery cell technology and an annual production of 1 million electric vehicles by 2015.

In addition, the Chinese government launched a two-year pilot program of subsidizing buyers 60,000 yuan ($8800) for battery electric cars and 50,000 yuan ($7,143) for plug-in hybrids in Shanghai, Changchun, Shenzhen, Hangzhou and Hefei to help cut pollution and reduce oil dependency. The country aimed to become the world's largest producer of electric cars by focusing on consumer choice rather than corporate subsidies (Bradsher, 2009). It also planned to expand a project of encouraging the use of energy-efficient and alternative-energy vehicles in public transportation from 13 cities to 20 (Lin et al., 2010). This incentive for electric car buyers has encouraged not only domestic production of electric cars, but also international auto makers such as Nissan, Volkswage, to produce their battery electric vehicles for the Chinese market (Shirouzu et al., 2010; Bloomberg News, 2010).

7. Energy Saving Program

Despite the difficulties in achieving the goals in energy saving and carbon reduction during the global economic crisis, China has made very serious effort to pursue its Five-Year Plan goals by fiscal, administrative, and market means. Through its effort, the country has already achieved remarkable progress in its carbon emissions reduction, many of these goals set in the 11th Five-Year Plan were achieved by 2010.

The Top 1000 Enterprises Energy Consuming Program: Under this program, the Chinese national government and the top 1,000 energy-consuming enterprises negotiated energy savings targets, which required the enterprises to conduct energy audits and establish energy savings plans to reach their targets. As a result of this program, 90 billion RMB ($13.2 billion) were invested in improving efficiency, which reduced energy consumption by 100 million tons of coal equivalent, which means that about 450 million tons of CO_2 emissions were avoided by the end of 2010 (Price et al., 2010).

Closing inefficient, Outdated Power Plants and Factories: To meet the energy and carbon intensity targets of the plan, the Chinese government used various police instruments, including administrative ones. For example, it closed down a combined capacity of 80 GW of inefficient small and inefficient coal-fired power plants with capacities below 200,000 KW and cut down hundreds of millions of tons of production capacity in China's heavy industry including steel and cement (Reuters, 2009; Finamore, 2010).

Building Meeting Energy Savings Targets into the Job Performance Rating System: Historically, Chinese provincial officials' and enterprise leaders' job performance benchmarks were GDP growth rates. The evaluation system established in 2007 monitored progress in meeting energy savings targets, and not meeting these targets would mean the loss of opportunities of promotions or annual awards. The new bureaucratic job evaluation system already has achieved expected results (Wang, 2008).

5. RE markets in China

Now many analysts see China as the world leader in several indicators of RE market growth: it was the top installer of wind turbines and solar thermal systems and the top hydropower producer in 2010. In 2010, China attracted approximately $56 billion investment in RE deployment as part of the country's economic stimulus strategy. Its RE investment accounted for more than a quarter of global investment of $211 billion that year, making it the global leader in RE investment for the second year in a row (Li, 2010; REN, 2011). China was followed by Germany with $43 billion and the United States with $ 35 billion (Pew Charitable Trusts, 2011).

International trade played an increasing role in RE development. There were continued trends in internationalization of the RE industry. International wind turbine manufacturers focused their attention on the Chinese market. For example, Gamesa planned to triple its investments in China by 2012. Solar PV manufacturers in China also sold more solar products in Europe than ever before (REN21, 2011).

China's RE markets grew to US$20.5 billion in 2010, a 15.5 percent increase from the previous year. The renewable electricity, including hydropower, wind energy, accounted for 25.64 percent of its total electricity generation.

a. Wind Power

According to China's Meteorological Administration's estimate, China has potential onshore wind power capacity ranging between 700 GW and 1,200 GW and a potential offshore wind power capacity of 250 GW (Zhang, 2009). Studies show that the country could meet its energy needs in 2030 by wind power alone (Zhang, 2009; Rutter, 2009).

China seems to be on track in this grand vision. It was the world's largest wind turbine manufacturer and became the world's top wind power consumer by the end of 2010. With a cumulative installed wind power capacity of 41.8 GW by the end of 2010, China surpassed its wind power target of 30 GW originally set for 2020 (NDRC, 2007) and the U.S.'s wind power capacity of 40 GW (REN21, 2011), becoming the world's biggest wind power installer. From 2000 to 2010, the annual growth rate of the annual installed wind energy capacity in China was 8.3 percent. As of 2009, China's small-scale turbines were providing electricity to an estimated 1.5 million people (REN21, 2011).

In 2010, China accounted for 50 percent of global wind power capacity additions, up from 4.4 percent in 2005. This significant annual installed capacity made the country "the single largest driver for global wind power development" (Steve Sawyer, Secretary General of the Global Wind Energy Council). The country plans to install more than 30 GW of wind power capacity during 2011 and 2012. China's 0.1 GW Donghai Bridge near Shanghai, officially began operation in July 2010. China began construction of four projects off the coast of Jiangsu in October, with a total installed capacity of 1 GW to be completed by 2014 (REN21, 2011).

There are more than 100 wind turbine manufacturers in China. Four biggest of them, Sinovel, Goldwind, Dongfang, and United Power, experienced strong growth driven by lower labor and manufacturing costs and continued political and regulatory support. The continued technology research and development of these companies also allowed them to narrow their technological gap with their overseas competitors; for example, Sinovel launched a five MW turbine model in 2010.

With a combined market share of more than 30 percent, these four Chinese manufacturers were among the world's top 10 wind turbine suppliers in 2010, posing an increasing challenge to the dominance of Danish manufacturer Vestas. At the same time, China's wind turbine sector might see consolidation, which was called for by a draft government policy. As a result of such a consolidation, the number of wind turbine manufacturers might be reduced to far fewer than the existing more than 100 companies. The major developers of wind projects in China were Longyuan, Datang, Huaneng, Huadian, CPI, and Guohua, which were all state-owned enterprises (REN21, 2011). The consolidation in China's wind power sector is expected to make the Chinese wind turbine manufacturing even more competitive on the international market.

Chinese manufacturers were learning quickly for systematic improvements in quality and product standardization. Most wind turbines China produced were installed domestically. China has started to export wind turbines to developing countries in Africa and Central and South America, regions with warmer climates where thermo-siphon systems can be sold. Chinese wind turbines have also begun to be exported to the European market (REN21, 2011).

According to the estimate of the Development Report of China Wind Energy in 2010, China will have an installed wind power capacity of 230 GW, an equivalent of the capacity of 13 Three Gorges Hydropower Plants. The cumulative wind capacity will reach 464.9 billion kWh, an equivalent of 200 power plants (Liu, 2010).

Offshore wind power remains in the early development stages due to complex operating environments for offshore turbines, high technological requirements and construction difficulties. However, China's offshore wind power potential is estimated at more than 750 GW, which represents about three times the estimated wind power resources onshore. The Chinese government is poised to accelerate the offshore wind power development. At a recent meeting on offshore wind power, the National Energy Board set a target for Chinese offshore wind power to complete 5 GW offshore wind power by 2015 and 30 GW by 2020.

Concessions for both onshore and offshore wind must be put up for tender offers with price offers to connect wind power to the grid. Tender offers must be made by Chinese-funded enterprises, or Sino-foreign joint ventures with majority Chinese ownership. China's National Energy Bureau has completed the first offshore wind tender in 2010 and will open the second offshore wind tender in the second half of 2011 to grant offshore wind concessions. While overall regulations in the wind turbine production sector have been quite restrictive for direct foreign involvement, China recently agreed to drop its subsidies to wind-power manufacturers because of a complaint the U.S. filed at the WTO (Haimowitz, June 2011). Many foreign companies have been able to get access to the wind power sector through mergers, acquisitions, and joint ventures (Wang et al., 2011).

b. Solar power

China's solar industry has started to take off. The two solar subsidy programs launched in 2009, the Golden Roof and Golden Sun programs, have achieved considerable results in boosting domestic solar installation, and have helped China become the world leader in manufacturing solar PV panels in just a few years (Finamore, 2009a; SNEC, 2009).

China was the world's largest producer of solar photovoltaic (PV) panels in 2010, which were mainly manufactured for export. The country's domestic solar panel market was still small. With less than 1 GW solar power installation, solar energy accounted for less than 0.01 percent of China's energy production. However, the country had 65 percent of the world's solar water heaters, including 80 percent of newly installed water heaters in 2010. With the global economic downtown came a slowdown of solar panels export, and China began to look at developing the solar power domestic market. Its updated targets for installed solar power capacity are10 GW by 2015 and 50 GW by 2020. In addition, China added an estimated 17.5 GWth (25 million m² of collectors) for a total of just under 118 GWth (168 million m2) for solar water heating (REN21, 2011).

China is the world leader in manufacturing solar water heaters and has dominated the world market for several years. Chinese solar water heater manufacturers produced 49 million m² of collector area in 2010. More than 5,000 firms were involved in the Chinese solar water heating industry. The largest manufacturers include Himin, Linuo, Sunrain, and Sangle. Around 20 percent of Chinese solar water heater manufacturers operated internationally and the other firms were active domestically at the national and/or regional levels (Tong and Warren, 2010).

c. Hydropower

With a 213 GW total installed hydropower capacity, mainly located in the western and southern provinces, China was the world's leader in hydropower at the end of 2010. The country's hydropower development has been greatly boosted by government support for the building of the Three Gorges Hydropower Station with a total installed capacity of 22.5 GW on the Yangtze River to be fully completed by 2015 (Shah, 2011, Xinhua, 2011a), and four hydroelectric dams, named Xiluodu, Xiangjiaba, Wudongde, and Baihetan, on the Jinsha River, which will have a combined capacity of 43 GW, almost doubling that of the Three Gorges Dam (Deng, 2011). Yet, the country is addressing the social and environmental issues connected to large-scale hydropower, such as population relocation, ecological disruption, and arable land disruption (Xinhua, 2007; Tullos, 2009; Fu et al., 2010). At the same time, local governments are involved in support for smaller, rural hydropower facilities with a 50 MW capacity or less. According to China's Water Resources Ministry, the total rural hydropower capacity will reach 74 GW by 2015, about 26 percent of total hydropower capacity by then (Xinhua, 2011b).

China's installed hydropower capacity is estimated to reach 380 GW by 2020, according to a 2011 analysis completed by China Research & Intelligence, and 450 GW by 2030, as called for by longer-term plans, more than double current levels (REN21, 2011).

d. Biomass

When biomass is used in digesters, the resulting biogas mixture can be up to 70 percent methane (Weisman, 2011). This renewable natural gas substitute from rudimentary small-scale digesters of solid waste is widely used in China's rural areas as a RE source for daily household cooking. Biogas methane can also be used to fuel engine generators and to produce electricity for single-home lighting, and heating households. Biomass heat markets are expanding steadily over the years. China was the world leader in the number of household biogas plants. About 22 million biogas systems were added between 2006 and 2010 and a total of 40 million systems were used in rural China in early 2010 (REN21, 2011).

However, with inefficiencies in transporting biomass feed stocks to centralized locations being a major hurdle, biomass has yet to realize its full potential as a source of grid-connected electric power in China. Its capacity rose about 25 percent in 2010 to 4 GW of capacity using a combination of sugarcane bagasse, solid biomass, organic waste, and biogas, including from livestock wastes (REN21, 2011).

Larger biogas projects from collectives can operate cogeneration facilities providing thermal energy for heating or hot water. Biomass-fueled electricity is generally considered to be carbon-neutral, but biomass is a very small part of China's overall centralized electricity production. Development of biomass projects connected to the grid is expected to be limited to areas with abundant biomass resources in order to promote direct-fired biomass electric power generation plants. But with modern technology and expanded capacity potential, current biogas engines manufactured by the likes of GE are capable of churning natural waste into large amounts of renewable energy. In Nanyang, Henan Province, for instance, a 36-megawatt power station running GE engines is being installed in one of the nation's largest ethanol plants to produce electricity for use on the regional grid within the plant itself. The station is expected to reduce annual carbon emissions by 1.1 million tons. Certain biogas processes are also capable of producing energy for chemical production and vehicle fuel (REN21, 2011).

As the world's second-largest consumer of corn and the producer of half the world's pork, China experienced wide-spread pollution from this industry and is in urgent need to install biogas digesters. The national pollution survey of 2010 estimated that 406 million tons of animal waste was dumped into waterways in 2007. Now biogas digesters are mandated for farms with over 1,000 cattle, 10,000 pigs, or 100,000 chickens. Despite the availability of multiple subsidies at state, provincial and local levels, only about 3 percent of China's large and medium-sized operations currently have installed proper biogas digesters to handle waste (REN21, 2011). According to statistics, the annual biogas output in China is 14.3 billion cubic meters, an equivalent to 21.6 million TCEs, which can reduce more than 52.6 million tons of CO_2 emissions (Wang et al., 2010; Zhao, 2011).

Research shows that desertified sandy land has been a significant contributor to CO_2 emissions (Duan et al., 2001). To combat this serious problem and arrest desertification in China, programs of generating biomass energy were developed and implemented. For example, planting fast growing willow trees and harvest them for energy sprang up in affected regions. A power plant in Inner Mongolia burns as much as 200,000 tons of willow annually, producing 210 million kWh of electricity (REN21, 2011; Zhao and Yan, 2011).

Renewable energy sector created more jobs in China. In 2010, wind power provided 150,000 jobs in China compared with 630,000 jobs worldwide; solar hot water 250,000 jobs in China, versus 300,000 jobs worldwide; solar PV 120,000 jobs in China, almost one third of 350,000 jobs worldwide (REN21, 2011).

The development of wind power generation is representative of the country's accomplishments, as installed wind power capacity has risen from 0.567 GW in 2003 to 41.82 GW in 2010 (Ryser, 2011). China has become the world's largest solar-panel manufacturer by output, which accounted for around 70 percent of the global solar-energy market with an installed capacity of around 18 GW in 2010 (Li, 2011). At the same time, the country passed the United States as the world's top builder and installer of wind turbines. It planned to further grow its wind power capacity to 150-200 GW by 2020 and to increase installed solar power capacity from less than 1 GW as of 2010 to over 50 GW by 2020 (Li, 2011).

6. Free Public Bike Rental: A Green Initiative in China

Once a famous "kingdom of bikes," China has experienced increasing problems of city air pollution, traffic congestion, lack of parking spaces with a sudden and sustained surge in private car consumption. To ease the problem, various green initiatives have been launched. One of them is free public bike rental.

Public bike sharing first appeared in Amsterdam, the Netherlands. In 1965, a radical organization placed un-locked white bikes on streets for public use free of charge. However, because of the lack of management, the project failed within a month, with all bikes either lost or destroyed in canals (Shirky, 2008). Thirty years later, public bikes reappeared in Copenhagen with designated public stations and some coin-based deposit system. However, because the bike borrowers were anonymous and deposits were insignificant, significant theft and loss remained a major problem for the public bike system. In recent years, the new-generation public bike systems appearing in many European cities such as Vélib' in Paris, the Vélo'v in Lyon and the Bicing in Barcelona, Spain started to use electronic, information integration, wireless communications and Internet technologies. North American cities such as New York, Washington, Montreal, also launched pilot or similar systems (DeMaio, 2009).

Beijing was the first city in China that launched a public bike system in 2005. Although Hangzhou was the second city following Beijing's example only three years later, the free public bike system launched by the Hangzhou Municipal Government was more successful and soon surpassed its first-mover counterpart in Beijing. The successful experience of the free bike rental program in Hangzhou then spread out to more than 30 other Chinese cities such as Suzhou, Wuhan, Tianjin, Shanghai, and Zhuzhou in Hunan (ITDP, 2011).

There are different investment models of public bike rental projects in China. The Hangzhou model is a public-investment model with the Hangzhou Public Bike Group as a subsidiary of the municipal public transit system, which was also responsible for building, operating and developing the Hangzhou public bike system. In contrast, the Wuhan's free public bike project was private-business model. It was invested by a private company, which operates based on proceeds generated from rentals of advertising kiosk spaces and other public resources at the bike rental stations (Xia, 2011).

Compared with public bike systems in other international cities, China's public bike programs stand out with features including free subscription and longer free rental times. The subscription fees are common for public bike systems in other cities in Europe, North America, and Asia. The Vélib' public bike rental subscriptions in Paris, for example, cost €1.70 per day, €8 per week or €29 per year. In China, except for the public bike rental cards launched in the preparation for the 2010 World Expo in Shanghai, there are no fees charged on the bike rental registrations or subscriptions in Chinese cities (ITDP, 2011).

In comparison to the free rental times for public bike systems in foreign cities, such half an hour for Vélib' public bike rental system in Paris, the free bike rental durations in Chinese cities are longer, for example one hour in Hangzhou and two hours in Wuhan (ITDP, 2011).

Some Chinese cities already have substantial fleets of free bikes. In Hangzhou, the first mover for free bike rental in China, already has a fleet of 60,600 rental bikes, which is significantly more than the Paris Vélib's fleet of 20,000 bikes. As a result, Hangzhou's 2050 free public bike stations are on average only less than 200 meters apart from each other while those in the Vélib' public bike rental system are about 300 meters apart from each other (ITDP, 2011).

Most free bike systems now use bike rental cards with refundable deposits. The Wuhan bike rental subscription was originally completely free of charge at the beginning and had 100 million subscribers. However, there were some serious managerial issues, such as "possessive rental," meaning some bike users did not return the bikes after use for extended hours. This sometimes caused a severe shortage of available rental bikes in circulation. Drawing on the common practices of other cities, Wuhan's public bike rental started to charge refundable deposits on bike rental subscriptions, at rates of ¥300 for local residents, ¥400 for non-residents, and ¥200 for low income families and students. Each rental longer than the initial 2 hours will cost ¥1 for one hour, and 3 consecutive late returns or one late return longer than 24 hours will freeze the bike rental card. This managerial change has been very effective. The charge of refundable deposit fees has virtually stopped the possessive rental and greatly reduced the problem of difficulty to rent bikes (Yang et al., 2011).

The bike sharing is already widely used in the early moving cities such as Hangzhou. A recent survey reveals that 30 percent of the public biking participants used the public service regularly as part of commute and 70 percent of them use it at least occasionally in their commute to work. 30 percent of the respondents replaced taxi trips. 78 percent of car-owner respondents replaced auto use; close to 50 percent of car households used it to replace bus transit. More than 80 percent of carless households used it to replace bus transit; 60 percent replaced walking, and 20 percent replaced taxi trips. This service caused some to use public transit more often and postpone auto purchase. The survey shows that the free public biking program reduced auto use, especially for car owners (Shaheen et al., 2011).

The increasing municipal free public bike rental programs in China can help reduce the needs of driving cars in the city, which can in turn ease many problems related to increased vehicle use in cities, such as air pollution, CO_2 emissions, traffic congestion, and the lack of parking spaces. The free public bike rental systems, when fully connected to and integrated in the municipal public transit systems, can also make the life in cities more convenient and healthy. However, there is an obvious need for dedicated bike lanes and improved managerial measures, such as providing real-time bike and parking availability information, more public bike stations and longer operation hours, and better bike maintenance to support and sustain these green projects in China and elsewhere.

7. Challenges to China's RE Industry

As part of the unprecedented environmental and ecological challenges, China also faces serious challenges in its greening efforts. Despite its recently gained leadership in wind energy deployment and in manufacturing wind turbines and solar panels, major challenges still exist and prevent the country's greening programs to become a quick and panacea solution to the severe environmental and ecological impacts of its rapidly growing economy. This section will focus on these challenges, which include among others the lack of research and development; RE market challenge; and the lack of local RE professionals.

a. Lack of Research and Development

As a developing country, China had virtually no financial resources and technical capacity for research and development of RE technologies when it embarked on implementing its RE support policy in 2005. Most technologies used for RE industry in China, particularly the key components of RE equipment, such gear boxes for wind turbines, have been imported. With the rapid deployment of RE technologies in the last few years, the lack of advanced R&D programs has become one of the main obstacles to meet the demand the rapid RE deployment and the new challenges resulting from the rapid RE deployment, such as low grid integration rate and related low efficiency of the installed RE capacities (Zhang et al., 2009).

For example, many installed wind farms could not be connected to the transmission grid because the installed wind turbines lack the capacity of supplying electricity on the low voltage power lines and many new wind projects could not start because utility companies did not have sufficient funds and technological capacity to modernize power lines to accommodate these projects (Kwok, 2009).

Facing these new challenges, China has begun to pay more attention to R&D of advanced RE technologies. However, most advanced R&D activities are carried out by individual RE businesses. The R&D capacity in universities, research academies and institutes is extremely weak, lacking RE technology innovation manpower and facilities.

b. RE Market Challenge

RE market challenge has been especially obvious for China's solar PV manufacturing sector because of the global financial and economic crisis. Its solar panel manufacturing was more severely impacted by the crisis than the wind sector for several reasons. First, solar energy technologies are more costly. Second, China's solar PV sector heavily relied on overseas markets before the financial crisis. Third, the overseas solar panel demand was significantly reduced during the global financial crisis (Solangi et al., 2011).

Facing these market challenges, China designed and implemented solar power support policies and programs to encourage China's solar PV industry to explore the domestic market. Recent solar FIT provision from China's national government, for example, is expected to create an interest in investing in a strong and stable domestic solar market. Increased deployment of the solar power technologies on China's domestic market can be seen as a turning point and a more sustainable solution for China's solar PV industry (Hook, 2011; Montgomery, 2011; REN21, 2011; SEMI PV et al., 2011; Solangi et al., 2011).

c. Lack of Local RE Professionals

The lack of local RE professional in the public and private energy sectors, including developers, senior strategist, planners, and technicians, is a major challenge for China's renewable energy sector. Introducing more professional programs and training courses on RE sources in universities, research institutions, technical schools, and other professional schools will help meet the current high demand for professionals and professional expertise in the RE industry.

d. Rare-Earth Conflict

The rare-earth conflict, in which China is involved with major Western countries, such the USA, the EU, and Japan, is a challenge for both China's solar energy sector and world solar energy sector. Rare earths are the core material used for manufacturing photovoltaic solar panels. The relationship of the supply and demand of rare earths has a vital impact on its price and the price of photovoltaic solar panels. China has approximately 36 percent of the world's rare-earth deposits, but produces currently around 97 percent of the global supply. In response to the falling demand for and the falling price of rare earth in the aftermath of the world financial crisis and in the anticipated shortage of meeting the annual 10–15 percent growth in rare-earth demand within two to three years, China started to implement more stringent controls over its previously under-regulated rare-earths industry.

Citing concerns over environmental impacts and overexpansion, China cut its rare-earth exports 72 percent in early 2010 and a further 11 percent in the first half of 2011 through tough pollution controls in late 2010 and rare earth export quotas (An, 2011) that are likely to further restrict rare-earth extraction and processing. This caused rare earth prices to rise of 300–700 percent for various rare-earth elements. The USA, the EU, and Japan filed a complaint with the WTO about China's rare-earth price manipulation and export control. The Chinese government, however, denies manipulation of rare earths prices, emphasizing the environmental impacts of re-earth mining and the need of correcting unreasonably low rare earths prices. (Xinhuanet, 2011).

Conclusions

This study explored the legislative, administrative, and fiscal tools China has been using to grow renewables and other sustainable activities, its greening accomplishments, and the challenges China faces as a developing country in its greening efforts.

It first examined the legislative, administrative green economic tools China utilizes to green its economy to solve the dilemma its faces in its economic development. The study found that Chinese decision makers have been well aware of the impact of CO_2 emissions-induced climate change on its sustainability and have become increasingly active in addressing the impacts of its rapidly growing economy.

To achieve this goal, China established the legislation promoting renewables development and generation. Various laws and five-year plans, such as the Electricity Law of 1995, the Energy Efficiency Law of 1997, the National Climate Change Program of 2007, the 11th Five Year Plan mandating the energy intensity reduction, the Law for Prevention and Control of Air Pollution of 1995 and 2000, and the Renewable Energy Law of 2005, established the necessary goals and mandates for a more sustainable economy, for example, by providing the improvement of its energy efficiency by 20 percent by 2010.

As a result of implementing these legislative provisions on greening China's economy, China succeeded in an annual reduction of over 1 billion tons of CO_2 since 2005 compared with a business as usual scenario despite its early lack of official quantified commitment to CO_2 emissions reduction. Guided by its new dedicated vision of carbon reduction, China recently established new carbon reduction goals, such as carbon intensity reduction by 40–45 percent by 2020 and 15 percent share of RE sources in the energy by 2020 and has initiated one of the world's most remarkable carbon reduction initiatives in recent years. However, the country has to improve its implementation mechanism significantly by more forcefully using market oriented tools such as taxes and incentives to achieve its greening goals.

At the same time, the paper also examined China's green research and development programs. It found that China has invested heavily in green research and development programs, such as the Key Technology Research and Development Program initiated in 1982 and implemented through four subsequent five-year plans, the "863" National High-Tech Program, the "973" National Basic Research Program created in March 1997, and the more recent renewable energy generation targets.

In this regard, China is considered having benefited greatly from its more effective policy-making processes and its recent insight that building and developing manufacturing capacity for its RE industry can not only increase its international sustainability competitiveness, but also help the country solve unprecedented environmental and climate challenges of its economic growth. It made serious legal, fiscal, and administrative efforts to promote a greener, low-carbon economy. In recent years, China set ambitious targets for developing its non-hydropower RE sources with a major push of laws, policies, and incentives. Because of these efforts, China has made remarkable achievements in its strategic shift from a quantity-based growth policy to a quality-based sustainable development policy.

The chapter examined China's use of incentives and subsidies to promote RE development. It found that the country acted aggressively at the height of the financial crisis in 2008. China invested $140 billion in renewable energy industry as its "green" stimulus packages, and implemented these RE Incentives and Subsidies through various tools, such as subsidies on investments and tax incentives for production, and feed-in tariffs (FITs) for wind power and solar energy. By using these policy tools, China has been able to achieve a widely acknowledged "global green leadership" in the major renewable markets and free urban bike programs.

The chapter also looked into China's weaknesses in RE as a developing country. It found that despite the worldwide recognition of its greening accomplishments, China faces significant challenges ahead to further improve its energy efficiency and reduce its carbon intensity. The main challenges include lack of research and development, RE market challenges, lack of local RE professionals, and rare-earth conflict.

In general, the chapter finds that the carbon-intensity reduction program China recently announced seems to be more suitable to meet the country's needs to both further develop its economy and to mitigate its expanding climate impact. Compared with its existing energy efficiency program, the program reducing carbon intensity adopted a reasonable quantified approach to its carbon reduction and is able to achieve better carbon reducing result because it consciously addresses the issue of relatively high GDP-based carbon emissions intensity and aims at reducing its carbon intensity over a planned period of time.

The findings in this chapter have multiple implications for our understanding and knowledge of green economics. First, this study can help scholars and practitioners evaluate China's policymaking choices on more effective strategic solutions to mitigate its ever-expanding CO_2 emissions in its ambitious economic development. China's greening experience shows that its green legislation, investments and programs have achieved, contrary to the common fear of negative effects, positive effects on its economic development and reduced the negative impacts of its coal-dependent economic development.

This experience provides a good lesson for researchers and professionals not only in the developing countries like China and India, but also in the developed countries like the USA, Canada and Australia, which are severely divided on and paralyzed in acting on greening policies for fear of their negative impacts on the economic growth. More importantly, China's success shows that its greening accomplishments have, like Germany's, increased its international competitiveness because the green technological capabilities and development meet the new market needs in the green transformation. Countries that have used proactive instruments in the greening transformation have shown more strength in resisting economic and financial crises and countries that were reluctant to do so have displayed a significantly larger vulnerability to economic and financial crises.

The findings of China's challenges in greening its economy call not only for avoiding the premature declaration of China as a green leader, but also for recognizing the necessity of collaboration between China and the developed countries like the USA in developing RE. The Greening collaboration is not only mutually beneficial to both developing countries' and developed countries' economies and the global economy, but also vitally beneficial to the planet's sustainability.

References

Bloomberg News. (2010) "VW to offer electric cars in China." *Toronto Star*, November 9, B9.

Buckley, Tim (2012) "How – and why – China leads in green economy." *Renew Economy*, February 1.

Campbell, Richard J. (2010) "China and the United States—A Comparison of Green Energy Programs and Policies." *Congressional Research Service*. June 14.

Center for American Progress (CAP). (2010) "Out of the Running? How Germany, Spain, and China Are Seizing the Energy Opportunity and Why the USA Risks Getting Left Behind." March.

Chan, Yvonne. (2009). "China sets FIT for wind power plants: Move will help struggling wind project operators boost profitability." 27 July, www.businessgreen.com/bg/news/1801182/china-sets-feed-tariff-wind-power-plants.

China Daily. (2010) "China sets on-grid price for 4 solar power stations." April 12, www.chinadaily.com.cn/bizchina/2010-04/12/content_9718668.htm.

Chinese Renewable Energy Industries Association (CREIA). (2011) "Sector Review of Renewable Energy in China and Its Potential for CDM Projects."

China Environmental Culture Promotion Association (CECPA) and the China Institute of Development Strategy Studies (CIDSS). (2008) "Research on China's Carbon Balance Trading Framework." November 10.

China International Investment Promotion Platform (CIIPP). (2011) "China Will Reduce Investment in Seven Emerging Strategic Industries." July 11. www.ciipp.com/en/index/view-437101.html

China.org. (1997) "Law of the People's Republic of China on Conserving Energy." Adopted at the 28th Meeting of the Standing Committee of the Eighth National People's Congress on November 1. www.china.org.cn/english/environment/34454.htm

Chow, Gregory C. (2007) "China's Energy and Environmental Problems and Policies." <u>CEPS Working Paper No. 152</u>, August JEL classification: O13, P28, Q5.

Cohen-Tanugi, David. (2010) "Putting it into Perspective: China's Carbon Intensity Target." *NRDC White Paper*, October.

DeMaio, P. (2009) "Bicycle-Sharing: History, Impacts, Models of Provision, and Future", *Journal of Public Transportation*, 12(4), 41-56.

Deng, Shasha. (2011) Nation to build new hydroelectric power plants, June 23, news.xinhuanet.com/english2010/business/2011-06/23/c_13945787.htm

Duan, Zhenghu; Xiao, Honglang; Dong, Zhibao; He, Xingdong and Wang, Gang. (2001) "Estimate of Total CO_2 Output from Desertified Sandy Land in China." *Atmospheric Environment* 35(34):5915-5921.

Electric Power Law of the People's Republic of China (EPL). (1996)

Fairley, Peter. (2009) "China's Potent Wind Potential: Forecasters see no need for new coal and nuclear power plants." *MIT Technology Review*, September 14.

Finamore, Barbara. (2009a) "Solar Subsidies in China." April 7, switchboard.nrdc.org/blogs/bfinamore/solar_subsidies_in_china.html.

Finamore, Barbara. (2009b) "Testimony before the Select Committee on Energy Independence and Global Warming USA House of Representatives." Hearing on "Preparing for Copenhagen: How Developing Countries are Fighting Climate Change." March 4.

Finamore, Barbara. (2010) "China Records Its Climate Actions By Copenhagen Accord Deadline." February 1, switchboard.nrdc.org/blogs/bfinamore/china_records_its_climate_acti.html.

Fu, Bo-Jie; Wu, Bing-Fang; Lü, Yi-He; Xu, Zhi-Hong; Cao, Jing-Hua; Niu, Dong; Yang, Gui-Shan; and Zhou, Yue-Min. (2010) "Three Gorges Project: Efforts and challenges for the environment." *Progress in Physical Geography* 34: 741.

Gnansounou, Edgard; Dong, Jun and Bedniaguine, Denis. (2004) "The strategic technology options for mitigating CO_2 emissions in power sector: assessment of Shanghai electricity-generating system." *Ecological Economics* 50(1-2):117-133.

gov.cn (2006) *11th Five Year Plan of China*, www.gov.cn/english/special/115y_index.htm.

Hook, Leslie. (2011) "China backing for solar power." *Financial Times*, August 1.

Howell, Thomas R.; Noellert, William A.; Hume, Gregory & Wolff, Alan. (2010) "China's Promotion of the Renewable Electric Power Equipment Industry Hydro, Wind, Solar, Biomass." Press release by the National Foreign Trade Council, March.

Hu, Angang. (2011) "Green light for hard targets." March 28. news.xinhuanet.com/english2010/indepth/2011-03/28/c_13801248.htm.

Information Office of the State Council (IOSC). (2011) "China's Policies and Actions for Addressing Climate Change." State Council, People's Republic of China, November, Beijing.

Institute for Transportation and Development Policy (ITDP). (2011) *Public Bike*. www.publicbike.net/defaulten.aspx.

International Energy Agency (IEA). (2011) *Clean Energy Progress Report: IEA Input to the Clean Energy Ministerial*, June, www.iea.org.

International Energy Agency Clean Coal Centre (IEA CCC). (2011) *Database*, www.iea-coal.org.uk/site/2010/home.

Kwok, Vivian Wai-yin. (2009) "Alternative Energy. Weaknesses In Chinese Wind Power." July 20. www.forbes.com/2009/07/20/china-wind-power-business-energy-china.html.

Li, Jing. (2010) "Carbon trading in pipeline." *China Daily*, July 22.

Li, Jingjing; Zhuang, Xing; DeLaquil, Pat; Larson, Eric D. (2001) "Biomass energy in China and its potential." *Energy for Sustainable Development*, 5(4) December.

Li, Mu. (2010) "China solidifying its lead in clean tech market", *People's Daily*, December 23.

Lin, Liza; Ying, Tian; Huang, Zhe. (2010) "China to Subsidize Alternative Energy Car Purchases." *Bloomberg*, June 1. www.businessweek.com/news/2010-06-01/china-to-subsidize-alternative-energy-car-purchases-update2-.html.

Martinot, Eric and Li, Junfeng. (2010) "Renewable Energy Policy Update for China." July 21, *Renewable   Energy   World*, www.renewableenergyworld.com/rea/news/article/2010/07/renewable-energy-policy-update-for-china.

Mehta, Shyam. (2011) "PV News Annual Data Collection Results: 2010 Cell, Module Production Explodes Past 20 GW." May 9. greentechmedia.com/articles/read/pv-news-annual-data-collection-results-cell-and-module-production-explode-p/

Ministry of Science and Technology of PR China (MOST). (2006a) "Key Technologies R&D Program."   *S&T*   *Programs*. www.most.gov.cn/eng/programmes1/200610/t20061009_36224.htm.

Ministry of Science and Technology of PR China (MOST). (2006b) "National High-tech R&D Program   (863   Program)."   *S&T*   *Programs*. www.most.gov.cn/eng/programmes1/200610/t20061009_36225.htm.

Ministry of Science and Technology of PR China (MOST). (2006c) "Mega-projects of Science Research   for   the   10th   Five-Year   Plan."   *Science   and   Technology   Programs*, www.most.gov.cn/eng/programmes1/200610/t20061008_36198.htm.

Montgomery, James. (2011) "China Stamps Solar FIT, But What Does It Mean?" *Renewable Energy World*, August 4. www.renewableenergyworld.com/rea/news/article/2011/08/china-stamps-solar-fit-but-what-does-it-mean.

Morales, Alex. (2011) "China Widens Lead over U.S. in Renewable Energy. Ranking by Ernst & Young." *Bloomberg Businessweek*, May 25. www.bloomberg.com/news/2011-05-25/china-widens-lead-in-renewable-energy-ranking-by-ernst-young.html.

National Development and Reform Commission (NDRC). (2007) "Medium and Long-Term Development Plan for Renewable Energy in China." September 4, *China Gate*, en.chinagate.cn/reports/2007-09/13/content_8872839.htm.

National Development and Reform Commission (NDRC). (2007) "The National Climate Change Program." *China.org.cn*, June 4. www.china.org.cn/english/environment/213624.htm.

National Renewable Energy Laboratory (NREL) and the China Renewable Energy Industries Association (CREIA). (2005). "Renewable Energy Policy in China: Overview." *NREL International Programs Fact Sheet*. www.nrel.gov/docs/fy04osti/35786.pdf.

Owen, Nick A.; Inderwildi, Oliver R. and King, David A. (2010) "The status of conventional world oil reserves—Hype or cause for concern?" *Energy Policy* 38(8): 4743-4749.

Pew Charitable Trusts. (2011) *Who's Winning the Clean Energy Race? G-20 Investment Powering Forward. 2010 edition*. March 29, www.pewenvironment.org/news-room/reports/whos-winning-the-clean-energy-race-2010-edition-329291.

Price, Lynn; Wang, Xuejun; and Yun, Jiang. (2010) The Challenge of Reducing Energy Consumption of the Top-1000 Largest Industrial Enterprises in China." *Energy Policy*, 38(8). August.

Qiang, Xiaoji. (2011) "Plans for emerging industries to be submitted to Cabinet: NDRC." *China Daily*, March 1, www.chinadaily.com.cn/business/2011-03/01/content_12097012.htm.

Renewable Energy Policy Network for the 21st Century (REN21). (2011) *Renewables 2011: Global Status Report*, Paris: REN21 Secretariat.

Renewable Energy Policy Network for the 21st Century (REN21). (2009) "REN21 Recommendations for Improving the Effectiveness of Renewable Energy Policies in China." October.
www.ren21.net/Portals/97/documents/Publications/Recommendations_for_RE_Policies_in_China.pdf

Reuters. (2009) "China to shut more small power plants in 2010." December 28.

Rhein, Eberhard. (2010) "Germany defines sustainable energy policy up to 2050." September 19, rhein.blogactiv.eu/2010/09/13/germany-defines-sustainable-energy-policy-up-to-2050.

Rutter, Michael Patrick. (2009) "China could meet its energy needs by wind alone: Study suggests wind ecologically, economically practical." *Harvard Gazette*, September 10, news.harvard.edu/gazette/story/2009/09/china-energy-needs-wind/.

Ryser, Jeffrey (2011) "Wind power installation slowed in 2010, outlook for 2011 stronger: AWEA." *Platts*, 24 January.

SEMI PV Group, SEMI China PV Advisory Committee, and China PV Industry Alliance (CPIA). "China's Solar Future. A Recommended China PV Policy Roadmap 2.0." April 2011.

Shah, Abhishek. (2011) "List of World's Largest Hydroelectricity Plants and Countries: China Leading in building Hydroelectric Stations." *Green World Investor*, March 29, greenworldinvestor.com/2011/03/29/list-of-worlds-largest-hydroelectricity-plants-and-countries-china-leading-in-building-hydroelectric-stations/.

Shaheen, Susan A.; Zhang, Hua; Martin, Elliot; and Guzman, Stacey. (2011) "Hangzhou Public Bicycle: Understanding Early Adoption and Behavioral Response to Bikesharing in Hangzhou, China." *TRB Annual Meeting*, January 25.

Shi, Jane; and Zhao, Shelly. (2011) "An Overview of China's Renewable Energy Market." *China Briefing*, June.

Shirky, Clay. (2008) *Here Comes Everybody: The Power of Organizing Without Organizations*. Penguin, 282–283.

Shirouzu, Norihiko; Liu, Li; Zhang, Kersten. (2010) "China to Subsidize Electric Cars." *The Wall Street Journal, Eastern Edition*, June 2, 255(127): B3.

SNEC. (2009) "China launches 'Golden Sun' subsidies for 500 MW of PV projects by 2012." www.snec.org.cn/Read_e.asp?ID=8582.

Solangi, K.H.; Saidur, R.; Rahim, N.A.; Fayaz, H. and Islam, M.R. (2011) "Present Solar Energy Potential and Strategies in China." *IPCBEE* 6(1): 184–187.

Sustainable Development Technology Foundation (SDT) and China's Energy Research Institute of the National Development and Reform Commission (NDRC-ERI). (2010) "Low Carbon City Forum Report." Beijing.

Tong, Ivan and Warren, Ben. (2010) "Quick Look: Renewable Energy Development in China." www.renewableenergyworld.com.

Tullos, Desiree. (2009) "Assessing the influence of environmental impact assessments on science and policy: An analysis of the Three Gorges Project." *Journal of Environmental Management* 90(3):208–S223.uk.reuters.com/article/2009/12/28/china-power-

United Nations Development Programme (UNDP). (2010) "China and a Sustainable Future: Towards a Low Carbon Economy and Society", *China Human Development Report 2009/2010*.

Wang, Hongjiang. (2008) "Green governance ranking list to come in months in China." March 11. news.xinhuanet.com/english/2008-03/11/content_7767853.htm.

Wang, Qin; Wen, Fushuan; Yang, Aimin; and Huang, Jiansheng. (2011) "Cost Analysis and Pricing Policy of Wind Power in China." *Journal of Energy Engineering, Technical Papers*, 137(3).

Watson, Jim. (2011) "China's low-carbon leadership headlines fail to capture the reality." *Guardian*, April 18.

Watts, Jonathan. (2011) "China to impose green tax on heavy polluters." *Guardian*, February 4, www.guardian.co.uk/world/2011/feb/04/china-green-tax-polluters.

Weisman, Warren. (2011) "Gas from the Past: Biogas 101." *Renewable EnergyWorld*.com, 4 January.

World Wildlife Fund, China (WWF-China). (2009) "Low carbon city initiative in China." www.wwfchina.org/english/sub_loca.php?loca=1&sub=96

Xia, Yi. (2011) "Value of Advertising Packaging for Public Bike Shelters in Wuhan." *Packaging Engineering*, December, en.cnki.com.cn/Article_en/CJFDTOTAL-BZGC201112024.htm.

Xie, Zhenhua. (2011) "Climate change challenge." *China Daily* (March 3).

Xinhua. (2007) "China warns of environmental 'catastrophe' from Three Gorges Dam." news.xinhuanet.com/english/2007-09/26/content_6796636.htm.

Xinhua. (2011a) "China's Three Gorges Project to be completed in five years." February 25, news.xinhuanet.com/english2010/china/2011-02/25/c_13750348.htm.

Xinhua. (2011b) "China's rural hydropower capacity to hit 74 million kw by 2015." May 7, news.xinhuanet.com/english2010/china/2011-05/07/c_13863961.htm.

Xinhuanet. (2011) "China denies manipulation of rare earths prices." July 21. news.xinhuanet.com/english2010/china/2011-07/21/c_131000442.htm.

Zhang, Peidong; Yang, Yanli; Shi, Jin; Zheng Yonghong; Wang, Lisheng; Li, Xinrong. (2009) "Opportunities and challenges for renewable energy policy in China." *Renewable and Sustainable Energy Reviews*, 13 439–449.

2.2 Strategies for a Sustainable City, Thimpu

By Jigme Tashi Tsering

Thimphu is the Capital of the Kingdom of Bhutan, a small kingdom situated north of India and South of China

Introduction
The rapid growth of cities has become the most striking feature of human civilization. Cities have depleted earth's resources by draining the fertility without replenishing it. They have exhausting the forests, watershed and in the process discarding vast quantities of waste and pollution.

Sustainability needs to be addressed if mankind is to continue to live in cities and continue to flourish on this planet. We need to find a viable relationship between cities and the living world – a relationship not parasitic but symbiotic, or mutually supportive (Girardet, 1992).

(c) Jigme Tashi Tsering

Photo: Bhutan (Photos kindly provided by the author of this chapter: Jigme Tashi Tsering)

In this article an attempt will be made to describe the situation of Thimphu city and the type of strategies that will make the city sustainable. While the city will never be entirely sustainable this attempt at reducing use of natural resources, reusing resources, use of additional renewable energy source aims to reduce the impact of the city on the environment and in the process also combat climate change.

Background

Geography
Bhutan is a land-locked country in the Himalayas having a population of 672,425 people (PHCB, 2005). Bhutan has an area of 38,394 Km^2 and borders China in the North and India in the South, East & West.

The Capital City Thimphu is located in the western region with a population of 98,676 (PHCB, 2005).

Environment
The Government has a policy of maintaining 60% of areas under forest cover. In 2005, 68% of total area was under forest cover (NECS, 2002).

Economy
The back bone of the economy is hydropower. Export of hydropower to India accounts for 60% of total revenue.

Kyoto Protocol
Bhutan is a signatory to the Kyoto protocol under the United Nations Convention on Climate Change. Bhutan's annual emission of CO_2 per-capita was 0.2 ton as compared to the world average of 4.5 ton in 2004 (UNDP, 2007).

While no targets have been set for reduction of Carbon Dioxide, Bhutan is committed to reducing GHG (NEC, 2000). Mitigation programs currently being implemented:

- Renewable energy technology options

- Improved technology to reduce fuel wood consumptions

- Introduction of fuel-efficient vehicles

- Improvement of imported fossil fuel quality

Bhutan has to date successfully constructed and commissioned a 70 kW Clean Development Mechanism micro hydropower project in Chendebji village with the objective to reduce GHG. The project commission in 2005 has reduced CO_2 emission by 593 tons, by replacing the need of kerosene, firewood and diesel by the villagers.

Energy

Bhutan generates about 1488 MW of electricity from hydropower of which it consumes 152 MW (BEA, 2005). However with global warming and glaciers receding fast, there is a need to depend on other renewable energy sources in the future.

According to the Population and Housing Census 2005, the main sources of fuels are firewood (37.2%), electricity (30.6%), LPG (25.5%) and the remaining from other sources.

While Bhutan has an abundant clean source of energy there is still abundant use of fuel wood. Even though Carbon dioxide is a GHG, fuel wood burning is not considered a GHG as it is absorbed when trees are planted. However, the burning of wood results in deforestation which damages the environment, effects the water shed (water source) and at the same time reduces the carbon sink potential.

It was found that most of the 6,982 households and over 1000 institutions in Thimphu still use fuel wood for cooking and heating purposes. For example on an average each school consumes about 15 truckloads of firewood every year (GEF, 2006).

Strategies to reduce fuel wood demand:

Replace traditional stoves with efficient improved cooking stoves will reduce the consumption of firewood. Such stoves can save up to 40% of fuel compared to traditional stoves. This puts less pressure on forest & energy recourses in addition to reducing GHG (Shrestha, S.K & Thapa, R. 1999).

- Use of sawdust briquette as an alternative fuel source

- Switch to electrical appliances instead of wood stoves (as electricity from hydropower)

- Use of alternative renewable energy source such as solar energy

- Most institution use fuel wood as a source of energy for heating water for having bath

- Switch to solar hot water system (SHWS) would result in decrease of demand for fuel wood

- For example a nunnery in Thimphu used to use five truck load of fire wood per year. With use of SHWS, three truckloads of fuel wood use is reduced a year (GEF, 2006)

- Solar power generation is considered a prominent form of clean energy that avoids GHG Emissions

- One KW of Solar power capacity avoids one MT of annual CO_2 emissions (Kaur, R. 2008)

Building Designs

Houses in Thimphu are poorly designed. Improving the designs of house can result in saving of energy and money in the long run.

One of the main sources of CO_2 is energy required for space heating. Improvements in building design can reduce energy consumption. In a new house, windows typically account for 15% to 30% of the total heat loss. With good design, large areas of glass window can save energy through passive solar heating gains. While initial cost of glazed window is high they will eventually pay for itself – for example, window with low energy coating cost about 10-15% more than conventional double glazed units, but they reduce energy loss up to 18% (Woolley, T & Kimmins, S. 2000).

In the same way using advance insulation materials can actually reduce the energy consumption of buildings by as much as 90% (Girardet, H. 1992).

Bhutan has a strict procedure to approve building designs prior to construction. In addition to checking structural integrity, the government agency should encourage eco-friendly practices. While initial cost might be more, building with good energy saving features can be viewed as an *eco-friendly* house and will eventually have greater market value as energy saving would compensate for the higher investment. This is in contrast the current practice of poorly insulated houses being constructed at the lowest possible cost. The result is that building owners also charging minimal rent but energy consumption of individual households are high. While the financial outcome may be same, there is more energy use in the latter.

The documentation of design and materials used in building now, is a good practice. This provides the ideal opportunity for incorporating building efficiencies. In addition during demolition of buildings it helps in efficiently sorting materials which can be later be used for recycling (Lawson, B. 1996).

Use of energy saving devices
Most buildings in Thimphu use incandescent bulbs. Switching to use of low-energy fluorescent light can save 70% power. Although they cost more initially they last longer and soon pay back the extra cost in the energy saving they make (Elliott, D. 2003).

Strategy for energy conservation
Environment preserved by:

- better fuel efficient stoves

- better building design

- reduced use of fuel wood due to use of alternate energy

- Social

- decrease in health hazard from indoor air pollution

- improved quality of life

- Economic

- While initial economic costs of these investments are high, in the long run they will pay back / benefit the community

- government can play a major part in influence the demand by affecting the supply cost by either taxation or subsidy such as by:

- No tax on electrical heaters and rice cooker appliances

- Subsidy on energy saving appliances

- Subsidy on briquette stoves to encourage use of sawdust briquette

- Subsidy on house insulation materials

- Increase in royalty on fuel wood

- Cost sharing basis by government for renewable energy

Transport

Bhutan imported about 70,047 metric tons of oil equivalent in 2005 which were used for *transportation*, lighting, cooking and heating purposes (DOE, 2005).

With inadequate public transport, cars have been an essential means of mobility by which individuals commute. As per the Road Safety and Transport Authority (RSTA), there are 19,000 vehicles in Thimphu in 2008 with the number increasing at 17% annually (RSTA, 2003).

A major source of air pollution in Thimphu is the combustion of fossil fuels from vehicle emission. Study conducted by the National Environment Commission (NEC) found that emission levels was found to be high in vehicles with 60% of petrol and 96% of diesel engine vehicles not meeting Indian emission standards (BSoE, 2001).

In fact, it was found that pollutants of vehicle as one of the main causes for acute respiratory tract diseases in Thimphu. A health study showed that acute respiratory tract disease had increased from 10.08% in 1990 to 14.02% in 1998 (BSoE, 2001).

More cars mean more pollution. In addition use of cars has a disadvantage to community. Cars not only pollute the atmosphere but also take away valuable space. It is estimated that "one hundred people in a bus need only 40 square meters of road space" whereas "one hundred people in cars travelling by themselves need some 2000 square meters" (Girardet, 1992).

Car based planning are destroying public spaces, and detaching bonds within community. High volume and speeding traffic causes people to retreat from street-based community. This results in social disintegration and isolation. Reliable public transport is therefore the only option to give back more public space to the community.

Vehicles not only need resources for production but also needs energy during operation. Pendakur (cited in Girardet, 1992) reports that "cars use 1860 calories per passenger mile, bus 920, rail 885, walking 100 and bicycles 35 calories per passenger mile". Hence we can see that the bus uses much less energy than car and should be the mode of travel.

From Pendakurs report we can see that bicycles use the least energy. To encourage bicycle usage, and to ensure that it is save and convenient as possible, it is vital that roads and facilities are of suitable standards. Hence Roads Authorities should constructed or rebuilt road with minimum recommended lane width so the bicycles can be safely included in the general flow of traffic (Healey, K. 1996).

The strategy for a sustainable city aims to reduce energy demand, reduce pollution & free more space for the community.

Strategy for transport sector

- Impose high tax on import of cars

- Policy to import fuel efficient vehicles

- Import good quality fuel

- Legal framework to control vehicle emissions

- Introduce reliable public transport system

- Subsidy for buying bicycles

- Improved footpath for pedestrians

A good public transport for Thimphu can be a bus or tram system that runs on electricity as the source of energy from renewable hydropower is within Bhutan.

Economic

- With less car pollution there will be decrease in health related illness, which will decrease health expenses of the government *as health care in Bhutan is free*

- Government health sector resources could be invested into the transport sector

- Higher tax on cars can help fund public transport

- Socially

- *class barriers* are not created, which will allow for an environment for interaction between people

- No financial pressure to invest limited resources in expensive vehicle. Hence it frees resources of people to be used in other meaningful ways.

Environment

- Use of public transport and bicycle will put less pressure on the atmosphere

- Decrease in demand for non renewable *petroleum* based fossil fuel

Water Demand

With a population of 98,676 people (PHCB, 2005) and with water demand at 125 liters per person per day (DUDES, 2006), Thimphu required 12,335.5 cum of water per day.

Thimphu's two water treatment plants supply of 15,000 cum per day is more than adequate currently.

However with the population growing rate of Thimphu of 10% per annum (NEC 1998), the current water supply of 15,000 cum per day will only be able to provide water for a population above 120,000. Hence water conservation measures have to be taken to ensure that water is available in the future.

Strategy for water sector

Rain water harvesting systems

- Thimphu is an ideal city for rain water harvesting as most building have Corrugated Metal Sheet roofing

- rainwater harvesting is sustainable as there is rainfall throughout the year

- Government needs to promote rainwater harvesting by inculcating social acceptance and pride in technology that preserves the environment

- Financial investment is minimal with building owners required to purchase *gutter* for channeling of water to tank, a tank, and an electric motor to pump the water from lower tank to existing tank

- Saving on water is an economic incentive for people

- Less energy is required to treat water thereby benefiting the environment

- The government can influence the demand by affecting the supply cost by either taxation or subsidy.

- Increasing the tariff on water to discourage use

- Subsidize water saving devices such as efficient shower heads, shower timers etc.

- Policies could be implemented such as all new construction being required to use dual flush toilets, water less urinals, all gardening to be done by grey water

Planning

Thimphu was establishment in 1955 as the capital of Bhutan. Since then Thimphu has undergone many changes. The town plan of 1998 was to make Thimphu a dream city with a vibrant culture which is people and environment friendly.

With rapid increase in automobile numbers and pressure on public health infrastructure in the town centre, a new plan called the Thimphu Structural Plan was implemented in 2003. This plan after implementation would ensure Thimphu to be a sustainable and livable city.

This new structural plan put restriction on plot coverage as well as building height. While the objective was the reduce pressure at the center this also allowed for other considerations:

- With residential buildings restricted to three floors, *lifts* are not needed thereby elimination the use of electricity
- Concept of elders residing on ground floor, middle class on second floor and young couples at the top floors encourages older generation to live in cities
- With no lifts *there is more free space*

The structure plan being implemented is aimed at improving the access of people to services. This structural plan requires the creation of 15 urban villages which is created through participatory land pooling. All villages will have its own village square with shopping centers, playground, gardens and an express bus link connecting it to the urban centre. This ensures a local communal environment where all activities are close together and walking and cycling can be the mode of transport (DUDES, 2003).

The urban villages provide communal public areas which are essential for people to interact. Young people especially require public meeting space where they can strengthen their links with people around them. Otherwise they may turn to crime and increasingly to suicide (Healey, K. 1996).

Strategy to improve the life of the community:

- Coordinate social gathering that ensures communal spirit and bonding
- Initiate communal service centers such as washing machine services. Instead of each individual buying a machine, communal washing machine can still serve the needs of people and ensure optimal use. These actions reduce GHG.

The establishing urban villages are being implemented. As the urban villages get completed the villages remove the pressure on the urban center, which will allow the city centre to also become more livable.

Solid Waste

Thimphu has grown rapidly in the last few decades. With rapid urbanization, rural-urban migration, change in consumption habits and the high population growth rate have resulted in increase of waste generated.

Thimphu which generated 10 tons of waste daily in 2000 (USPS, 2000) is currently generating 64.5 tones of waste daily (Penjor, 2008). The waste generation of 0.3 kg per capita per day in 2001 (BSoE, 2001) has risen to 0.56 kg per capita per day in 2007 (Penjor, 2007). These wastes are being disposed of at Thimphu's only landfill site.

The tariff charged by the Municipal Corporation for the disposal of Solid waste is low. There is no limit restriction to the amount of waste disposed. Being a cheap method for waste disposal, there is no incentive for other viable economic methods of waste management.

As per a survey by Penjore (2008), the composition of waste by weight was 25% organic, 14% cardboard, 12% paper, glass 10%, plastic 5%, metal 4% and other the remaining. This revealed that recycling of waste at household level was minimal. In addition organic and green wastes are not composted. The decay of organic matter in absence of air also releases methane a harmful GHG.

The success of management of solid waste is crucial in the attitude and behavior of humans to the environment. The strategy for solid waste management should be to *reduce waste to the landfill:*

Strategy for solid waste sector

- Tariff for the waste for landfill should be charged based on quantity

- Increasing tariff would result in people reducing waste to land fill. Only waste with no value will be disposed as it cost people money to dispose of it. Waste such as paper, glass, metal, organic waste which have value could either be sold off for recycling

With increased tariff for waste disposal, recycling option can become economically viable. Recycling will:

- preserve the environment as the recycled resource does not require new raw materials

- uses less energy in processing recyclable materials than processing from raw materials

With increased tariff for waste disposal composting options can become economically viable

- Composting of organic matter and greens can produce manure

- Composting done properly would not generate methane, a GHG

- Manure can be sold

- Effective composting requires a right Carbon to Nitrogen (C/N) ratio of about 25-30:1. For example the mixing high C/N ratio such as sawdust, with low C/N ratio such as glass clippings or vegetable peels resulting with C/N ratio of 30 would allow compost activity to take place at optimum rate (Mason, J. 2003, p.43, 44).

- Waste such as sawdust from sawmill could be used in composting or converting to alternate source of fuel such as briquette.

- This would also encourage reduction of waste disposed into landfill and in the process promote value from waste material

Government should finance and provide technical expertise to encourage private business to take up recycling and composting

Cost of purchasing different bins for different waste should be subsidized. This will encourage segregation of waste at source

Increase in cost of disposal of construction waste will have positive impact on initiative to reuse old material

- most current industrial practices and systems are currently ecologically unsustainable

- Tucker and Treloar (1994) recommends that from an energy conservation and CO_2 emission viewpoint, recycling of building materials should be encouraged based on research

- It is essential to make use of resources a more natural systems, which are typically characterized by cyclical process (Lawson, 1994) and symbiotic, mutually dependent relationships (Allen,1994) for sustainability

These methods will:

- conserve materials and energy;

- generating less waste for landfill

Economic

- With the increase in tariff of disposing waste to the landfill, it becomes economically viable to compost which is valuable nutrient that has economic value

Social

- people can eat food from natural nutrients and not artificial fertilizers

Environmental

- With composting, valuable nutrients which could other wise have been lost is replaced back into the soil, closing the nutrient cycle

Sewerage

As per L. M Austin and S. J. Van Vuucen, human being excretes 500 liters of Urine and 50 liters of faeces per year.

While 50 liters of faeces is not difficult to manage, the mixing of faeces and urine when flushed with water as sewerage becomes a problem. That means 50 liters of faeces becomes 550 liters of polluted and unpleasant sewage.

The sewerage of Thimphu is piped into a sewerage treatment plant which currently has a treatment capacity of 3,060 m3/day (TCC, 2005). With increase in population, there is increase in demand of water for flushing and increase in energy needed for treating sewage.

Strategy for sewage sector

One strategy to reduce water demand for flushing in toilets and reduce energy demand for treatment of waste is to introduce the Urine Separating toilets (UST). What UST does is that, it separate urine (nutrients N,P,K) from mixing with faeces matter.

Advantage of the UST is:

- Lower water use with 0.1 to 0.3 liters of water is required to flush urine (Johansson et al., 2002) which is 90% reduction compared to half flush from standard 3/6 dual toilet

- Nutrients from Urine (N,P,K) can be used as concentrated fertilizer with only limited treatment prior to land application

- Energy consumption for nutrient removal at Sewage treatment plants can be reduced by source separation technology resulting in lower nutrient wastewater for treatment.

Based on calculations presented in *Annex A*, there is potentially a saving of 2250 m^3 of water per day. In addition there is a reduction of 2250 m^3 of sewage that does not require treatment per day and hence less energy use.

In addition to water saving and energy reduction, a life cycle analysis of different removal and recovery technology (Table 1) found that nutrients can be recovered energetically at *source* more efficient that either their *removal* at the Sewage Treatment Plant or from *new* production from natural source (Maurer et al. 2003).

Nutrients	Specific Energy required (de-nitrification and precipitation) at Sewage Treatment Plant	Specific Energy for production of traditional fertilizer
N	13 kWh/kg	13 kWh/kg
P	14 kWh/kg	8 kWh/kg

Table 1: Comparison of energy required for treatment at Sewage treatment plant & production of fertilizer

Source: Maurer et al. 2003

Hence, nutrient segregation at source is the most environmental friendly approach as it requires the minimal energy demand, which reduces GHG emission which otherwise would be emitted during the sewage treatment or during production of new fertilizers.

In effect UTS closes the nutrient circles as nutrients can again be put back into the fields as fertilizer.

Economic

- Practical problem is difficulty in collection of urine separately. With the existing sewage network, what can be done is that the urine is stored separately during the day. At night, the urine could be released and collected separately at the sewage treatment plant. This *method does not require infrastructure investment*

- Concentrated Urine with minimal treatment can be sold as fertilizer

- Urine separating toilet with flush provision can be easily retrofitted in standard toilet

- Additional land not required for expansion of sewage treatment plant

Social

- Urine separation with flush provision will make it more appealing

- *Reduces demand for water*, making it cheaper for people

- While use of urine as fertilizer may seem revolting, people are very adaptable in Bhutan and cheap cost will be a major incentive for use

Environmental

- *Reduces discharge of nutrients* to sewage treatment systems

- *Reduce volume of water demand*

- *Reduces demand for energy to treat waste*

- It potentially closes the nutrient cycle by returning nutrients to the field, which contributes to sustainability

Conclusion

According to the International Union for the conservation of Nature, "sustainable development improves people's quality of life within the context of the earth's carrying capacity'.

While Thimphu is a relatively small city by modern standards, the demands and impacts of the city's existence is clearly visible. This essay has identified issues that are crucial in making the city more sustainable:

- Energy efficiency

- Energy and water conservation

- Use of more renewable energy

- Efficient public transport

- Urban planning and livability of citizens

- Recycling of solid waste

- Solid waste composting

By reducing the demand on the natural resources and improving the living condition of people, the city will not only have a circular metabolism existence for sustainability but also have a liveable city where people can live in harmony with the environment.

Photo: Bhutan. (Photo: kindly provided by the author of this chapter

Annex A – Water saving and sewage reduction

(Note: Volume of water required and volume of sewage generated is calculated in Annexure B)

<u>Water saved</u> and <u>sewage reduced</u> when <u>comparing full flush toilet and urine separation toilet</u>

(for Thimphu city population per day)

Toilet type	Volume of water required per person per day (liters)	Population of Thimphu	Total water saved (liters)	Total water saved (cubic meter)	Remark
Full flush toilet	30				Total toilet use is 5 times per day x 6 liters of water = 30 liters
Urine Separation toilet	7.2				toilet use is 1 time for faeces and 4 times for urine = 1 x 6 liters + 4 times x 0. 3 liters = 7.2 liters
	22.8	98676	2249813	**2250**	

Toilet type	Volume of sewage per day	Population of Thimphu	Total sewage reduction (liters)	Total sewage reduction (cubic meter)
Full flush toilet	31.54			
Urine Separation toilet	8.74			
	22.8	98676	2249813	**2250**

Annex B – Calculation for water use and sewage generated

(Note: Calculation of water use in toilet and sewage generated is per person per day)

Assumption (taken from L. M Austin and S. J. Van Vuucen):

a) 1 human uses toilet 5 times daily (1 time for faeces and 4 times for urination)

b) each human being urinates quantity is 0.35 liters each time (500 liters / 365 days / 4 times daily)

c) each human being faeces quantity is 0.14 liters (50 liters / 365 days / once daily)

d) each full flush requires 6 liters, half flush 3 liters and use of urine separation 0.3 liters

Toilet use: Full Flush

Toilet use type	volume of human waste (liters)	Volume of water for flushing	Total volume of sewage per toilet use	Number of times toilet was used	Total sewage = Total volume of sewage per toilet use x no. of times toilet was used
faeces	0.14	6	6.14	1	6.14
urine	0.35	6	6.35	4	25.4
					31.54

Toilet type: Half flush

Toilet use type	volume of human waste (liters)	Volume of water for flushing	Total volume of sewage per toilet use	Number of times toilet was used	Total sewage = Total volume of sewage per toilet use x no. of times toilet was used
faeces	0.14	6	6.14	1	6.14
urine	0.35	3	3.35	4	13.4
					19.54

Toilet type: Urine Separation Toilet

Toilet use type	volume of human waste (liters)	Volume of water for flushing	Total volume of sewage per toilet use	Number of times toilet was used	Total sewage = Total volume of sewage per toilet use x no. of times toilet was used
faeces	0.14	6	6.14	1	6.14
urine	0.35	0.3	0.65	4	2.6
					8.74

Photos: Bhutan (Photos kindly provided by the author of this chapter Jigme Tashi Tsering)

2.3 Green Development: Modern Service Industry in Tianjin

By Shuhan Liu

1 Introduction

With the global development of information technology, the modern service industry is characterized by high technology, high added value, high human capital and low resource depletion and pollution. It has taken the place of manufacturing industry and has been the main impetus for world economy. With the adjustment and shifting of global industrial structure and the transition of developmode in China, how to adjust economic structure has been the key issue in post crisis era. development of service industry of metropolitan cities is imbalanced. The progress of service industry in Tianjin drops behind other cities in terms of service industry output and employment rate. The lagged development of service industry in Tianjin is becoming the bottleneck for future. However, the rapid growth of Tianjin economy paves the way for its further progress.

2 The Problems of Modern Service Industry in Tianjin

2.1 Small Scale of Total Volume and Slow Development of Emerging Service Industries

In spite of the rapid speed of Tianjin service industry, there are still obvious gaps compared with Beijing and Shanghai. The absolute added values of service industry of Beijing and Shanghai are two and three times the amount of Tianjin respectively. The proportions of service industry in GDP in three cities are 75.9%, 59.3% and 43.5% respectively. The proportion of traditional services like transport, storage, hotels and restaurants is high, reaching 50%, while percentages of finance, information, design and education are comparatively low. These reflect that the tardiness and disperse of emerging service industry without scale and conglomeration effect. The knowledge intensive services like information consulting, manufacturing design and medical care are still to be improved. The connected effect, diffusion effect, interactive effect and united development among service sectors have not yet been integrated.

2.2 Low Level of Structure and Weak Strength of Producer

The process and tendency of global service industry demonstrate that knowledge and technology intensive services with high added value are the mainstream besides the fast speed and continuous upgrading of service industry. The statistics show the output of producer services in developed countries account for more than 50% of the total service industry. However, in spite of the fast industrialization in Tianjin, producer service industry is lagging behind. The scale advantage of producer service industry including finance, insurance, business, law, R&D, consulting and asset evaluation has not constructed.

2.3 Low Marketization in Service Industry

Service industry is quite competitive with high marketization degree and its globalization has been seen in the world. With service products transferring to developing countries from developed countries, innovation, knowledge based and internationalization have been the dominant tendency. Many emerging developing countries divert to "world office" from "world factory" in order to undertake a new round of international industrial transfer. Some core cities have owned "headquarter economy effect" in international industrial competition. Compared with 707 MNCs' headquarters attracted by Shanghai, Tianjin possesses less 1/7 than Shanghai. Though Tianjin Binhai New Area evelopmentPlan has been brought into the national overall development strategy, less publicity to international consortiums and MNCs, the monopoly of some service sectors and low level of private economy restrict the process in modern service industry.

The reasons for the above gaps can be concluded. First, concept and system restrict. Second, Tianjin's own advantages have not been exerted. Third, income level and consumption structure upgrade slowly. Last, the input in service industry is insufficient and lack senior talents.

The Construction of Modern Service Industry Development in Tianjin

The Developing Design

Firstly, it is necessary to promote the industrial structure shift from "manufacturing type" to "service type". The sweeping-world economic crisis brought about new tendencies in adjustments and changes of world economy and great pressure on Chinese economic restructuring, which formed anti-driving mechanism. The main focus of restructuring is to complete the transformation from manufacturing economy to service economy by virtue of policy supporting. The focus of service should divert to Bohai Rim and international market from Tianjin and domestic market. Accelerating service industry will enhance the radiation and influence of Tianjin as an international metropolis.

Secondly, we should promote the integration of modern service industry and advanced manufacturing with reference to international experience. The integration of modern service industry with advanced manufacturing is the objective law of industrial evolution. With the intensified competition, concentrating on intensive specification rather than scope economy has become corporations' universal demand. In order to be the advanced manufacturing R&D center, it is essential for Tianjin to separate some service functions as design, marketing and consulting from previous complete process of manufacturing and to accomplish the services by independent market. In this way, the internalization of producer service can be transformed to externalization. Some foreign integrating modes can be used for reference. Combination integrating mode refers to the inputs and market research for new product R&D connect together. Computer and operation system is the example of binding integration. The derivatives consumption brings to manufacturing industry by movie, animation and sports are extended integration.

Thirdly, optimizing internal structure can help transit to high-end service industry. The added value of traditional service industry (transport, storage, postal service, wholesale and retail) occupied 40.03% of total service industry while finance sector, as the high-end service industry, 12.92%, and its contribution to GDP was only 5.6% in 2009. The proportions in Beijing and Shanghai were 14.5% and 12.2% respectively in same period. The added value of creative industry in Tianjin was RMB33.45 billion, while 325.07 billion and 272.54 billion in Beijing and Shanghai. It is obvious that high-end service industry in Tianjin is far behind. Therefore, the focus should be put on accelerating high-end service sectors like finance innovation, modern logistics, service outsourcing, creative industry, and headquarter economy.

3. Constructing a Modern Service Industry Developing System

3.1 Public Administration Service Industry System

Urban public administration services include elementary education, public health, medical care, transport and communication, etc. Most fields are government agencies, public institutions, with large proportion of state-owned and high monopoly degree. They are still adopting planned economy instead of market economy and industrialization and their operation and management have common problems such as insufficient service supply, lack of humanization and low efficiency management level. Though the municipal government has adopted a series of strategies to improve the environment, Tianjin still lags behind other cities in the aspect of soft environment. Therefore, the key to upgrading soft strength is to optimize public service system. To accomplish the goal, it is necessary to break the system barriers and introduce competition mechanism to display the role of market allocation. Meanwhile, widening market access, breaking monopoly and constructing service evaluation system are other effective ways.

3.3.2 Producer Service Industry System

Producer service is the fastest growing service industry and is the focus and breakthrough of modern service development in Tianjin. Though having formed some scale, differences still exist compared with other cities. The main problems lie in unreasonable structure, insufficient emerging service industry and low degree of marketization and specialization. At present, the proportion of producer service industry in manufacturing is about 60% in foreign country, while less than 40% in Tianjin in 200. Therefore, the construction of Tianjin producer service industry should externalize manufacturer activity and professional service as well as strengthen the specialization and integration of services. Taking manufacturing as axis in production and market, the effective way is to form all round service system integrating R&D, consulting, logistics, finance and insurance, human resource training, marketing, law and intermediary service. At the same time, it is indispensable to expand new service fields and to establish cross-regional service system around Bohai Rim.

3.3.3 Consumer Service Industry System

The financial crisis not only impacted global entity economy, but also challenged China's economic growth mode led by exporting. The dependence degree on foreign trade has increased form 34.87% in 1980 to .3% in 20 and the average growth rate is 11.1 points higher than world average level. The change of external environment will undoubtedly result in serious consequences on China's exports, especially on coastal cities like Tianjin. In 2009, under the situation of GDP growth rate at 16.5%, the year-on-year growth rate of foreign trade decreased 20.6%. The export trade volume declined to USD30 billion in 2009 from USD 42.23 billion in 2008. Transforming economic developing mode and driving domestic demand are the inevitable choices for keeping economic growth. The consumer service industry is the largest potential and innovative service field in Tianjin. In addition to overcoming insufficient effective supply, it is necessary to dig potential demand in emerging industries so as to meet the needs of different consumers in different living standard. The practical way at present is to foster advantageous products in education training, health service, culture, and tourism sectors.

4 Policy

4.1 Key Fields of Public Administration Service Industry Policy Suggestions

4.1.1 Executing System and Mechanism Innovation

In spite of the large scale reform on modern service industry, reform-legging is still a problem. The imperfect modern property right and corporation institution and low proportion of private enterprises have resulted in weak competitiveness. The private and foreign capitals are limited to enter market due to the low level of industrialization and marketization in some key fields. The reforms should be made on three aspects. First, introducing competition into monopoly industries, such as gas, water, electric power, and heating supply. The government should break the administrative barriers and widen the market access standard as well as push non state-owned capital to possess shares. Second, further improve the charging and monitoring of public and commonweal institutions, intermediary and other services. Third, push the reform on socialization of the rear-service of public organizations. Fourth, standardize the service industry criterion and establish strict charging and monitoring system in culture, education and medical care departments.

4.1.2 Improving the Implementation of Polices

Some imperfect policy effects can be seen in aspects as uneven policy support on service industries and tax preferential concentrating on infrastructure and hard environment. So we should adapt to the changing situations and social development and improve policy system. First is to review and old policies and abolish or liberalize the unreasonable ones. Second is to make policies clear and executive so as to carry out smoothly. Third is to develop E-government and improve the efficiency.

4.1.3 Introducing Competition and Evaluating System

The key to improving the service quality of public administration is to introduce competition system due to the high state-owned proportion and monopoly. First is to permit different economic entities to participate in the competition and operate in market economy. Second is to evaluate the service quality by third party. The last is to regulate market and industry standard to keep fair market order and environment.

4.2 The Key Fields and Policy Suggestions on Producer Service Industr

Generally speaking, it is necessary to execute financial and logistic innovation, to develop headquarter economy and service outsourcing as well as the exhibition economy.

4.2.1 Deepening Financial Reform

The global crisis triggered by American subprime mortgage crisis has exposed the excessive financial innovation and weak financial regulation which make virtue economy far beyond the capability of entity economy. Therefore, financial innovation and modern financial system must be established based on the scientific and cautious principle to control the risks. The measure is to widen financing channel and perfect modern financial service system. In virtue of the experimental edge of financial innovation in Binhai New Area, various types of industrial investment fund can be developed. By trial operation of private equity, leasing, risk investment and venture investment fund, it is dispensable to regulate financial market transactions and perfect multi-level capital market and OTC market. next is to deepen financial institutional reform and build sound financial organization system. The system innovation and preferential policy can attract MNCs' headquarters and transnational financial groups enter Tianjin and can encourage local legal person financial institutions to enhance core competitiveness. Meanwhile, by establishing and introducing trust corporations, factoring, assets management, insurance broker and assets evaluation, Tianjin can construct multi-level, compound, modern financial organization system. The third is to create financial services and products. Innovation can be executed in the fields like fund, factoring, leasing, private equity and offshore finance. The fourth is to perfect financial regulation and enhance risk management. Through the way establishing united credit managing platform and regulating financial products and services, fair, reasonable and transparent market can be built.

4.2.2 Developing Modern Logistics

To correlate logistics with manufacturing, business and agriculture can shape complete industry and supply chain and can reduce costs. Extending the construction and service of "anhydrous port" and establishing electronic declaration system and one-stop service can make Tianjin be a modern logistic base. The next step is to build the logistic platform to cooperate with logistic enterprises home and abroad and to integrate with manufacturing industry and businesses. Further, based on TEDA, Tianjin Bonded Area and Dongxiang Bonded Port Area, logistic park can be built and will improve the intensive operation. By expanding logistic function, logistic services can be upgraded to supply chain finance from payment collection, settlement agency and pledge of warehouse receipts.

4.2.3 Developing Headquarter Economy

Headquarter economy is a service economy symbolizing with the characteristics of manufacture industry upgrading and advanced industrial level. It is suggested that we should take the transfer of high-end service industry in developed countries as an opportunity. The government should increase the strength on preferential policy, investment environment and talent pool reserve in order to attract headquarters, R&D centers, purchasing and marketing center.

4.2.4 Facilitating Exhibition Industry

Due to the lack of nationwide high quality exhibitions, it is essential to boost exhibition economy in Tianjin. By undertaking international well known exhibitions, business negotiation, tourism and trade can be expedited. The brand effect of universal acknowledged exhibitions can improve city image.

4.3   The Key Fields and Policy Suggestions on Consumer Service Industry

With the increase of income level, the demand to consumer service tends to be diversified and individualized. Besides satisfying popular demand, consumer service industry needs to seek breakthrough in innovation.

4.3.1 Education Training

With the scientific progress and faster speed of renewable knowledge, the demand for further education, enterprise training, re-employment training, vocational education and professional technology education has increasdramatically. Starting from vocational and technical training, the effective way is to foster skillful compound talents for Binhai Area. Aiming at various certificate examinations, perennial training institution or base with favorable brand should be established. In addition, it is helpful to introduce famous training organizations to cultivate high quality talents.

4.3.2 Tourism

With increasing living standards, consumption of tourism has froms an increasing proportion of individual consumption. Compared with Beijing and Shanghai, Tianjin is short of tourism resources. How to make attractive tourism highlight is the key to promoting tourism. Establishing large sized business mall integrating shopping, entertainment and hotels without influence of season and climate change will attract tourists and enhance city strength. Another approach is to upgrade the original brand tourism resources (city tour, Hai River tour, and Binhai New Area tour and mountain attractions tour).

Perfecting the tourism incentive and punishment mechanism will improve the quality, supervision and management of tourism services.

4.3.3 Business Service

Based on urban characteristics, creat characteristic business areasis the effective way. Different from Gold Street Area, the construction of New Italian Street and Ancient Culture Street should establish international business area, traditional brand business area and consumption flagship shops area to demonstrate particular features. addition, to build community business service areas combined with the large business centerswill construct "spider web" developing mode. Meanwhile, the government should reinforce infrastructure and regulation and introduce competition mechanism in order to achievewell-acknowledged image.

Conclusion

Expediting a modern service industry is not only the main tendency of urban modernization but also can reflect the economic position of Tianjin. The exploitation and opening of Binhai New Area creates the opportunity for developof modern service industryin Tianjin. Borrowing foreign and home experience and based on resource endowment and advantages, new measures and actions should be carried out by focusing on idea innovation, system innovation, management innovation and development mode innovation.

sources of energy are being increasingly used to power the transmission towers. Secondly, advanced batteries, which consume fraction of the energy consumed earlier, are used for providing the backup. Thirdly, operators are going in for sharing of mobile towers and other resources to lessen the number of mobile towers. Fourthly, greener data centers, and more energy efficient networking and telecom equipment are being used. Additionally, efforts are being made to make the mobiles and other equipment free of hazardous and toxic substances. Moreover, systems are also being put in place for proper disposal of the e-waste generated and also for the recycling of products.

Information Technology (IT) is an important sector, which has brought about a revolution. IT is the acquisition, processing, storage and dissemination of vocal, pictorial, textual and numerical information by a microelectronics-based combination of computing and telecommunications. The increasing dominance of computers, laptops, tablets, music players, scanners, printers, servers, other networking and storage equipment, in our lives, is due to information technology only. How these products and the IT services add to the emission, is something which is not unknown. However, importantly, this is changing. A lot of research and development is taking place which has lessened the impact of the technology on the environment. The datacenters which brought the digital revolution are being made greener. They are being increasingly powered by alternative sources of energy like solar energy, wind energy etc. and natural ways of cooling are being used to reduce the energy consumption by the cooling units. The networking and storage equipment too are being made more energy efficient. This is being coupled with smart building techniques, wherein sensors are being used to detect and reduce the wastage of electricity and water. Advanced technology has also resulted in smart grid technology, which increases the energy efficiency on the electricity grid and in homes and offices. Green IT has also enabled advanced video conferencing solutions which are being adopted by the corporate to reduce the emissions and spending due to air travel. Additionally, virtualization of servers is taking place to reduce the number of servers used. Moreover, IT has also made possible development of tools to calculate the carbon footprint, to monitor and control energy usage in homes and offices, besides providing utilities like ERP tools which aid a company to optimize their financials as regards to green concerns like energy efficiency, water, and waste and greenhouse gas emissions. Furthermore, several new systems and solutions have been put in place for effective traffic management. Initiatives have also been taken to reduce the use of toxic substances in IT products and to have better e-waste management and recycling solutions.

Not to be left behind is the automobile industry. Automobile industry designs, develops, manufactures, markets and sells motor vehicles and is one of the world's most important economic sectors. As per statistics, a total of 77,857,705 vehicles were globally manufactured in 2010. Adding to this, the number of vehicles already on road, the amount of fuel consumed is substantial. Apart from the fuel consumption, the vehicles also contribute to the pollution. Moreover, the manufacturing process too adds onto the greenhouse gas emissions.

Efforts have been made to make the automobile industry greener and more sustainable. These measures include, design and production of hybrid vehicles, electric vehicles, alternative fuel vehicles etc. These vehicles use electric energy or biofuels to power the cars, hence decreasing the use of conventional diesel and petrol. Other measures include greening the supply chain, wherein parts and components used for manufacture are procured from vendors who themselves adopt green practices, thus reducing the carbon footprint. Additionally, the vehicles manufactured are made in compliance with strict emission norms, to reduce the pollution and emissions. Moreover, other practices like carbon offsetting are also followed, wherein, a small fee is charged from the consumer to offset the carbon emissions incurred in the manufacturing process. This money is then used to fund other green projects or to plant trees. Furthermore, the government is also doing its bit in greening this sector by providing tax sops and other incentives for such green projects.

Banking is another important sector, which surprisingly contributes to the emissions equivalently. Daily electricity consumption, fuel consumption due to air and road travel etc. adds to the emissions. Moreover the huge amounts of section used results in the felling of trees. To make this sector more greener, one of the major initiatives has been the internet and mobile banking. Now, the banking transactions are being done through internet and mobile, and this has reduced the need for people to travel to bank. Secondly, core banking solutions have been implemented, which have minimized the amount of paper used, through the use of technology. The banks have also started sending customer banking statements through mail, further reducing the use of paper. Moreover, solar powered ATM's, and incorporation of smart building techniques in the office building has reduced the electricity consumption in a big way.

Apart from the Green technology and initiatives, the carbon credit policy also helps in minimizing the impact of technology on the environment by providing an incentive to invest in and adopt green technologies. A carbon credit is a generic term to assign a value to a reduction or offset of greenhouse gas emissions. A carbon credit is usually equivalent to one tons of carbon dioxide equivalent (CO_2-e). A carbon credit can be used by a business or individual to reduce their carbon footprint by investing in an activity that has reduced or sequestered greenhouse gases at another site. Carbon credits are bought and sold in the international carbon market - much like any other commodity. Of the total number of carbon contracts signed in the world so far, India has the second largest portfolio with a market share of 12 percent, behind China which had a market share of 61percent. In India, the Delhi Metro Rail Corporation has been certified by the United Nations as the First Metro Rail and Rail based system in the world which will get carbon Credits for reducing Green House Gas Emissions as it has helped to reduce pollution levels in the city by 6.3 lakh tons every year thus helping in reducing global warming.

Green Technologies in India's Four Emerging Sectors

Telecommunication : Airtel which is one of the leading global telecommunications companies has launched a comprehensive program in saving energy. The main motive behind the entire program is to reduce energy and diesel usage leading to carbon emission reduction. One initiative of the program is the Green Towers P7 Initiative. It aims to cover 22,000 tower sites with a priority given to the rural areas. The program is for 3 years and at the end of the 3 years period it will bring down the diesel consumption of 66 million liters per year and carbon dioxide of around 1.5 lacs MT per year.

The Initiative includes the following:

· Alternate energy sources: Airtel has encouraged the use of clean energy solutions. These have proved to be the strong alternative to conventional sources of energy. The deployment of such alternate sources of energy at around 1050 sites has helped the company to save around 6.9 million liters of diesel and around Rs. 280 million.

· IPMS and DCDG: the installation of Integrated Power Management System (IPMS) and the variable speed DC generators (DCDG) at around 900 sites has been able to reduce diesel consumption by 1.2 million liters and saved Rs. 47 million.

· FCU: The use of Free Cooling Units (FCU) in place of air conditioners at around 3400 sites has saved diesel consumption of around 4.1 million liters.

In addition to the Green Towers P7 initiative, Airtel has taken up other measures to reduce energy consumption such as:

· The installation of solar hot water generators at its main campus in Gurgaon for filling hot water requirement in the cafeteria.

· Lighting Energy Savers (LES) are installed across NCR region which has reduced energy consumption to the amount of 10 – 25% in the lighting system.

· The installation of Variable Frequency Drives at its campus in AHU (Air Handling Unit) has increased the efficiency of cooling system by 10%.

The above three measures have helped the company to save around 8.5 lakh units of electricity per year. The other measures taken up by Airtel are:

· The implementation of the 'Secure Print' solution which has saved about 8 MT of paper per annually. The drive of sending e- bills to the post – paid customers leads to the saving of 12,840 trees per year.

· BhartiInfratel, a subsidiary of BhartiAirtel has installed around 3 MWT of solar capacity which has generated more than 5 million units of electricity annually.

Vodafone, another leading player too has launched a series of green initiatives. It has introduced solar chargers and handsets that make extensive use of recycled plastic and have energy efficient features. They have reduced packaging material, and have introduced e-billing. They also collect handsets for reuse and recycling and have researched capacity to manage electronic waste.

IT Services

Wipro, an IT company and also a leading provider of IT services has taken up a number of initiatives leading to greener and sustainable environment. Some of the important measures are:

· *Ecological Sustainability*: This includes reduction in Green House Gases emission by:

- using alternative sources of energy for lighting like the LED lights

- implementing car – pool policy for employees

- reducing business commute

- generating wind/solar power in campuses

- running air conditioning plant on solar thermal

- by planting trees on unused campus land

·*Water Efficiency*: The use of Sewage Treatment Plans for recycling of water. The solid waste generated from treatment is converted to bio fertilizer for use in the campus garden. Approximately, 76% of waste generated is either recycled or composted.

· *E Waste Management*: Under e waste management, Wipro has adopted e waste take back program by following WEEE (Waste Electrical and Equipment) guidelines. Under this initiative, plastic and carton boxes are reused; the metallic parts are sent to European countries for treatment.

· *Elimination of Toxic Chemicals*: Under this initiative the Company has implemented 100% RoHS (Restriction on Hazardous Substances) compliant desktops and laptops and elimination of 21 hazardous chemicals. Additional products are free from toxic chemicals like PVC (poly vinyl chloride) and BFRs (Brominated Flame Retardants).

· *Greener and Ethical Supply Chain*: Under this measure, the suppliers are expected to supply products and services meeting environmental standards.

Other initiatives are Clean Energy, Green IT Infrastructure, IT for green products and services.

Infosys, another IT giant too is not far behind. It has implemented database archival, and document sharing to minimize the use of paper. It has procured electricity through mini hydel plant, and has plans to install bio gas generation facility in its campus. Besides efficient building cooling solutions, smart power management tools, cloud computing solutions and greener data centers it also has effective waste management strategies in place.

Automobile

Hero MotoCorp has adopted a number of initiatives and tools in its organization to minimize the use of resources and to take care of the waste product leading to sustainable development. Some of the initiatives are:

·   *Green Technology*: Hero MotoCorp has introduced a special painting process known as Acrylic Cathodic Electro Deposition (AECD) for the frame body. This new process leads to 99% paint transfer efficiency as well as minimizes effluents. The Company also used water soluble paint which is environment friendly ensuring quality and product.

· *Cleaner Processes*: Raw materials and chemicals are first tested on their impact on environment before introduced them in the process of production. Hero MotoCorp has eliminated the use of harmful substance like Hexavalent Chromium, Asbestos, and Phenolic Substances for many years now.

· *Green Roof program*: This program saves huge amount of energy by moderating temperature of roof and surrounding areas. It also helps in reducing storm water runoff volume and peak flow rate. In this way this eco – friendly method restores ecological and aesthetic value.

· *Green Supply Chain*: In the supply chain, the Company has launched two programs, The 'Green Dealer Development Program' for the front end and the 'Green Vendor Development Program' for the backend of the supply chain. In each of these programs, the partners are made aware of the importance of environmental issues as well as managing material resources, energy resource, industrial wastes, pollution and other effluents.

· *Rain Water Harvesting*: The Company has introduced Rain Water Harvesting at both its plants in Dharuhera and Gurgaon of Haryana, one of the driest states in India. In both plants, 16 rainwater harvesting catchments have been set up covering an area of 31540sqmts saving around 18 million liters of water annually.

Maruti Suzuki, another Indian automobile giant, has introduced fuel efficient engines, which gives greater mileage. They have also introduced vehicles which are factory fitted with dual fuel engines, and comply with European ELV norms, which mean that nearly 85% of the car is recyclable. They have strict adherence to BS III and BS IV emission norms and have brought reduction in landfill waste, reduction of groundwater consumption, reduction in CO_2 emission through processes like installation of solar panels, LED lights.

Banking

Reserve Bank of India acknowledges the term *green banking* in its publication, Policy Environment, 2009 – 2010. This report also provides the outlines for the implementation of Green IT in all areas of work in the financial sector. Subsequently, financial institutions are taking up a number of philanthropic activities under the CSR banner. In an emerging market such as India, projects which focus on clean production, good corporate governance, and sustainable energy are considered attractive business opportunities for the financial institutions.

The Indian financial institutions have incorporated sustainability by incorporating in their functions. They have embedded the concept of sustainability in their core business processes like decision making and risk management. Generally, in India, a separate organization or foundation is set up with the main purpose of giving back to the society. The main activities of such an organization relate to under privileged, education and social initiatives, partnering with an NGO or charity house, organizing employee engagement drives, in which employees donate part of their income, volunteer their time and share their knowledge for various community services.

Disclosure of sustainability performance helps in the ranking of financial situations based on global indices such as the Dow Jones Sustainability Index (DJSI), which tracks sustainable – driven companies worldwide on their financial performance. According to Ernst & Young Report, the steps that a financial services organization can take towards sustainability reporting are:

· develop a sustainable strategy

· identify a sustainability reporting roadmap

· develop and implement sustainability management systems

· assess sustainability relating to risk and opportunities

· obtain assurance on sustainability reports including on health and safety aspects

ICICIBank has promoted a number of green programs and technologies as part of giving back to the system. Some of these are:

· *Home Finance*: Under this program, the Bank offers reducing fees to customers who purchase homes in 'Leadership in Energy and Environmental Design' (LEED) certified buildings.

· *Vehicle Finance*: Under Vehicle Finance, the bank offers 50% waiver on processing fee on car models uses alternative mode of energy. These cars include Hyundai's Santro Eco, Maruti's LPG version of Maruti 800, Civic Hybrid of Honda, Omni and Versa, Reva Electric cars, Mahindra Logan CNG versions and Tata Indica CNG.

· *Instabanking*: This refers to Internet banking, i – Mobile banking, and IVR banking.This helps to reduce business commute.

ICICI Bank has also launched programs for employees such as follows:

· Fully utilizing power saving settings when in use and turning off lights and electronic equipments when not in use

· Use of CFLs bulbs

· Using online Webinars to save travel cost and time

· Use of car pool and public transport system

ICICI Bank has also initiated and promoted a program in making institutions, corporate, banks, and government agencies aware of environment issues like biodiversity, wildlife habitats and environment.

IndusIndBank, another local bank has initiatives like solar powered ATMs, thin computing, e-archiving, e-learning, e-waste management, paperless fax, energy conservation and also supports finance programs with incentives to go green. With the solar-powered ATM, the bank expects to save around 1,980 Kw of energy annually besides reducing carbon emissions by 1,942 kg. It also expects to save power bills of around Rs. 20,000 per year in urban areas, where it replaces diesel generators with solar panels.

Application of Green and Eco – Friendly Technologies in Rural India

India at present has promoted and facilitated a number of green and eco – friendly technologies in the rural sector. These technologies are implemented at the national level, regional level, and at the state level as given below:

At the National level:

·   *SOLECKSHAW*: CMERI has developed a Solar Powered Electric three – Wheeled Vehicle, named as SOLECKSHAW. This vehicle transporting people through small distances, especially in busy streets of cities. It is an environment – friendly car since it is free from toxic emissions. The novelty of this invention is the use of Brushless Direct Current (BLDC) hub motor instead of Permanent Magnetic Direct Current (PMDC) motor. The electric drive has been separated by installing BLDC motor directly on to the front axle and the mechanical drive on the rear axle. This system has also eliminated the use of mechanical devices like spring loaded frictional plate and couplings.

·   *Cabinet Dryer and Washing Unit for Ginger and Turmeric*: CMERI has developed an Improved Cabinet Dryer with higher drying rate. The availability of the sun is uncertain and hence the cabinet dryer serves as a useful device for preservation of ginger and turmeric produced by rural farmers. Likewise, CMERI has developed a continuous type washing unit where waste water is being filtered and re – circulated.

·   *Cultivation of Medicinal and Aromatic Plants*: The cultivation and processing of aromatic and medicinal plants have enriched the bio – diversity of North Eastern Region as well as opening new opportunities for income generation in the rural sector. IIIM has developed and standardized cultivation and processing technologies in the case of rose, lavender, clarysage, rose geranium and others.

·   *Low – Cost Oxygen Monitor*: The system is useful for measuring the oxygen percentage in the stack gas monitoring which in turn improves the combustion efficiency of the oil fired boilers used in various industries, ultimately to a cleaner and friendly environment The successful models taken by the State Science and Technology Councils in India are as follows:

Technologies for Water Purification and Waste Management

·   *Plastic and hospital waste management system*: Four plasticand hospital waste disposal demonstration plants based on indigenously developed plasma incineration technologies were set up at ecologically fragile locations having tourist influx at Goa, A&N Islands, Himachal Pradesh & Sikkim and other locations in the states of Andhra Pradesh, Haryana, Uttar Pradesh and Tripura.

With a view to provide safe drinking water, *water purification technologies* are adopted to remove contaminants from drinking water. These technologies are installed in different states in India.

·   *Pilot demonstration plant* for treatment of hard/brackish water based on indigenously developed Reverse Osmosis Technology was installed at UttarlaiAirforce Station, Barmer. The project is successful and has been providing drinking water to inhabitants of air – base as well as nearby villages.

· *A sea – water desalination plant* based on 2 – Stage desalination process development indigenously was installed in Nelmudar village, Tamil Nadu.

Distributed Energy Systems

In order to promote decentralized energy generation based on locally available resources, the following technologies are demonstrated at various places:

· *Bio – Diesel production plant* (100L/batch)set up at Orissa with IIT Delhi Technology.

· The Bio – Fuel Plant developed at JSS Academy of Technical Education, Bangalore has been installed at Utthan Center for Sustainable Development and Poverty Alleviation, UP & Raipur Institute of Technology, Raipur Chattisgarh.

· *Biomass Gasifier Project* using 30kg woody biomass per hour with 100% producer gas based engine has been installed at village Bagdora, Chattisgarh. The plant is operated by the Village Energy Committee (VEC). The plant is operating in the morning for commercial activity for 2 hours and in the evening for lighting purpose for 4 hours.

· *Biogas enrichment plant* to meet the electricity requirement has been installed at Rajasthan Go – SewaSangh, Jaipur, The plant has a biogas enrichment system used to get 95% Methane for power generation based on water scrubbing technology developed by IIT, Delhi.

· *Ferro Cement Roof Top Rain Water Harvesting Technology* constructed by Himachal Pradesh State Council of S&T, which was installed at Shimla.

At the Regional Level with Reference to North Eastern Region

In the North Eastern Region of India, the North – East Institute of Science & Technology which was established in the year 1961 has promoted a number of green initiatives. Some of the initiatives are as follows:

· *Agro practices of medicinal plants* like dioscorea, solaniumkhasianum, annatto, bhringaraj, kalmegh, punarnava, agechtachitrak, vedailota, and iswarmul which are used in treating diseases.

· *Bio – Organic Fertilizer*: It is an ecofriendly product of bioactive and organic compound. It enhances the soil fertility and plant growth, and it protects the soil and soil beneficial microbes. This fertilizer can be used for all types of cultivation.

· *VERMICOMPOST*: It is well recognized as an important organic manure for plant growth and development. It improves the physical conditions of soil, and helps in biodegradation of organic compounds and therefore improves the soil fertility.

· *Bacterial Culture for Crop*: It is a new formulation based on plant growth promoting rhizobacteria. It is used for all types of crops and it protects the plant from fungal diseases and enhances the microbial biodiversity. In this way, it increases crop yield.

· *Ceiling Board*: It is an environmental friendly product. The process is based on agricultural waste and by – products. Its main raw materials are agricultural wastes like paddy husk.

· *ACRYLAMIDE*: It is an environmental friendly product. It has a great demand a starting material for production of various polymers to be used as flocculating agents, stock additives and polymers for petroleum recovery.

· *Electronic Grade Potassium Silicate*: It is used for fixing TV tubes and screens. The product is an electronic grade and purity is very high. It is free from environmental hazards.

· *DEOILER*: It is used in oil industry for removal of oil from large volume of associate water effluent. It is an environmental friendly chemical and can remove as much as 90% of the oil present in the water.

· *Banana Fibers*: Fibers from banana pseudo stem can be used for manufacture of ropes and twines for packaging industry and also for manufacturing hessian clothes. It can also be utilized for making dolls, bags, table and door mats, baskets, and other products. Its process is eco - friendly with less disposal problems.

At the State Level with reference to Meghalaya

In the state of Meghalaya, the State Council of Science, Technology & Environment has adopted a number of green and eco – friendly technologies. The innovative technologies are:

· Improved Chula and Water Filtration

· Solar LED Lighting

· Stabilized Mud Block

· Fire Retardant & Life Extended Thatch Roof

· Low – Cost Sanitation

· Rain Water Harvesting

· Organic Chapter 10Composting

· Pedal Pump

· Hydraulic Ram Pump

· Low – Cost Oven

· Low – Cost Cold Storage

· Leaf Plate Making

· Paper Re-cycling

There is no denying the fact that India has done a lot of work in saving resources, environment preservation and in giving back to the system, but there is a lot more for India to achieve in this regard. At present, there are no strict regulations that mandate sustainability reporting.

However, certain measures are taken up by Government of India to make Indian corporations environmentally and socially responsible. One of such measures is a policy that will cause all PSUs, companies and financial institutions to invest 50% of their CSR funds in afforestation initiatives. Secondly, the Confederation of Indian Industry (CII) is coming up with a *green rating system* for the companies. Thirdly, the Institute of Chartered Accountants of India is working on a new set of rules on CSR. The urgency to adopt sustainability has been intensified with the launch of Sustainable Development Funds and Indices in India such as CRISIL, S&P ESG Index.

The chapter concludes by seeking suggestions from the other learned international speakers to address crucial issues of India like the recycling of huge amount of waste resource and empowering the law enforcement authority, which at present is weak.

References and notes:

1. Annual Report 2009-10, Department of Scientific and Industrial Research, Ministry of Science and Technology, Government of India.

2. State Science and Technology Program (SSTP), 2010, Ministry of Science and Technology, Government of India, New Delhi.

3. Annual Report, 2010, North Eastern Institute of Science and Technology, Jorhat, Assam.

4. Annual Report, 2006, RRL Jorhat Technologies, Assam.

5. Newsletter, September 2010, State Council of Science, Technology & Environment,   Meghalaya.

6.Maruti Suzuki Sustainability Report 2009-10

7. Infosys Sustainability Report 2009-10.

8. Finesse, Financial Service Newsletter, Nov 2010-Feb 2011, Ernst and Young.

9. http://en.wikipedia.org/wiki/Automotive_industry

10. http://www.oica.net/category/production-statistics/

11. http://en.wikipedia.org/wiki/Information_technology

12.http://www.airtel.in/wps/wcm/connect/About%20Bharti %20Airtel/bharti+airtel/media+centre/bharti+airtel+news/corporate/pg-statement-   from-bharti-airtel-green-initiatives

13. http://ibnlive.in.com/news/icici-goes-green-makes-offices-ecofriendly/861407.html

14. http://business-standard.com/india/news/for-banks-green-isnew-black/395561/

15. http://www.icicibank.com/go-green/Index.html

16.http://www.wiprogreentech.com/recycled_plastic_content.html

17. http://www.businessstandard.in/india/news/indusind-bank-launches-first-solar-powered-atm/81456/on

18. http://www.indusind.com/indusind/wcms/en/home/top-links/investors-relation/analyst-meet/QIPInvestorPresentationAugust2010.avsFiles/PDF/QIP   %20Investor %20Presentation.pdf

19. http://www.epa.vic.gov.au/climate-change/glossary.asp#CAM

20. http://climatechange.worldbank.org/node/3828

21. http://www.delhimetrorail.com/whatnew_details.aspxid=LrHUclpD03glld&rdct=d

22.http://www.vodafone.com/content/dam/vodafone/about/sustainability/reports/vodafone_sustainability_report.pdf

2.5 Introduction – Green Economics, protest and renaissance in social and environmental justice and gender

By Miriam Kennet and Michelle Gale de Oliveira

Most of the worlds poor are women and most women are poor! Any serious discussion of poverty must include gender discussions as this is where the worst poverty is to be found.

The aim of the article is to bring together voices and people from all walks of life from all over the world in many different situations, from farmers, dispossessed in developing countries, in countries where women cant go to school for fear of death, to Harvard Professors, all of whom have faced discrimination in their professional lives and who have sought to rise above it. The article combines this with information about scientific and academic methodological tools to enable the reader to contextualise their own work in attempting to campaign for change and to make such work much more effective.

In compiling the article it helped us see where we had hit the glass ceiling as one of the authors Miriam Kennet had worked for 20 years in engineering and often was top of the department and then would be ruthlessly stabbed in the back and often told – we are not promoting a woman! This book has reassured her that it wasnt her at fault but rather that we are socialised to do this to women and to accept it when it happens to us. However our network is full of very talented women and its vitally important that such women are free to make the innovative contribution they want to make. We must help them do it.

Women make up half of all the people on the planet, and yet they are not really represented in policy making or in politics in a way commensurate with that at all.

**Miriam Kennet at the House of Commons
A woman's Place is in the House (of Commons!)**

The UN has identified that a lack of political representation is a reason for economics difficulties as lacking a voice in decision making the decisions that are made dont include their considerations or worries or interests. Financially men own *99%* of the worlds assets. In many countries women can still be stoned to death for adultery and in some countries they still don't have the vote and are not allowed to drive or to go to school. Women form half the world's population, but are enormously under represented politically, almost everywhere, and this is one key factor, along with women's education, that needs to change urgently to rectify these huge imbalances.

It wasn't always like this and some scholars believe that up to the era of our so called "civilisation" 10,000 years ago, women held the power in what has been termed a "matriarchy." In fact in our closest cousins, the bonobo or pygmy chimpanzee, the relationship to the mother determines a male's status in a group. Females are firmly in charge.

In years gone by, according to archaeologists, iconography always seemed to show women. Dieities seem to have been female as well and it is believed that the Virgin Mary is a continuation of some of these earlier cults. The idols that Abraham destroyed in Ur were in fact of women! This continued globally, right up to the **domestication** event of agriculture around 10,000 years ago when it all changed and became male. This domestication was of wheat, animals and women! There are some wonderful books charting women's and men's history of the world -including Rosalind Miles, *A womens history of the world,* and a *Men's history of the world.* Bryan Sykes, an Oxford geneticist in the *Curse of Adam.*(2008) writes about the disintegration of the y chromosome which makes suggestions about what is happening to correct the imbalance on a subconscious genetic level which makes shocking reading!

However we find in our campaigning, that although green economics is our innovation and challenges the main stream status quo – in many many different sorts of ways- it is our work on gender which gets people the most angry and resistant. We even had a trustee resign over the very idea that women could be working in construction in Bangladesh for half the wages for the same work in the same jobs. We went to the Government spy centre, GCHQ, allowed in a most bizarre day, (at the onset of recession),for a brief moment, to radicalise the staff- and the only resistance we had, was not about the green issues, but rather it was the idea that women might not be paid the same as men. We find people also get extremely heated about whether women should be zipped on political lists- or whether women should go out to work and all sorts of equality issues.

In 2009, one of the authors Michele Gale D'Oliveira, ran a campaign at a London university to raise awareness of women´s unequal pay in the UK and internationally. The responses to the campaign included support from some young women and most – if not all – young men. Strangely enough, it was many of the young women who felt threatened by the campaign, citing their offense at posters and language they termed `women´s rights rubbish.´ The vast majority of the statistics on the gender pay gap were unknown to any of the students, however the young men reacted in astonishment by taking offence to the idea that their colleagues should be paid so unfairly, while the young women were offended by the information itself, tearing down flyers and stating that ´the women´s rights movement is *over*.´ Their reactions suggested to us that a significant percentage of the younger generation of Western women, aged 15-25, place little to no value on resolving or even acknowledging gender-related issues. Yet the abstract concept of equality and its necessarily concrete interpretation have been so widely embraced by the younger generation of Western men, that a blatant threat to that equality – in the form of a pay gap, for example – is seen as shocking and unacceptable.

At the moment we are running a campaign where we found symbolically in both the economics reform and the protest movements, the green movements, and the climate change movements- often the platforms of experts are either 4 men and a male chair and recently we find there are 3 men experts and a female chair- as if women are not experts in anything but can organise an event to showcase male superior knowledge.

This all male panel was at the House of Commons and had a female chair and was experts discussing High Speed Rail Train service January 2012

This all male panel was at a climate change symposium at Oxford University January 2012 and each one was asked about new paradigms and thought they had found one.

It is also well known that most Professors are men and most women are found in the academic hourly paid teaching which has no stability, no long term contract and is paid a fraction for a much shorter time than men in academia. we even have female Chancellors of Universities paid less than the equivalent men. In one of our books we have a female Nobel nominated Lauriate who was paid less than far less productive or well known men in her department. Her story is given in the book, Womens Unequal Pay and Poverty (2012) and makes heart breaking reading and is very shocking as it indicates that discrimination exists at every single level. Further when women do shine, they often attract negative comments from others and have to endure resistance and jealously and back stabbing as if somehow powerful women deserve to be treated thus. As Chichilnisky tells us -***the more you succeed the more you get punished!***

This all male panel was in the bank of England Feb 2011

Miriam Kennet, one of the authors herself had a very successful career in engineering and got to create the innovation of Voice over IP globally and the technology behind it. She set up the global outsourcing for the French government and Orange and Equant the largest global network and she got absolutely stabbed in the back..

When she came top in her class for her Masters studies, the men, who had previously been happy to help her, claimed she had slept with the tutor to get the high marks! She had never even met him outside of class!

When she did her undergrad studies her personal tutor locked her in the library to molest her, and in her first job the MD stuck his hand down her blouse- and broke her necklace during a meeting!

 At Nortel network where she was the only woman - working on Digital networks, the others in the department gave her a really hard time but when it came to promotion the men told her that although she was the only one fit for promotion -she couldn't have it as " they would never give it to a woman." They told her she was no good at science and technical things. Time and again she has been told to stick to domestic things. She was determined to prove them wrong and went and got   a science degree from Oxford University with very high exam results!

In fact she was put forward for a Director's job at Hertz Europe and the same thing happened. The Global VP said she should have it and sponsored her for it, but there was an man in charge in the UK and he prevented her having the job and gave it to a man who was not qualified and didn't know the work! The company lawyer told her to sue as there was a cut and dried case but as she had a young child at home and couldn't afford the disruption she didn't pursue it. . At Orange -France Telecom, she was in line for a bonus for creating multi-million pound contract with Finland and they gave the money to a man, a friend of the boss and ousted her so they could keep the money between them !

We have found that the lack of access and affordability of access to law is the single most important reason why women don't pursue many claims.

We have found people also tend to quote and cite male writers and even male artists far more than men- even in the green movement. We need to tell other women about this stuff so when it happens it doesn't discourage them

This advertisement above would also be laughable if it was not so serious- a dialogue about the future of the Post office ! All male, not a woman in sight! Called the BIG RETHINK follows a narrative very common at the moment where people are talking about new paradigms and once more we have usually have 4 white western men talking about how they see things differently!

As something concrete readers can do, we would like all readers to take pictures of any panel which has a really ridiculous imbalance and to send it to us so we can create a gallery exposing this. Send them by email to us at greeneconomicsinstitute@yahoo.com. Expert women speakers on almost any subject really are available and we need to promote them ourselves as part of this campaign. One issue is that people often dont " hear " when a woman makes a suggestion and when a man brings it up effectively repeating it- and claiming the credit, if its good then they praise the man. We find lots of examples of this and we are nearly all socialised to do it- to get behind a narrative or an alpha male and his entourage missing the contribution of the women. It has been described as the clashing of antlers. Nowhere has this imbalance itself been more ridiculous than in the economics Nobel prize where only one woman has ever won it.

Climate change discussions are something that are more tangible than some other parts of green economics as the science can be measured and changes, the delta, can we described. This means that most of the acknowledged climate scientists and economists that get analysed and reviewed are men- even though it was a woman that invented sustainable development and a woman who invented carbon markets, but we find most panels on climate change are full of men with no women – although at Durban it was significant that the UNFCC Kyoto Protocol was actually saved by two women – one from Denmark and one from India. The significant people in the green movement are Rachel Carson, Gro Harlem Brundtland, Petra Kelly and Professor Graciela Chichilniski. However many people don't know who they are and are more likely to quote a male contributor even though it was women who framed the movement.

The Green Economics Institute has been arguing that no claim to be green can possibly be accepted unless it addresses and encompasses a gendered perspective as we stated in our piece in the New Scientist. In fact one of the biggest issues of our time and the cause of many of the difficulties we face in the geological era of the Anthropocene, is too many people. The empowerment of women would help everyone on the planet and would be more likely to ensure our survivability. It is no longer just a cosmetic imperative, it is something we all need. The costs of womens unequal pay and poverty are now threatening all of us. It is women's lack of power which often leads to so many children being born as an insurance policy for their parents. It is known that when women are educated and empowered, they produce far fewer children and then men help with child care as they start to aspire to get on with other things in their lives. There are many other reasons why its not economically efficient and why it is now too costly not to allow empowerment for women and not to give them equally deserved salaries or positions in public life.

Reduction of those costs has been estimated by the OECD *Gender and Sustainable Development* Stevens (2009) as the equivalent to adding 2-3% onto GDP in the Uk alone! Goodness knows we need that so this is a really short sited omission.

Also women are bright- it has just emerged that they are actually even better at parking cars than men – where the received wisdom is that they cant do it. So we need to change the rhetoric – that people regard women's abilities as a joke- women are highly intelligent and full of common sense both in pure processing terms and also in emotional intelligence and so their power really needs to be harnessed and used especially as we find ourselves in an economics crisis.

Additionally, in many countries, India being an example women's lack of access to health care and economic benefits directly affects the outcomes of processes such as pregnancy which of course affects the whole country and the whole community. Their overall health is compromised and so this means that their economics contribution is reduced. Weakening half the population will also lead to a weakening of the men that are born from women. So this inequality affects everyone in India and the detailed analysis of the figures is provided in a special chapter in this book.

The Millenium Development goals provide an important benchmark and it is those about women and girls which are most likely not to be realised! We need to ensure that this situation is reversed.

The green ideal -and sustainable development is about economic, social and environmental. In Kennet Womens *Unequal Pay and Poverty* (2009) I gave the indicative figures for why woman have a better environmental record. They are more likely to be directly dependent on nature- to be more aware of nature in their own bodies- and to see themselves as connected to it- rather than constantly vainly hoping to conquer it or destroy it. They know it is more powerful than they are and so live within its bounds much more.

Sustainable development, and the gendered perspective of greens – extends right through from theory into practice- so that if large multinationals want to claim to be " green " then they need to get on board to this an absolutely core principle. They need to recruit and train and promote and reward women equally.

If half the population is women then countries need to find a way to have equal representation of women in their parliaments. The UN keeps statistics on this. Readers might like to familiarise themselves with these figures. Women need to be encouraged to participate in political life. Only by being equally represented can those women help other women in their country. Even Margaret Thatcher had to make 24 attempts to be adopted by her party as a candidate for parliament as she faced such discrimination.

Today, women in the UK for example are facing four new challenges. Firstly as documented by Rugieri (2010) women are affected most by the cuts, as it is the public sector which is being cut first, especially those areas which are dominated by women numerically. This includes health education and social care- all of which are subject to very deep cuts and other political constraints which will limit their size. The literature also charts that in addition to the Austerity Packages aimed at womens jobs- (as women are more compliant and known to complain less) the stimulus packages are mainly aimed at heavy manufacturing jobs where women are not represented or welcomed at all. So in fact they miss out twice in this rapidly emerging scenario. You may wonder - Are they well represented in the " cleaner" industries?(such as banking and finance) and in fact here we find the very worst of gender inequality of the lot! So the men are helping themselves to immoral and economy threatening bonuses and the women have far less gender equity there almost than any other sector of the economy. Only yesterday I went to an event at the Bank of England- and the panel of expert bankers – although it had a woman chair. It seems we like our experts to be men. It has been widely criticised that the city has too much testosterone and the former Deputy Prime Minister Hariet Harman, said that if *Lehman Brothers had been Lehman sisters then we would not have had the crash at all*. Women tend to be more careful and to consider the next generations far more than short term greed. The country Iceland was the best example, where the men brought the national banks and the economy to its knees and the women sorted it out.

Gender Budgeting is a methodology which ensures that womens perspectives and economics angles are considered and this is an important contribution and should happen for all major projects, policies and initiatives.

A unique geography of gender issues is provided with voices from around the globe, from China to Africa to India and South America, giving a truly inclusive perspective from those most affected. The final section deals with implementation of inclusive policies and diversity and the practicalities of this process.

As we have seen in the UK, child benefit -once regarded as a really good modern way to ensure that at least some money ended up in women's pockets directly to help them with child care- is now being removed. Also pensions, are being changed so that they are based on life time average earnings rather than final salary so women loose out as they are paid hundreds of thousands less than men over a life time (Kennet 2009.) Women gain but then can fall back easily.

So its vital we continue with the struggle – that each woman who reads this volume takes something from it on which she can make a difference.
We were very pleased that we won an award for our work in this important area of change. Last autumn we were recognized for our womens work and campaigning at an event with top journalists in London.

Gender balance starts in our own work even in our academic journal. It is very successful but in each issue about 20 men happily send their work in – and exhibit a range of qualities- women – we like to have gender balance – we nearly always have to ask -to remind and reassure and some of the best articles have been written by women but I think they are so used to either being pressured -as women are doing much of the worlds work -according to statistics- and also being kicked back or ignored so they are not used to receiving encouragement to publish. We need more women to publish and to be noticed. Please do write something for the academic journal!

Further one of the new campaigning ways to make a difference is to ensure that companies have equal representation on company boards. In the Green Economics Institute we have managed to do this. However in company boards in the UK the figure was 9%- and in Norway a big campaign was started as they were the world leader but still only had 27% of boards having women. This means that in the private sector women's views and concerns didn't make it into the board room at all- since people seem to promote people in their own image this meant that women had no role model and no mentor or promoter at all in most of the big companies or even the little companies. This is something every reader can get involved in. Most companies have the names and biographies of the Directors on their websites. Check out all the companies in which you invest or have shares or a pension or buy from regularly. Check they have gender equality and if not then write to the board and ask them how they are going to change it.

We personally raise this issue at everything we go to so that people know it matters. Ensure you check and ask when you buy things and when you attend events. If there are no women speakers on a panel – ask – not just why not- but ask what the next event is like and which women they will put onto it- do they need help finding women to participate?

Actions for our Readers:

1. Check all panels of experts and speakers you see and start asking them to include women next time or even this time-

2. Check all new policies you hear about for their impact on women -and ask the policy maker what they propose to do about it

3. Check company boards for equality in their Directors Board Room and if its not equal write and ask them what they are going to do about it or attend their shareholders meeting and raise the question in public.

4. For books it is known that its more difficult for women to get published- and on a panel we went to of all the major large book buyers in the Uk for example we found not a single woman. So women's perspectives, concerns and writing has much less access to market right from the early selection but worse than that- publishing in a way is an arbiter of truth and so if that is completely without women in it then women wont be part of the creation of that narrative of truth -please check the companies whose items knowledge and books you read and ask them how they will create gender balance.

5. If you are a woman, get on the boards of companies and ensure your perspectives get heard.

The Green Economics Institute has so far run 6 events on women's unequal pay and poverty and economics, as well as publishing a special issue of our academic journal *International Journal of Green Economics,* Inderscience Vol. 3 issue 3 2008, and also *Proceedings (2006, 2009,2010, 2011)* of all the events and conferences available from the Green Economics Institute and sees it as a core issue. We hope you do to and we look forward to welcoming readers to join with this most worthwhile of activities.

Women hold up half the earth, we are sailing into unchartered waters, literally and in terms of the economy and climate change and biodiversity loss, which will cost us dearly and our survivability is for the first time scientifically open to question. We need to reduce the costs of women's unequal pay and poverty and empower this half of the world to take its equal and rightful place on our planet and in our economy.

Part 3: Challenges in today's economic methodology

London City building, 2012 Photo by Tone Berg

"The frog does not drink up the pond in which it lives"

(Chinese Proverb)

3.1 The Tragedy of the Commons

Why we are not being careful enough

Clive Lord

"The Tragedy of the Commons" was the title of an essay published by Garrett Hardin in *Science*, 162 (1968):pp1243-1248.1 I first read it in *Towards a Steady State Economy*, edited by Herman Daly, (1973). It made a profound impression on me at a time when I was new to environmental politics, and my whole view of life (my 'paradigm') was in the melting-pot.

Hardin starts by asserting that there is a class of problems to which there is no technical solution. He uses the example of what he, an American, calls 'tick-tack-toe', and in Britain we call noughts and crosses. If neither player makes a mistake, then no one can win. (Some may remember this being used to dramatic effect in the film *Dr Strangelove.)* He then argues that world population and pollution are problems in this class. Technology can take us so far, but ultimately a finite world can only support a finite population, or absorb a finite amount of waste matter. Sooner or later we must make choices between maximum and optimum, having given those terms meaningful definitions. Remember, Hardin was writing in 1968, four years before the beginning of the sea-change made possible by *Limits to Growth,* and at a time when there was utter confidence in technology to solve all or any problems.

Hardin quotes a pamphlet published in 1833 by an amateur mathematician named William Foster Lloyd, *Two Lectures on the Checks to Population,* to explain what he calls 'the tragedy of freedom in a commons'.2 Hardin uses the term 'Tragedy' in the sense of Greek tragedy - not unhappiness per se, but the remorselessness of a given chain of events, and the futility of trying to escape it. He explains:

The tragedy of the commons develops in this way. Picture a pasture open to all. It is to be expected that each herdsman will try to keep as many cattle as possible on the commons. Such an arrangement may work reasonably satisfactorily for centuries because tribal wars, poaching, and disease keep the numbers of both man and beast well below the carrying capacity of the land. Finally, however, comes the day of reckoning, that is, the day when the long-desired goal of social stability becomes a reality. At this point, the inherent logic of the commons remorselessly generates tragedy.

As a rational being, each herdsman seeks to maximize his gain. Explicitly or implicitly, more or less consciously, he asks, "What is the utility *to me* of adding one more animal to my herd?" This utility has one negative and one positive component.

> 1. The positive component is a function of the increment of one animal. Since the herdsman receives all the proceeds from the sale of the additional animal, the positive utility is nearly + 1.

2. The negative component is a function of the additional overgrazing created by one more animal. Since, however, the effects of overgrazing are shared by all the herdsmen, the negative utility for any particular decision making herdsman is only a fraction of - 1.

Adding together the component partial utilities, the rational herdsman concludes that the only sensible course for him to pursue is to add another animal to his herd. And another... But this is the conclusion reached by each and every rational herdsman sharing a commons. Therein is the tragedy. Each man is locked into a system that compels him to increase his herd without limit -- in a world that is limited. Ruin is the destination toward which all men rush, each pursuing his own best interest in a society that believes in the freedom of the commons. Freedom in a commons brings ruin to all.

After discussing the limitations of some apparently easier or more obvious answers, the solution which Hardin proposes is 'mutual coercion mutually agreed upon'. He cites taxation as an existing example of this, and uses parking charges backed up by fines as an illustration of how access to a commons can be regulated. So far so good. Unfortunately that is as far as Hardin's essay takes matters. He does not deal with the formidable difficulties on the way to agreeing effective mutual coercion world-wide over the vast range of topics where the Tragedy of the Commons is already a serious problem. In particular, Hardin does not address the excessively competitive ethos inherent in an expanding economy which prevents co-operative attitudes from emerging quickly enough to avoid serious problems when scope for expansion comes to an end. The whole phenomenon of globalization, and the drive for global competitiveness follows naturally from Hardin's thesis. A series of summits starting with Stockholm in 1972 have predictably failed to address the perceived environmental threat. These attempts, are charted in Chapter 28, but according to Oliver Tickell2, even the measures purporting to implement the 1997 Kyoto Protocol have done more harm than good. At the time of writing there is widespread disappointment at the outcome of the Copenhagen summit in December 2009 which has not been allayed by the muted expectations and results from Cancun in 2010.

In order to explore these difficulties I propose to start from the situation outlined in the parable just quoted. I shall call this 'Scenario One'. Each herdsman with access to the commons will approach the situation differently. One, let us call him Alfred, fears over-grazing sooner than all the others. They smile, and tell him that if he wishes to solve the problem that exists only in his mind by reducing *his* herd, no one will stop him. If he does so, he will have the least power to influence events when the crunch really does arrive.

But the parable assumes that everyone is acting rationally. Alfred swallows his misgivings and carries on as before. In due course more and more herdsmen recognize that although Alfred was unduly pessimistic to begin with, the time is approaching when he may be right. So long as they are in a minority nothing changes, but eventually most of the herdsmen accept that they will have to do something. Rational - i.e. rationing - solutions are proposed, but a significant minority, led by the ebullient Bernard, will have none of it. They have centuries of common sense on their side. They do not accept that overgrazing is going to happen. Not yet at any rate. The problem may be solved in the ways it always has been. Besides, there are all sorts of new strains of grass being developed. They could chop down more forest and extend the common pasture, or perhaps they could even...

At this point, coercion could be brought to bear by the majority on themselves as well as the objectors. Remember, everyone is assumed to be acting rationally according to the situation as they see it. It would not be a happy ending, because it is unlikely to be peaceful. It is not too fanciful to guess that the Alfreds of this hypothetical world are by nature quiet, self-effacing types, and the Bernards are more aggressive and accustomed to being tactically astute in their dealings in the cattle market. Even an overwhelming nominal majority may not be enough. Above all, it would certainly not be mutual or agreed upon.

Another scenario could be that some herdsmen do exercise restraint.3 But if they do, Bernard and his friends will grow relatively richer and more powerful, so that when the crisis does break, it is the worst offenders who are in control. No, we are dealing with a rational community. No one will allow that to happen to themselves as individuals. Either everyone is subject to enforceable restraints, or everyone carries on headlong into Tragedy. This is 'Scenario Two'.

A variation which cannot be ruled out is that Bernard is not being entirely honest. His aggressive manner has worked well enough in the past, and at the back of his mind is the determination that if things *do* go wrong, he will make sure that he is in a position of strength, so that he is not the loser. There are basically three, not two logical responses to an imminent 'Tragedy'. Firstly, there are those who recognize the problem, and would like to co-operate with plans to avert it, but whose efforts would be pointless until all other members of the community participate. Secondly there are those who genuinely believe that technological solutions will be found, certainly in the short term and possibly indefinitely.

It is understandable that entrepreneurs who correctly perceive that ecological-rules will inhibit their opportunities will cling to a 'techno- fix' view longer than most. It is serious enough that such entrepreneurs will have been generally successful, and hence as a group they will (do) exert powerful economic influence. But the problem is much worse than that. It will be impossible to distinguish entrepreneurs with a genuine belief in infinite human ingenuity from a third, and most dangerous group: those who do recognize the problem, but who are in a dominant position, or who believe they can be before the crisis occurs. Unbridled competition does make sense as a basic feature of a society with scope for expansion. When the number of sheep on a pasture which will support 10,000 increases from 9,999 to 10,001, it is not immediately obvious that the interests of each individual shepherd suddenly reverse from being identical to those of society as a whole to being diametrically opposed. Given the difficulties in switching to a consensus to set limits due to the lack of unanimity, those who think they are the probable winners are more likely to decide that it is in their interests to *pretend* to be in the denial camp. But to make this strategy work, logic requires that they behave *badly* in the here and now in terms of ecological sustainability where necessary to ensure dominance economically - or militarily.

The behaviour of the George W. Bush administration in the USA would fit this hypothesis, but rather more worrying is the behaviour of corporations such as Exxon as documented by George Monbiot4, which is likely to be less transient. Exxon has poured millions into obfuscating the evidence for climate change, and creating the impression that there is considerable doubt within the scientific community, where this is almost non-existent.

Earlier I referred to a community, but the parable mentions no community, only herdsmen. I have implied that all the characters in this 'Tragedy' do at least meet and talk. Even if we assume that they all know of each others existence, as do nation states in the real world, not until all conceivable users of the common pasture are fully involved in a real community can we be sure of either effective coercion or mutual agreement. As long as any significant players, be they groups of people, corporations or nation states deny that there is a problem, Scenario Two proceeds apace.

Unfortunately this is no parable. It may have seemed theoretical when it was first written, but it is happening in reality. The pasture is the biosphere - the thin shell within which life is possible which surrounds a ball only 8,000 miles (13,000 Km.) in diameter. The community must include everyone, and every nation on Earth. The collapse of the Grand Banks fisheries off Newfoundland followed almost exactly this course. Scientists' warnings to the local fishermen had gone unheeded for years, but it was boats from other countries that precipitated the final swift destruction of what had been a truly enormous resource. Two decades earlier, the same Tragedy was enacted at the expense of the blue whale - the largest animal that has ever lived on Earth. Despite these precedents, the same play is currently being performed on the European side of the North Atlantic. It probably has some of the same actors.

In case anyone doubts the determination and ruthlessness of the real life 'Bernards', let me quote again from Elizabeth Brubaker, on the collapse of Newfoundland fishing stocks:5

The fact that this ecological and economic disaster could have been avoided makes it even more tragic. For too much of the history of the Atlantic fisheries, the wrong people have been making the wrong decisions for the wrong reasons. Politicians have permitted catch levels far beyond those recommended by their own scientists. They have subsidized expansion of the fishery despite countless warnings of overcapacity. Like political piranhas, they have cleaned out the fisheries in their greed to snatch the next election; this species of leader leaves nothing behind to sustain those who will soon follow.

Canada's fisheries managers tried desperately to blame the groundfish collapse on forces beyond their control. Colder water temperatures, they suggested, had driven the cod away, while an exploding seal population had eaten both the cod and the capelin, the cod's favorite food. In fact, such environmental factors played minor roles. The real problem, scientists now widely agree, was that the politicians and bureaucrats in charge not only permitted but actually encouraged overfishing.

There is a body of opinion which rejects Hardin's 'Tragedy' thesis on the grounds that there are numerous examples of perfectly well managed commons6, 7. These examples are not relevant to the dynamics inherent in an expanding society. This rejection is coupled with the allegation that the 'Tragedy' was used to justify the enclosures of common land in Britain in the eighteenth century, which caused appalling hardship to displaced crofters. That the 'Tragedy' may well have been misused in this way does not affect its validity., as the example of Easter Island demonstrates. As Professor Diamond points out:

It is clear from all the cases discussed in this book that precisely such a failure has happened repeatedly.8

Indeed, in another book, Diamond adduces evidence for the proposition that in *all* instances where humans first colonized uninhabited territory, they reduced its population carrying capacity by deforestation, or exterminating species which could have been hunted sustainably.9 He suggests a 'road map' of four stages at which such failures of group decision-making: may occur:

First, a group may fail to anticipate a problem . . [for example] . . because they had no prior experience of it. Second, when the problem does arrive, the group may fail to perceive it. Then, after they perceive it, they may fail even to try to solve it. Finally, they may try to solve it, but may not succeed. 8

Professor Diamond's discussion demonstrates how incredibly easy it is to fall at any of these seemingly low fences. Extrapolating his penetrating analysis to our current global situation becomes especially chilling. However, like Garrett Hardin before him, his discussion does not include the relevance of competition having extended beyond its normally limited role where a society has escaped ecological constraints for too long. Even in the halcyon days prior to 1400, competition between clans on Rapanui was clearly evident, though it was no doubt friendly enough at first. The statues for which Easter Island is famous steadily grew in size and number, in effect constituting an expansion of economic activity as a multiplier of the population growth. However, not only did construction abruptly cease when trees and ropes were no longer available, but one by one, all those erected were toppled during inter- clan warfare. Those now standing are latter-day resurrections, presumably with tourists in mind.

Agriculture is perhaps worth a special mention in the context of the 'Tragedy of the Commons'. The quotation in Chapter 6 by Clive Ponting points out that agriculture, far from being a brilliant idea, was more likely to have been a desperate remedy for over-population or habitat destruction. Humans with all our astonishing capabilities have existed for at least 100,000 years, yet it is only 10,000 years since anybody bothered to plant things, or to use animals. Remember, the first farmers did not start with succulent cereals, brassicas, yams or potatoes, but with the grasses and scrawny forbears still to be found in the wild. The same goes for domestic animals. For, me, it follows that any community which has adopted some form of agriculture must have passed through at least one 'Tragedy' at some point in the past.

Once the principle is recognized, the 'Tragedy of the Commons' can be seen at work at all levels. The principle underlying Scenario Two applies to all kinds of situations. It is why limitations on arms sales to unpleasant regimes are difficult to pin down. "If we don't, somebody less scrupulous will." There is no doubting the loss of prosperity when a tank factory in East Leeds closed. Which car manufacturer is expected to be the first to reduce production on the grounds of climate change? The same argument applies across the whole range of consumer durables. Such battles have already been fought, for example in the steel and shipbuilding industries. But that is the point. They have been decided by conflict with winners and losers, not by mutual agreement in advance of a crisis which was clearly looming. Perhaps a moment of wisdom after the event is in order here. The behaviour for which bankers are condemned is simply a typical example of the 'Tragedy'. Even if an individual banker did see the economic collapse coming, what should he do? Certainly he should not moderate his excessive lending criteria unilaterally. The answer can already be found earlier in this chapter.

Scenario Two made a dramatic entrance in Europe in September 2000 in the shape of fuel blockades which swept through most countries in the European Union. First France, and then Britain was paralysed by farmers, fishermen and road hauliers blockading oil refineries. The blockades were effective because the apparent victims and even the public at large supported them wholeheartedly,10 despite the inconvenience and indeed sheer panic. There were distinct echoes of the events leading up to the Grand Banks fisheries disaster. There was a brilliant cartoon in the *Independent* newspaper, of a Third World flood victim marooned in a dead tree holding up a placard which said, "The price of petrol is too high". But that did not stop me 'panic buying' petrol when I had the opportunity, along with all the other car drivers. Once again collective insanity resulted from each of us acting rationally in pursuance of our short-term individual interests.

The same forces are at work over the question of housing on green field sites, but here another factor could be involved, to which I shall have to return later: population pressure. Population increase in Britain is localized in its effect, and is only one of a whole range of pressures driving the housing market. But in some areas resistance is increasing to encroachments of any kind - evidence that we may be approaching a perceived saturation point. Volatile house prices are due to other causes, but population pressure will not help. In a room which will comfortably hold 100 people, as long as there are say 98 or fewer, one leaving or entering will not be noticed. But over 100 each extra person - or for that matter any other normally insignificant added pressure, will create discomfort out of all proportion for everyone. This is just another aspect of Garrett Hardin's concept of the 'carrying capacity' of a commons.

But it is the global examples of the working of the Tragedy of the Commons which are of the greatest concern: those whose effects ignore national boundaries. Commercial considerations dominate environmental ones in the nuclear power and waste reprocessing industries. Genetically modified crops have the potential to affect the environment worldwide in unpredictable and irreversible ways. Yet just as in Garrett Hardin's parable, the benefit to the GM manufacturers is +1, and they estimate the harm to themselves as only a fraction of -1. This has been compounded in Britain by government support for GM crops. Its reasoning was quite understandable. If there are immense profits to be made, the government wants them to be made and taxed in Britain, rather than for the technology to be exploited elsewhere. Scenario Two again.

Specific areas of concern against which all others pale into insignificance include the energy industry, transport generally and the rise in air traffic in particular, and rainforest destruction. In the case of the energy industry, although the same pressures are clearly at work, there is a gleam of hope that it will be less intractable than most examples of the 'Tragedy'. If governments really do start to take their Kyoto commitments seriously, a shift to renewable sources of energy could happen

Limits to Growth correctly predicted that pollution would threaten to be the most serious problem associated with expanding energy use, but 'peak oil' – whether we are approaching, or may already have passed the point at which oil consumption worldwide must inevitably decline – and the sheer traffic congestion in urban areas the world over are major problems in their own right. A move towards public transport and pool cars would help to ameliorate this last mentioned. However aviation is the fastest growing sector now. It has been estimated that the fuel consumption and exhaust produced by each and every plane carrying passengers from Britain to Australia is the same as if each of those passengers had driven a car for the same distance. But much of that pollution is water vapour and greenhouse gases in the stratosphere which was previously devoid of them. As there is no rain at that altitude, these accumulate, and will take years to dissipate.

Despite the scientific evidence, governments continue to subsidize airlines, so that anyone who does not fly on environmental grounds subsidizes those who do. This is a straightforward case of Scenario Two, with the USA again in the role of Bernard. Other countries remonstrated, but naturally, their rational response to the USA's refusal was not to put themselves at a disadvantage. The rationalizations employed during the fisheries disaster were being writ large. Airlines not only offer cheaper fares than surface travel, an environmental scandal in itself, but all are in fierce competition with cheap fares as the selling point. As with fishing, increases are still planned.

In the same vein, the USA has probably the cheapest petrol prices in the world. So it stood out at Kyoto against tighter targets. At least Europe had made some attempt to introduce environmental factors into fuel prices, hence the backlash, but apart from some state taxes, there has never been the slightest question of such a move in the USA. The reason is of course that no politician dare suggest otherwise as long as 'Bernards' heavily outnumber 'Alfreds' there, which they clearly do. I shall discuss this problem in later chapters , including the reason why Al Gore has been a member of a government or an environmental campaigner, but not both at the same time. Meanwhile, efforts to reduce greenhouse gases elsewhere are nullified.

Rainforest destruction speaks for itself. There are comprehensive accounts of the appalling scale and speed of this, extensively catalogued in *The Stern Report11*. Not only is it a prime example of the Tragedy of the Commons, it is yet another illustration of how Scenario One inevitably deepens into Scenario Two. The rainforest is a crucial part of the biosphere which affects us all. There are two factors in the destruction of the rainforest - transnational companies, and subsistence farmers on the margins who do it simply to survive for another year. The transnationals claim that in Brazil it is poor farmers who are responsible for more of the damage than they are. This is of course no excuse, but there is a grain of truth in it. Both problems must be addressed if hopes of an ecologically sustainable future are to become a reality.

Quite apart from specific examples, the 'tragedy' is driving the whole dynamic of globalization. Some of us are appalled at the rapacity with which mega corporations are sucking the life out of peoples without the power to resist, not to mention the ecosphere, and the specious arguments used to justify such behaviour. But what would be the point of one or more of them giving up their hard fought advantage, if the way is simply cleared for the next wave of predators?

Paradoxically, for me the most worrying aspect of this threat to mankind lies with those who are trying to respond to it. It is not clear that the Green movement fully recognizes the significance of the Tragedy of the Commons, especially the sheer enormity of the dynamics driving Scenario Two - the principle that in general the worse the ecological behaviour the greater the perpetrator's economic strength in conventional terms. Schumacher's dictum was "Think globally, act locally".12 Perhaps the latter half is better observed than the former because it is only at the local level that Greens can have a significant impact, certainly in Britain. But what is the point if British good behaviour is puny alongside uninhibited economic growth in China, India, or the USA? Of course decentralization is right in principle. Decisions should be taken as locally as possible, and individuals should feel empowered, not controlled. But how are we to dovetail these ideals with the need for 'mutual coercion mutually agreed upon' - worldwide?13

This is clearly a huge problem. Certainly localization and carbon taxes have a vital part to play.. Does it entail some form of democratically elected *world* government, with effective powers of enforcement? If so, then most aspects are beyond the scope of this book, which merely offers a possible basis for a worldwide consensus. How might such a government arise? Are there lessons in the experience of the European Union? Because economic expansion was their primary concern, the influences of the IMF WTO or the World Bank have usually been disastrous from an ecological point of view. How are these influences to be circumvented? Gaia has always successfully re-established equilibrium after environmental disturbances *without* any vestige of world government, but we have yet to learn how she does it, or whether her methods would be acceptable in the context of human society. But somehow we must achieve Garrett Hardin's prescription. Until this is in prospect, what hope can there be of those who do not share the Green paradigm taking any notice? They will go on demanding cheap petrol, over-fishing, building entertainment and shopping complexes, selling arms, expanding car (and other consumer durable) sales, exploring for oil (and flaring off the inconvenient bits into the stratosphere), promoting air travel and felling rainforest for profit *until it is too late.*

For anyone who still has difficulty in taking this threat seriously, please read *A Green History of the World,* by Clive Lord Ponting.14 The Tragedy is *not* inevitable, but a theme which I shall develop is that the whole of the human race (except a tiny minority) has been on a course of expansion for many millennia, accelerated by the introduction of permanent agriculture. For all except a pre- agricultural minority, the Tragedy has been a constant threat requiring progressively more difficult evasive action, not always successful.

As we have seen, the Tragedy can operate at any level, from the personal to the global, but it is in the context of globalization that the Tragedy becomes devastating. Wherever there is unrestricted competition, each competitor must disregard the long term common good if it conflicts with his immediate interests. The rule is whatever the risk, it is outweighed by that of losing market share. The first competitor to throw in his hand in this deadly poker school ensures not that the world will be preserved, but that others will gain at his expense. If primary resources are added to Garrett Hardin's population and pollution, everything else comes down to these three basics. Sooner or later each must come uncomfortably close to the limits of its 'carrying capacity', and with the exponential principle at work, the moment will, as we have seen in the examples where it has already happened, tend to come rather more suddenly than conventional wisdom anticipates.

As Jared Diamond says in *Collapse:*

The parallels between Easter Island and the whole modern world are chillingly obvious. Thanks to globalization, international trade, jet planes, and the internet, all countries on Earth today share resources and affect each other, just as did Easter's dozen clans. Polynesian Easter Island was as isolated in the Pacific Ocean as the Earth is today in space. When the Easter Islanders got into difficulties, there was nowhere to which they could flee, or turn for help. . . . Those are the reasons why people see the collapse of Easter Island society as a metaphor, a worst-case scenario for what may lie ahead of us.

Despite the foregoing, Professor Diamond ends on a hopeful note, and indeed, I hope in subsequent chapters to make such optimism more realistic. But as expansion comes up against limits, the Tragedy ensures that unless there is a better strategy in place, each participant can see no alternative but to hasten and worsen the crisis. This book attempts to suggest such a strategy. It is possible that the fishermen off the east coast of North America and the Easter Islanders were more stupid than the rest of us. But is it not just as probable that like us, including even some who are trying to take evasive action, they simply underestimated the speed with which the exponential principle finally snaps shut the trap set by the Tragedy of the Commons?

References

1. Hardin. Garrett (1968) *The Tragedy of the Commons* Science 162 (1968) pp1243-12482.

2. Tickell, Oliver (2008) *Kyoto 2)* Zed Books 7 Cynthia St. London N1 9JF

3. An actual example of this occurred in 1999 when the British pig industry was subjected to regulations which did not apply to imported products

4. Monbiot, George (2006) *Heat* Allen Lane

5. Brubaker, Elisabeth, *Cod don't vote How politics destroyed Atlantic Canada's fisheries.* An Internet discussion. Email ElisabethBrubaker@nextcity.com or PerspectiveCDV@nextcity.com.

6. Ostrom Elinor *Governing the Commons* (1990): *The Evolution of Institutions for Collective Action* Cambridge University Press (and later work)

7. Shiva, Vananda (1989) *Staying Alive: Women Ecology and Development* Zed Books London

8. Diamond, Jared (2005) *Collapse: how Societies choose to fail or survive* Allen Lane

9. Diamond, Jared (1992) *The rise and fall of the third chimpanzee* Random House

10. Opinion polls put support for the blockades at 88% in France, and between 78% and 84% in UK.

11. Stern, N (2007) *The Economics of Climate Change: GThe Stern* Review Cambridge University Press

12. Schumacher, E. F: (1973) *Small is Beautiful: Economics as If People Really Mattered* Abacus. London

13. See Axelrod, Robert (1984) *The Evolution of Cooperation* Basic Books inc., New York; (1990) Penguin Books, London W8 For a discussion of this topic

14. Ponting, Clive (1991) *A Green History of the World* Sinclair Stevenson Ltd London

3.2 How useful is econometrics for Green Economics?

By Sophie Billington

In this chapter, I shall address the contentious issues relating to the use of econometrics within the field of green economics and I will argue that, in many cases, econometrics *could* prove to be a useful tool for analysing specific problems in green economics. I shall start by defining the key terms, 'green economics' and 'econometrics' and then go on to suggest some of the reasons why econometrics could be of use as well as some of the reasons why it may be applied inappropriately in the context of green economics. I will conclude by reflecting upon the future for econometrics within the discipline of green economics.

Green economics is an alternative approach to thinking about economics in a world where our actions are beginning to have huge implications for the natural environment. This developing field of economics highlights the inter-dependence of human civilization and natural ecosystems, and considers the impacts that our own decisions have on all aspects of life on earth. Research in green economics typically aims to find solutions to problems such as, climate change, resource depletion, poverty, damage to ecosystems, loss of biodiversity and population pressure (Kennet, 2007). The research tends to be based around instinctive and practical ideas; it rarely makes use of econometric models, which are often thought to be too narrowly defined for the issues which are dealt with in green economics.

Econometrics can be described as the application of statistical techniques to economic theories. It can be used for modelling purposes i.e. to test hypotheses and infer the relationship between a set of variables. It could also be used for forecasting purposes, in order to predict future trends in the data.

Let us now consider a simple econometric model, $Y_i = \beta_0 + \beta_1 X_i + \varepsilon_i$. That is, for each individual observation, i, and with fixed parameter values, β_0 and β_1, the dependent variable, Y_i, is determined by the value of X_i, plus a random component, ε_i. For the model to be unbiased, the expectation of ε (its mean value) must equal zero. Furthermore, to find the most suitable estimator to use, we must also minimize the variance of ε. Therefore the primary aim is to find the estimator with the minimum variance, subject to the condition that the model is unbiased. This will be our best linear unbiased estimator, and will be used to obtain an estimate of the parameters in the model (in this case β_0 and β_1).

Why might this type of analysis be useful for green economics? Let us, for example, consider the model $Y_i = \beta_0 + \beta_1 X_{1i} + \beta_2 X_{2i} + \varepsilon_i$ and define Y as the number of people living in absolute poverty, X_1 as government expenditure on education, and X_2 as government expenditure on social security benefits. We are then able to use either time-series data (taken over a period of time), or panel data (from a sample of different countries), to determine the effect that expenditure on education or social security has on the level of absolute poverty within a county. We can establish whether these variables are statistically significant in the model and can evaluate their parameter values to find the effect they have on the level of absolute poverty. This analysis would therefore be extremely useful for informing decisions related to government policy. Should a government invest in education or social security if their primary objective is to reduce absolute poverty and they only have a limited budget? The model I used is, of course, highly simplified, and therefore our estimates are likely to suffer from problems such as omitted variable bias, which is referred to later in this paper. We could add more variables, which may improve our model, provided that they were statistically significant.

Other examples of using statistical models to make informed decisions on green issues include regressions to find out: how significant is the effect of a carbon trading scheme on carbon emissions reduction; to what extent are rising sea levels affecting the seagull population; what effect do democracies have on the level of absolute poverty within a county. Using similar regressions to these, we may determine crucial relationships between variables which may not be obvious or instinctive if the analysis had not been carried out.

There are, however, various problems with the use of econometric analysis, many of which are indeed acknowledged by mainstream economists. In the next few paragraphs, I will briefly describe some of these issues before expanding my discussion into further concerns which are held by many supporters of the green economics movement.

The most obvious fault with most econometric and mathematical modelling is that the models are often highly simplified. For example, there may sometimes be a case of omitted variable bias, where explanatory variables from the true model are omitted, either because no data for that specific variable was available, or because the relationship between the variables was not recognized. This will therefore bias the estimates of the parameters in the model. As a consequence, the results will be incorrect and therefore, the conclusions drawn will be wrong. This is a classic example of when critics describe econometrics as being precise, but wrong; whereas they often claim that a more intuitive or philosophical approach will be less precise, but closer to the truth. Moreover, supporters of green economics believe that the world is characterized by extremely complex and inter-dependent systems and relationships between human and ecological factors.

Furthermore, the models used in economics can often depend on questionable assumptions which can affect the 'practicality' of the model. We need to ask ourselves whether these assumptions are realistic enough to be acceptable in the model. If the assumptions are not satisfactory, then when too much emphasis is put on the models, we can end up with significant economic consequences. An example of this is the recent financial crisis. The financial models used by the banks were established on the assumption that house prices would continue to rise. When this key assumption broke down in early 2007, a huge 'credit crunch' led to a global economic recession, the effects of which are still prominent 3 years on.

Green Economics Methodology : An Introduction

A further critique of econometrics is that it deals with variables which must be measured quantitatively. There is, however, considerable difficulty in measuring many variables this way. For example, what value do you put on the loss of the entire Amazon rainforest? What value would do you put on the entire elephant population becoming extinct? Economists' answer to this is to apply CBA (Cost Benefit Analysis) to these situations, whereby a monetary value is assigned to each and every social, environmental and economic aspect which may occur in a specific situation. The values are typically calculated by considering how much people would be willing to pay, to prevent one of these scenarios from occurring. Inputs are evaluated in terms of their opportunity cost. The effect that the scenario will have on GDP is also commonly used as a way of measuring total cost. Surely though, some of these scenarios are impossible to valuate. Indeed, money, our own invention, is too narrowly defined to be used to evaluate the impact of major a disaster, one which could, for example, wipe out the entire human population. This is an extreme example, but it illustrates why many supporters of green economics have criticised the use of econometrics as failing to deal with these issues in a practical way.

Furthermore, economists have often discussed the fact that some variables which we use in econometrics are inappropriately employed as a proxy for a variable which is more difficult, or even impossible, to measure. The alternative variables which are used can sometimes prove to be a poor substitute.

One final observation is that econometrics is very good at showing us the relationship between specific variables in the past, but it tells us very little about future solutions to problems which we are only beginning to experience now. We have not yet compiled enough data to calculate the extent to which we have already been affected by climate change and predicting the magnitude of future climate change involves a very high degree of uncertainty. It is these types of issues which are at the core of green economics and perhaps a more creative wisdom is necessary in order to find possible solutions and ideas before it is too late.

In conclusion, I do agree that there are certain problems with using econometrics to analyse issues in green economics. Using statistics in the practise of economics is very different from analysing statistical relationships in most other sciences, where conditions can be appropriately controlled and inputs carefully monitored. In economics, it is more difficult to create these perfectly controlled conditions in order to conduct a 'social experiment'. Tony Lawson (2007) questions whether human behaviour is predictable and queries whether the same results would occur if we were to repeat a social experiment in the exact same conditions.

However, I think that econometrics should not be dismissed when considering its usefulness for green economics. It is a fact of life that we must make decisions. Choices must be made and trade-offs will be involved. From deciding whether to invest in solar power or wind-turbines, to deciding what rate the Bank of England should set interest rates at, the only current method of objectively analysing their impacts in order to make an informed decision is to apply econometrics to the problem.

3.3 Cost Benefit Analysis, superficially an elegant tool but in reality a path to wrong decision making

By Juliane Göke

Cost-Benefit Analysis, Discounting and Social and Environmental Justice

Cost-Benefit Analysis is a widespread tool, helping governments and businesses to not only evaluate the attractiveness and feasibility of projects and policies, but also to make investment prospects more comparable. As the name already indicates, the analytical tool outweighs the cost of a project against the expected benefits (Mishan, Quah 2007). The assumption that a project is viable if its benefits outweigh its costs appears reasonable. However, looking at the actions of many international corporations today, one might argue that the benefits are unilateral (Sumaila, Walters 2005). This is further visible in many policies implemented by governments, which appear to be biased against long-term benefits, thus neglecting Peter Drucker's "Primum non nocere" (First do no harm) principle.

Using a Discount rate, the Cost-Benefit Analysis transforms future cash flows into present values. In the choice of an appropriate discount rate the effects of the actions on non-reproducible resources, such as biodiversity, as well as the effects on climate change, poverty creation and health are often disregarded. Therefore a social discount rate has been developed especially for the investments in social projects. The social discount rate compares projects in order to find those that have the largest aggregate benefits for the public money which will be spend on them (Sunstein, Rowell 2007). The flaw in the system is that it only compares quantitative outcomes of projects, even if they are from different natures (Varian 2006). It is thus possible that a government will not invest in emission reductions if the cost is higher than the value of climate change, but rather invests in its own welfare state, completely neglecting that the harm for future generations, and possibly other more vulnerable countries, is in need for investments in these particular areas.

The Stern Review on the Economics of Climate Change drawn up by former World Bank chief economist Nicholas Stern on behalf of the British government is a well-known example of an attempt of applying the discounting principle to climate change. The report concludes that climate change is an increasing threat, but that taking action henceforth on an international level it is still possible to stop the most harmful risks at reasonable costs. The annual cost for stabilizing the Greenhouse Gas concentration is estimated to be one per cent of the world's gross domestic product. Using a starting discount rate of 3.3 per cent, which Stern reduces to two per cent in a hundred year period, he finds that, if no action is taken, the annual cost of climate change will be equivalent to at least five per cent of the world's GDP (The Guardian 2006).

The Stern review faced support as well as criticism, especially due to the choice of the discount rate. While several mainstream economists claim that the discount rate is too low, thus overestimating the risk of climate change, environmental economists such as Frank Ackerman and Thomas Sterner believe the numbers Stern uses are in fact underestimating the danger of climate change (Cole 2008). Ackerman et al. (2009) in fact propose to use a discount rate of 10.8 per cent instead of the 3.3 used by Stern due to the importance of the matter.

After the release of the Stern review Tony Blair said that "the earth is warming at an alarming rate, we are running out of fossil fuels, and it is long past time for us to take action to correct these problems" (NY Times 2006). Six years later the debate about how much money to invest in which kind of projects has still not evolved. Despite increasing investments in areas of renewable energies, emission reductions, protection of biodiversity and poverty alleviation we have still not reached their aspired outcome, mainly due to poorly implemented projects (Easterly 2006). The loss of biodiversity and the change in ecosystems which has already taken place is severe and climate change cannot be denied anymore. Further exploitation of these resources is not just to following generations (Chong 2006). Past generations have failed to make enough of a difference. It is now up to our generation – the young people – to make a difference. To innovate, where old systems failed. To implement new ideas, technologies and knowledge. Young people around the world have a universal responsibility to take action!

References

Ackerman, F., Stanton, E., Hope, C., Alberth, S. (2009) Did the Stern Review underestimate U.S. and global climate damages? Energy Policy. Volume 37, Issue 7, Pages 2717-2721.

Beckerman, W., Hepburn, C. (2007) Ethics of the Discount Rate in the Stern Review on the Economics of Climate Change. *World Economics Journal*. Volume 8, Issue 1, Pages 187-210.

Chong, C. (2006) 'Restoring the rights of future generations.' *International Journal of Green Economics*. Volume 1, Issue 1/2, Pages 103-120.

Cole, H. (2008) The Stern Review and Its Critics: Implications for the Theory and Practice of Benefit-Cost Analysis. Natural Resources Journal. Volume 48, Issue 1, Pages 53-90.

Easterly, W. (2006) The White Man's Burden – Why the west's efforts to aid the rest have done so much ill and so little good. Gosport: Oxford University Press.

Mishan, E.J., Quah, E. (2007) Cost-Benefit Analysis. 5th Edition. Oxford: Routledge.

NY Times (2006) Bill Clinton Debuts $1B Renewable Energy Fund. Last accessed 12.01.2011 at: http://www.nytimes.com/aponline/us/AP-Clinton-Global-Initiative.html

Sumaila, U., Walters, C. (2005) Intergenerational Discounting: A new Intuitive Approach. *Ecological Economics*. Volume 52, Issue 2, Pages 135-142.

Sunstein, C.R., Rowell, A. (2007) On Discounting Regulatory Benefits: Risk, Money and Intergenerational Equity. *The University of Chicago Law Review*. Volume 74, Issue 1, Pages 171-208.

The Guardian (2006) Stern Report: The key points. Last accessed 02.07.2012 at: http://www.guardian.co.uk/politics/2006/oct/30/economy.uk

Varian, H.R. (2006) Recalculating the Cost of Global Climate Change. The New York Times. Last accessed 01.07.2012 at: http://www.public.iastate.edu/~bkh/teaching/505/cost_climate_change.pdf

3.4 Rewriting Economics

By Edward Goldsmith

Economists identify their discipline with the study of its subject matter rather than with what it is trying to achieve. As the highly respected economist Kenneth Boulding notes, it studies "prices, quantities of commodities exchanged, produced and consumed, interest rates, taxes and tariffs, etc." The assumption is that it is only by studying the interrelationships between these variables that one can determine how to achieve the economic goal modern society has set itself - the creation of "wealth" (material wealth), and hence the growth of Gross Domestic Product in terms of which it is measured. For economists, behaviour that contributes towards the achievement of this goal is judged to be "economic" and thereby "rational" while that which even slightly reduces economic growth in the interest of satisfying social, ecological and moral imperatives, is judged to be "uneconomic" and hence "irrational". Unfortunately, as I shall try to show in this short article, the most important things we need to do today if we are to have any future at all on this planet, are "uneconomic" and hence "irrational".

Let us see why modern economics produces such a distorted view of our relationship with the real world in which we live. The main reason is that modern economics has been developed in total isolation from the disciplines that seek to understand the living world. The late Professor Nicholas Georgescu-Roegen, a dissident economist at Vanderbilt University, shows how "the economic process is depicted as a circular diagram, a pendulum movement between production and consumption within a completely closed system", hence, by the way, the nature and the narrowness of the range of variables that make up the legitimate subject matter of modern economics.

As a result, Georgescu-Roegen observes the fact that there is "a continuous mutual influence between the economic process and the natural world that carries no weight with the standard economists. In Marx's famous diagram of production, too, the economic process is represented as a completely circular and self-sustaining affair."

If we consider "this continuous and mutual influence between the economic process and our physical and environment" we are forced to face the seriously negative effects of the "economic process". We can see it, in effect, as giving rise to a new organization of matter: the technosphere or world of human artefacts, or the surrogate world that is rapidly supplanting the ecosphere or world of living things, or the real world on which we ultimately depend for our welfare, and for our very survival. Unfortunately in terms of modern economics, this systematic annihilation of the real world does not qualify as a cost.

For Professor Samuelson, author of the best-known university textbook on economics, the reason is that to acquire value, things must "become scarce". On the other hand, "the more there is of a commodity the less the relative desirability of its last little unit becomes, even though its total usefulness always grows as we get more of the commodity. So, it is obvious why a large amount of water has a low price, or why air is actually a free good despite its vast usefulness. The many units pull down the market value of all the units."

In other words, neither our forests nor our soils, anymore than our wetlands, our rivers, our seas, or our coral reefs, have any value until the economic process has so degraded and destroyed them that they become sufficiently scarce to acquire an economic value. But even when this has occurred it does not mean that what still remains of the natural world is now protected from the destructiveness of economic growth. Thus US agriculture is the most destructive in the world and agricultural land in the USA is being compacted, eroded, desertified, and salinized, at an incredible rate. However, it is uneconomic and thereby "irrational" to return to sounder, and hence more ecological farming practices. As we are told by economists Earl R. Swanson and Earl O. Heady, "an adequate soil conservation" plan that would meet "soil loss tolerance levels for 20 years into the future" would increase "annualised private net farm income by only one percent". This is too little for there are "more profitable investments that can be made in the farm business". So in purely economic terms, and that is what counts for economists who study the economic process in a void, and for governments and in particular corporations that, within the context of the global economy, are increasingly in control, soil conservation is not economic, and is hence totally "irrational".

Lester Brown, founder of the Worldwatch Institute, points to the dreadful problems that face Africa today. But for him there is little we can do about them until we desist from applying to them solutions that are based on "narrow economic criteria such as the rate of return on investments". To continue doing so, Brown cautions, "is in effect to write Africa off."

Of course, economists will tell us that social and ecological costs can be internalised. For Professor Herman Daly, the father of Ecological Economics, this can be a reasonable procedure "when the externalities involved are of a minor nature", but once it is "the very capacity of the Earth to support life that must be internalised, it is time to restructure basic concepts and start with a different set of abstractions that can embrace what was previously external." This, of course, means little less than rewriting economics in the light of a unified theory of the living world.

Edward Goldsmith kindly wrote this article for the Green Economics Institute when it was launched.

3.5 What is Green Economics? A new discipline

By Volker Heinemann

Green Economics is a new academic discipline that is based on the innovations in the society that started to emerge in the 1960ies and attempted to replace the consensus based on traditional values and aims for society that existed at that time. The 'Green' agenda developed into a new set of thinking similarly to the conservative, liberal and social democratic/socialist traditions already existing.

A common misunderstanding is still that 'Green' is primarily focused on the environment, which is not the case. The ecological issues raised are part of a wider set of concerns that have at its core a rejection of conventional values and aims for society, the environmental issues follow from this core request for change in attitude similarly to the emergence of other movements like peace, feminism, social justice and human rights economic development. All those new and already existing subjects were combined to a new holistic strategy based on the unifying concern for a new consensus for society beyond conservatism.

Over the past 30 years this new set of thinking has matured and comprises a wide variety of issues and disciplines. Green Economics is a newly founded discipline within academic economics that is systematically assessing problems and questions in that original spirit. These new ideas have a defined set of basic principles that are particularly important as far as economics as a key social science is concerned. Green Economics is influenced by its historic roots concerned with the problem that existing structures are defined or seen as value free and objective whereas they are in fact a particular value or ideology based concept that just happened to be the starting point for the development of the society.

A strong belief in the benefits of evolution of society renders this new discipline truly innovative and it works to replace the existing ideologies and conventions with a wider set of options. It does so by accepting that ultimately a value free social science is not possible but in accepting this fact the discipline is therefore less normatively biased than conventional economic thinking which bases its claim to be value free because it is predicated on maintenance of the status quo and reflects majority thinking. Furthermore, all innovations in society were once in a minority position.

The outcome of such conservative thinking is a strong normative bias in economics towards explanations and concepts that have no longer any future.

As a consequence of this awareness of normative influences Green Economics is set up in the most holistic way possible. Discoveries from other sciences are actively incorporated into the own work to really make sense of the complex phenomenon called society. This stands in sharp contrast to the reductionist and overly quantitative mathematics and assumptions on which conventional mainstream research is based. Conventional economics creates an artificial world of how things could optimally be, based on the values it inherently includes. Green Economics tries as an alternative to incorporate a wider set of potential behaviour and allows for systems and institutions to be designed so that this degree of freedom is maintained and rather than a particular set of rules accepted as unavoidable. Along this way the language, methodology and terms used are reassessed. Freedom, optimal, growth and justice are all terms that have a surprisingly intentional use in conventional economics. Terms like competition, are used as if competition itself is freedom, something that is desirable, where in fact competition only occurs when people cannot achieve all their goal simultaneously. Green Economics gives people back the sovereignty over their decisions and life rather than pushing the language used, not to mention the methodology, into areas where an objective assessment of the matter considered is no longer possible.

Green Economics is practically focused and deals with all economically relevant phenomena of the modern society. Significant findings from other areas of science like for example the awareness of absolute limits to resource use are comprehensively incorporated in the approach taken, rather than a continuous attempt to rescue as much from conventional methodology and definitions as possible.

There are some similarities of Green Economics with Ecological Economics. But Ecological Economics remains focused on the environment and Green Economics does not. This is the basis for calling Green Economics a new and independent discipline from all other existing economic disciplines so far.

As it appears to be the case that the original spirit of the new value set, that gave rise to the wider green movement and finally to Green Economics, is as relevant as ever considering current issues that require addressing, it is of prime importance that this new discipline is developed further in the near future to balance the views and opinions publicised that are based on conventional thinking. It is of particular concern, as conventional economic thinking is always surrounded by scarcity up to the point that scarcity is actively promoted. This is in order to maintain a reality that can be explained within the existing framework and concepts. People are advised how to behave accordingly, so that with such outdated methods the current economic challenges will not be met. It should be emphasised that Green Economics is as a consequence not only developing an alternative view to economic issues that might or might not be normatively desired depending on the viewpoint.   The research develops the tools and methods that are required to master today's economic problems in society. This is because conventional economics evolved in the nineteenth century in a different set of circumstances and was designed and is still designed to meet those previous needs and is unable to solve the problems of today. Green Economics is truly the future of economics not just a niche addition to the discourse.

3.6 Methodology Tools and Instruments:

Green Economics: Research: Disciplinary developments: Background: Instruments and tools

By Miriam Kennet, Volker Heinemann and Michelle S. Gale de Oliveira

Green Economics has become the focus of much interest over the past year. It is increasingly clear that the standard neo-liberal model of economics is in urgent need of not only a major overhaul but a replacement with more sophisticated concepts.

These new concepts, that still need to be developed fully, are however beginning to emerge in more detail and a significant increase in alternative, pluralistic contributions is emerging against the persistent strong hostility from mainstream economics. One particular area has been the pioneering field in economics where changes to traditional concepts have been demanded and were developed already some time ago. It is the area where ecological principles were introduced into the economic discourse, where much ground has been covered in identifying the deficiencies and limitations in scope, methodology and contents of conventional economics. This area of economics is transforming itself at the same time and more recently a newly emerging concept of 'Green' or 'Progressive' economics is widening the scope of the search for an alternative economic framework even further, extending the scope and methodology of environmental and ecological economics. In doing so it is trying to reform mainstream economics, rather than adding a discipline too mainstream economics regardless of how critical this discipline might be of the existing conventional thinking. Green Economics is not niche economics, and is likely to be a major contribution to the development of a more sophisticated understanding of economics as a social science and our current economic situation and prospects for the future. There will be some examples of how economic concepts can already now influence the economic debate and transform existing policies and decision-making and will explain some of the new approaches and methodologies that have developed in this field.

Evolution towards 'Green Economics'

For quite a number of decades, environmental concerns have had a significant influence on public debate, including economics, which have recently, with the recognition of climate change as a global and highly significant environmental problems, enhanced their importance.
The significance of such environmental problems for economics is in fact very simple. It introduces absolute limits into a science that has traditionally been based on the concept that

more is better than less and which was considered as a permanent given and undisputed as the basis of all economic thinking. People have now realized that the world has an end and this existence of an absolute limit introduces the concept of evolution of society into economics. The world cannot continue forever on the basis of unchanged principles or paradigms, linear thinking has to come to an end and new concepts are required. As a consequence environmental issues are still one of the most profound areas of criticism of mainstream economics as in the standard discourse, typically referred to as 'environmental economics' the tendency persists that ecological questions are seamlessly incorporated into existing economic thinking with the aim to preserve as much as possible from the standards concepts. Conventional economics attempts to explain all ecology related decision-making based on standard economic assumptions about human behaviour assumed without looking at the impact of the newly recognized absolute boundaries that might well require people to change their behaviour, rather than just aggregating the observable human activity and presume optimal solutions from it.

Such deficiencies in the conventional 'environmental economics' approach where the environment is costed and introduced with that price into the unadjusted decision-making procedures was quickly criticized as it is in many areas missing the point that made the whole subject relevant in the first place, namely that ecological limits require a reassessment of how economic decisions can be derived based on an objective assessment of what is required rather than taking unadjusted opinions for granted. This environmental economics approach was soon criticized and led to the development of ecological economics, which aims to address the above mentioned deficiencies and to a certain extent widens the scope of its analysis by including similar issues like social justice into its discourse.

A great number of important insights can be derived that consider the natural environment and other related spheres in the discourse of Ecological Economics. There is however growing awareness that even this wider scope is still not sufficient, and that there are other issues, unrelated to ecology, that are of equal importance to make their impact in economics. There are issues of strategy, of how to implement change in mainstream economics given the fact that ecological economics concerns are experiencing a backlash or widely ignored. Most importantly that ecological economics cannot fully explain the reason why such resistance persists and the necessary reform of mainstream economics has still not taken place, despite clear deficiencies that become right now in the current economic crisis caused in part by deregulation and is very apparent.

What is required is a more comprehensive understanding of current mainstream economic thinking and of how only one specific discourse, the neo-liberal agenda, could become so dominant despite an apparent lack of sophistication in many areas. The answers to this are very complicated and require a detailed historical assessment as to how the economic discourse is formed and how it is influenced.

Green Economics is the term given to this progressive approach that is developing an alternative to conventional, conservative economics based on a more fundamentally holistic approach that identifies economics as a social science, as well as a natural science. It shows that economics as a whole cannot be explained by simplistic, typically linear, mathematics and fixed preferences of individuals.

Green Economics searches far beyond ecological economics and in fact ecological issues to wider considerations of ideology, history of thought, evolution of society, the level of objectivity and the time specificity of solutions in a social science environment to be taken into account that provide a much stronger basis to criticize current mainstream economics and eventually lead to a replacement of this doctrine. Green Economics is, with this approach, not only a very recent and advanced form of criticism of conventional 19th century economics, in addition, it has the potential to enact a comprehensive reform of this science which could and is starting to equip political decision-makers with a much more sophisticated and ideologically unbiased set of tools and insights to manage the economy more successfully. It has the capacity to widen the scope to include all relevant stakeholders rather than continuing the narrow focused reductionist economics of the past. Green or Progressive Economics results from the acceptance of society as an evolutionary process an inherently innovative and undogmatic exercise. It will help to develop true economic freedom for a much wider range of individuals including non human species concerns and those of the natural environment, nature and the planet as well as its systems. . As such it is an innovative approach to economic theory and an extremely timely and relevant contribution to the development of economics as a social science which incorporates natural and biological science data. This is in sharp contrast to the extremely un-innovative and repetitive contributions from mainstream economics. It is becoming a most significant contribution to a reform of economics, most importantly, because it does not try to reform economics by introducing ecological concepts into economics but by reforming economics in a much wider sense so that this science can correctly assess economic realities, and is as a consequence embracing a wider set of values including ecological values. -The conflict is not between economics and ecology but between the conservative conventions that have shaped a specific economic discipline that is narrow minded and those wider ecological and social and physical science concerns that are by definition not part of the conventional science of economics.

Scope, methodology and contents

Ecological and green, progressive economics are contributing to changes in economics as far as scope, methodology and contents is concerned. The contents side is of the highest relevance from a practical point of view and here we focus on some of the issues and changes in practical economic policy making. We summarise a selection of such methods that are currently shaping the discourse and already contributing to a gradual shift away from neo-liberal objectives.

We can summarize the main criticisms, concerns and areas that require change to give an overview of how the practical examples fit into this progressive framework and why the changes are necessary. In respect of the scope of economics, the major issue is methodology and the contents of economics itself, and a sample of reforms will be discussed for each category.

Green Economics Methodology : An Introduction

Scope

Economics can no longer only deal with goods and services in a narrow sense, it has to embrace a wider set of values. Ecological, cultural and social values have to form an integral part of the science.A less anthropocentric view is required to incorporate the concerns of non-human species as ultimately humans rely on the wider web of life.

Economics needs to be aware of the historic dimension. Economic models may work at a certain time but as society moves on, such concerns and concepts become irrelevant and others take their place. Non appreciation of this evolution makes models dogmatic or even worse, reality is changed or restricted -unbelievably simply to fit with the models. Efforts are made to make people behave in a certain way so that the conventional wisdom remains correct! It is this process which causes some of the disasters from economics. Reality is messy, fuzzy and complex. Economics as a discipline has attempted to be tidy, limited and linear. The two are currently mis -matched.

Economics is a social science, as well as a natural science but not a formal science like mathematics. This gives rise to a very complicated issue of what is fact and what is normative and how the normative views that influence human behaviour change over time. Economics cannot be blind to such considerations in its reasoning.

Methodology

Many economic phenomena are qualitative in nature rather than quantitative. This needs to be reflected properly and limits the usefulness of especially simple mathematics. Considerations on the quality of data are neglected. In physics it is of prime importance to get proper unbiased data. In economics very vague datasets are used as the foundation of highly formalized models without concern on how sensitive the findings are in respect of the assumptions.

Empirical data in a social science is not the same as measurements in physics. What is measured is the current activity and behaviour of human beings. This can however change and the empirical data now is not indicative on how the future of society might be, nor whether the activities of human beings based on their opinion are in any way objectively right. Empiricism has a tendency to be conservative, explaining that the world has to be as it is because this is how it currently is.

Related to this, economics requires a higher level of objectivity rather than just using current observations. Such demoscopic economics is able to identify how people behave now or what people think, but opinion is not equal to facts. Precisely an objective science has for example to be able to identify necessary changes to human behaviour to, for example balance an ecological deficit, regardless whether the public opinion accepts such a problem.

Contents

Most of the above deficiencies result in a very simplistic picture of society and very crude suggestions of how people behave and why. As a tendency a wider set of values is off the radar. The price (not the value) is the prime variable, or it is assumed that the price is always a correct approximation for value. This however ignores any intrinsic values of incorrect reflection of the full scope that should determine decision-making. The theory of external effects can obviously rectify this partly but precisely such findings are pushed to the side as soon as important proposals are made. The main criticism by Green Economics is the ideological bias of mainstream economics with the aim of using it to derive a conservative society which ignores current important trends as far as ecological, cultural and social limits or considerations are concerned. Mainstream economics is not pluralistic and it is the aim of Green Economics to add to the pluralistic and progressive spectrum by focusing on and incorporating facts derived from other sciences to overcome this bias.

In relation to this concern, current economic discourses are still highly influenced by battles between political concepts from the past. The axis of the battle with socialism is still contributing to retention of to a tendency that markets need to be deregulated ever further. This is contrary to the evidence available and can be regarded as political propaganda rather than objective science about the differentiated advantages and disadvantages of particular methods that contribute to the advancement of society.

Modern, highly sophisticated developed societies require a high level of investments that appear to be mainly 'public' in nature or are for various reasons provided publicly. Under those circumstances it appears questionable to continuously argue for the trend of reducing the public involvement and suggest that tax reductions will always contribute to economic development. Such arguments are designed to avoid all shaping of society, which is done by economic policies, and they suggest that a simplistic competitive market outcome is all that is needed. This is an attempt to prevent a simplistic materialistic economy from developing into any culturally or socially higher state, and it thus most importantly excludes any and all options which would be able to initiate any responsible lifestyle changes to balance ecological or social imbalances.

Photo by Miriam Kennet- the economics of doing, the economics of sharing, the economics of supporting each other! 2010

Part 4: Criticism of the traditional theories of Growth

The Pier at Pacific Beach, San Diego, California. 2012 Photo By Tone Berg

"Earth provides enough to satisfy every man's need, but not every man's greed."

Mahatma Ghandi

4.1 The Green Economy: Rethinking Growth,

After RIO + 20 2012

By Volker Heinemann and Miriam Kennet

Lower or zero growth could offer a realistic scenario, particularly for the future of the economy of advanced societies. This might arise from a variety of possible causes ranging from overt attempts to reduce growth in order to achieve sustainable development in society as a whole, or from the natural or cyclical levelling out of conventional, unadjusted economic growth, without any deliberate action being taken for whatever reason. Growth forecasts in many western economies have become bleak recently and the prospect of higher growth is unlikely in the shorter term at least, It seems to be the beginning of a longer lasting trend. Growth forecasts from the Treasury in the UK Budget 2008 were 1.75% in 2008 and 2.75% for 2009, but this was revised downwards by the IMF and the Eurozone is in trouble currenntly too.

Growth , post WW2, was based on high mass consumption which is unsustainable in the longer term as it would overshoot the earth 's capacity and so exeeed actual physical limits. This factor was not taken into account in the designing and execution of the economic strategy of ever higher GDP gowth but is now very apparent and the strategy is now being questioned in all quarters even in the current powerhouse of glboal growth,, China. On a finaite planet other means of generating and conceptualising wealth need to be found. The economy needs to put itself onto a sustainable footing to provision for all people everywhere , nature, other species , the panet and its systems and those groups as beneficiaries, not just as thow away imputs to the economy. That ought to be the aim of the economy of the 21st century and so we need to do different things differently and use the word growth to mean growth not destruction as it currently actually means.

The IMF World Economic Outlook, reported on what it termsed " a major financial crisis, especially in advanced economies, with global expansion now loosing speed" (IMF 2008:1) and was predicting global growth of 3.7 percent in 2008, down from 4.9 percent in 2007 and with little pick,up in 2009—at around 3.8 percent. Moreover,t here was a 25 percent chance that the growth will be 3 percent or less in 2008 and 09. Currently even growth in G ermany is less than 2 %.

The cost of the global credit crunch from over lending in the US is expected to reach 945$ US billion, and total losses so far declared are $193 billion. It is yet uncertain how growth rates will recover in the post credit crunch era.

This has come at a time of changes to the economic structure of the global economy, the highest rise ever in the price of many raw materials, including petrol reaching 100 US $ a barrel, with the US$ falling and the US economy being on the brink of recession. Competition between land for biofuels and land for food and has pushed up food commodity prices significantly causing unrest.

Economic growth is still an integral part of peoples' expectations from government economic policies. Growth has up to now, generally been accepted as a essential, critical and viable constituent of economic policies, especially at times or situations where not only short term economic prospects are worsening. However, but due to a lack of cheap resources a new sense of a possible fundamental limitation to growth potential is emerging, that growth rates globally might start to reduce in the long term.

Aims of economic growth

Very recently it has become apparent that the justification for a continuing policy for ever increasing economic growth, defined conventionally as measured as increases in GDP, has undergone a remarkable transformation. Consumption was specifically encouraged in order to stimulate markets, rather than to meet people's needs, and this ignored the limits or requirements of other species or the planet. Demand was all the time, managed upwards - Predict and Provide, an example has been the policy for transport. Managing demand upwards has been considered good economic management for decades and has been artificially stimulated by advertising.

In the aftermath of the Hyperinflation of the 1920s and the destruction and hardship of WW2, new aims for economic policy were established. It was believed that the provision of increased volumes of goods for consumption would tend to halt the rise of communism and would lead to more stability and well being. (W. Rostow)

The perception of the evolving economy influenced by Darwinism, developed into a linear progression from "primitive economies" of indigenous peoples and subsistence conditions, through an economic "take off period" and towards the end goal of "High Mass Consumption" (Rostow). The idea was that lack of economic growth was equated with primitivism and under-development and that economic growth would lead everyone out of poverty. (Sachs)

On a theoretical level, the drivers of such growth are considered to be an evolutionary improvement in the quality of human capital stimulating an increase in the rate of technological progress. Galor and Moav (2001, 2002).

Social security can create faster growth via new technological advances

Sharing of common processes occurs as generic basic knowledge spreads and converges in the population. The development of Open Source is an interesting example for other reasons. This most profitable sector was largely developed during a cyclical downturn when most of the "anoraks" were out of work and not paid. They were living on benefits paid for by society. When the market picked up again, the whole economy was able to capitalise on this expertise, and Open Source has made a serious challenge to the market leaders.

The lesson here is that using all the expertise in society is important, without creating boundaries between the formal and informal economy or the paid and unpaid as in the end society wins from all its developments and all its evolutions. Therefore there is a possibility that supporting everyone properly in their social activities – not just in the formal economy is a huge win for everyone, which is totally contrary to current thinking on incentives. This is one main thrust of argumentation in this chapter, that with a careful design,pre-- supposed or pre-alleged trade offs between ideas or incompatibilities of aims and objectives have a good chance of actually being found to be incorrect and therefore opening up the possibility of overcoming them.

A report was published last week showing that women around Europe are not paid for up to 20% of their work and this work is not then recorded as a contribution to GDP. This means that we now know that current GDP and growth figures are therefore highly inaccurate and misleading in terms of an indication of value in the economy. Some of the worst offenders include the UK paying women 20% less and Germany paying 22% less. There are many consequences for today's economy of this situation including possibly women having to actually work longer in the formal economy than men for equivalent reward and also other research shows they also work longer in the informal economy. Direct results may be causing some of the very poor youth dissatisfaction figures the UK is registering.   So in fact harbouring a nostalgia for our golden age of economic growth and well being is partly illusory. This is an area urgently needing economic adjustment, but has been delayed as it has been regarded as politically unobtainable. (Der Grosse Unterschied, Die Welt,15th April 2008,WSI- Frauenlohnspiegel, Eurostat, Hans- Boekler-Stiftung.)

The suggestion we would make is to include all work which benefits society within the GDP figures. This would have the additional benefit of increasing reports of growth, just at a time when a down turn is occuring. The mechanics of how this might work, is attracting more interest. Degrowth or 'Decroissance', (which is a more positive idea than its equivalent expression in english) or *serene downscaling* is becoming fashionable in France. Latouche (2003) questioned if the only way to happiness is more growth, more consumption and more productivity, and complains that growth for its own sake becomes the actual aim of society. He claims it's unsustainable as it pushes the limits of the biosphere, and that each person should really only require 1.4 hectares as their ecological footprint, not the 4.5 currently in use in Europe.

He argues that eco efficiency has been created to decouple growth from resource use, but that in accelerating economic growth as a result - the "rebound effect" actually means people simply use the same resources or more with the increased economic buying power they thus create.However the world population has now increased to 6.6 billion people and the Earth itself cannot support 6.6 bn people based on a high mass consumption at the levels of developed countries.(Limits to Growth).

The power houses of world growth China and the US are currently challenged by both ecological and economic limits.

Trade off between ecology and economics: eco innovation

Porter and van der Linde 1995, argued that a fixed trade off between ecology versus economy is false and if environmental standards are correctly devised, the resulting standards will spur innovation, and actually increase productivity, making firms more competitive. Environmental protection and competitiveness are not trade offs. Eco innovation is actually driven in an environment of regulation.

INSEAD (European Business Summit 2008) has just produced a report showing that the best way for European business to grow is to attract venture capital to finance Eco innovation and to take the lead in this fourth industrial revolution, which will lead to smaller more local units founded as previous revolutions on energy and knowledge, with a fusion of these factors into knowledge and energy products created at the point of use. (Jeremy Rifkin 2008 European Business Summit 2008)

The New scientist has just carried a fascinating article, which argues that the very interconnectedness of the global economy carries within itself the seeds of its own destruction. It argues that civilisation is too complex which makes it too vulnerable, and she describes why the demise of our civilisation may now be considered to be inevitable (Debora MacKenzie 2650 New Scientist. 2 April 2008.) A more localised and grounded system is more likely to last, because once a society gets beyond a certain level of complexity, it becomes increasingly fragile to with stand outside pressures.

Over decades our economy has been designed to incorporate growth at its centre. Where such growth is not achieved, this particular structure of economy will encounter severe problems and additionally political actors will face strong pressures from the public and from various interest groups to reinstate the situation everyone is used to.

It is those fears of loss of political power, stability of the society and fear of changing our own habits that have more and more contributed to growth becoming almost entirely a goal in its own right. Society continues to maintaining growth paths even if the underlying activity becomes more difficult to justify or even contradicts more recently recognised foundational issues like climate change or environmental degradation on a global scale.

There are some 'trade-offs' between economic activity and ecology in direct comparison, but most of the alleged 'trade-offs' are actually at the level of these conventions, suppositions and beliefs rather than at the level of factual problems.

Green economics assumes that there is no contradiction between economics and ecology. (Kennet and Heinemann 2006). Eco-nomics and eco-logy both originate with the same root concept , (oikia the household) and therefore Green Economics always includes ecological considerations and argues that no economics can exist without ecology.

The problem is that currently a narrower definition of economics is prevailing that prevents such comprehensive considerations being part of mainstream economics. The economic structure, the population got used to, is difficult to change for the very reason that people are afraid of change.

In addition a social system such as the economy is almost entirely governed by self fulfilling prophecies, or less strictly, there is scope to change many things in the longer term that appear impossible to adjust in the short term.

Furthermore precisely the same properties of social systems can be used by political forces for the deliberate manipulation of public opinion and to guide the way the economy can or cannot be transformed. (The growth economy encounters *problems* in cases of no growth, hence all effort is then geared towards growth. Policy makers and economists have not engaged in envisaging what the eventual structure, effects and benefits might be of a change to a fundamentally lower growth scenario, as it will need to develop with   different structures and circular loop-backs but of a completely changed nature or composition. Suddenly, this has become are more realistic prospect and the task is more pressing.

A successful political strategy will require a careful assessment of where there are real 'trade-offs' between core economic aggregates and sustainability concerns and where the degrees of freedom are, and where it is actually possible to change the structure and composition of economic activity quite significantly.

This chapter will argue that there is significant freedom for change, far more than conventional economic research tends to suggest.

Separating growth from stabilization

It is furthermore proposed that it is entirely possible to reduce opposition to changes in the economic structure using a a specific political design strategy.

This political strategy would split the task into two periods, the transitional period and the advanced period. During *transitional period* where the emphasis is placed on the problems arising from facilitating change and on gaining evidence of how economic actors react to the initial political changes implemented.

During the consecutive *period* involving more fundamental adjustments to the economy and implementing benefits from the information obtained in the transitional period. It should be possible to clearly separate growth issues from stabilisation issues in this period.

It should be clearly possible to focus on the true final goals of the economy and incorporating all ecological issues simultaneously. This means an end to tweaking growth into ever different purposes which are not in line with the most important objective of the economy of providing people with a higher quality of life.

Transitional period

In this period the emphasis is on relatively straight forward substitution processes. (product A for B or production process A for B) The economic structure is as almost everything in the economy, a product of self regulating market forces. As those market forces do not take into account a large number of phenomena they are never optimal in any objective way. They reflect the current economic activities of the economic actors and are efficient in co-ordinating detailed production and consumption. During this initial period sustainability considerations can be implemented by focussing on substitution of one economic activity for another including promoting research into further alternatives.

The outcome of such substitution should be designed to ensure that the overall level of economic activity provides for enough employment opportunities for people and earning activities for businesses. The economy will effectively change but only by technical fixes where one area where economic activity ceases will be replaced by other economic activity in a way that is less harmful.

It is intended to keep the overall level of activity roughly similar to the conventional path and it might even be the case that economic activity measured in conventional GDP terms increases as low quality and cheap products are replaced for higher quality, longer lasting items etc.

This period will help to convince the general public in particular that the changes in the economy are required even in conventional terms, as otherwise it is very likely that the economy will continue on a growth path of not more than 2% p. a. for most of the developed world.

Changing the structure of the economy will require higher investments and will provide earning opportunities for the businesses involved in such a change.

The main difference is that a new more wider defined economic scope and goal will become the basis of the economic action and the basis of policies that shape society. The methods to move towards those goals are designed to make this first step less painful.

For every industrial activity that is abandoned, new industrial activities are selected that ensure that the balance of employment is at least maintained. There is no need for any more sophisticated adjustments to the economy. Where for example overall activity has to be limited, and under the assumption of further productivity increases, adjustment need to be made so that the remaining, limited amount of available work has to be more evenly distributed among all potential employees.

Even under conventional economic development the increases in productivity require a constant increase in economic activity to maintain even the same level of employment. This is the most important driver to promote ever further economic growth as it appears to be difficult to gain support for shorter working hours among the general public, hence if all people want to work the same increasingly productive hours the resulting higher volume of goods produced need to be sold.

The substitutional options are however limited, as at some point all benefits that can be derived from switching materials or processes but not the intention and aims will have been exhausted. Any efficiency gains will have themselves come to an end and correspond to the law of diminishing returns. The problems are shifted into a different more abstract area of debate where political aims are disguising the real   economics facts and necessities and these political aims are delaying or hindering change.

When this transitional period comes to an end, which is determined by the lack of availability of substitutional solutions (forced exit) or the fact that society has already been convinced that a stable path via different means and with different objectives is possible, the issue of economic stability without growth will have to be tackled face on.

It will now no longer possible to move along traditional lines of economic development by increased activity but it will be necessary to stabilise the economy (employment, income, profits etc) directly.

The following main economic areas require changes and policy adjustment that are however less difficult than is is conventionally thought. Over longer periods, perceptions and attitudes can be easily adjusted even though they are often presumed in conventional model building to be fixed. There is no fundamental economic reason, why the current methods of maintaining economic activity should be the only way possible and why   society is condemned to ever increasing GDP growth activity.

It is however required that specific adjustments to the mindset of the public and how economics is viewed are needed that are nevertheless achievable if a carefully designed strategy is selected. The following main areas are of particular concern:

Employment

As has been identified above, the maintenance of a high level of employment is one of the driving forces behind the political and economic desire for continuing growth.

In the forseeable future it is highly likely that there will be continuing productivity gains in the economy. Not all the existing technologies have been fully absorbed by businesses and further technological advances mainly in the area of micro electronics are likely.

Micro electronics in particular has structure that is different to other areas of technical change, the new inventions do not only lead to **new products** but to **new production processes** that have been replacing labour with machinery (capital).

The question that now arises is whether a change toward sustainable development makes this situation worse or whether it contributes to an improvement in opportunities for employment. Effectively examples exist both ways. Reducing excess packaging and recycling of goods obviously reduces the material flows and will therefore reduce employment in raw material producing industries, but recycling itself is relatively labour intensive and therefore creates significant employment opportunities.(Murray Zero Waste)

In this context it is interesting that the public and even sometimes academic debate about economics realises that environmentally friendly products or processes are more expensive, and identifies this as entirely negative, but fails to see that this higher price is due to the higher labour contents in the products or processes concerned, which is clearly a positive as far as employment opportunities is concerned. Organic farming produces high value products that are more expensive than conventional produce because they are produced to higher standards and with less machinery and more labour. Every unit of GDP generated will result in a higher level of employment created.

In this respect it is important to identify that particularly the price relation between capital and labour provides great scope to mitigate any potential loss of employment due to the deliberate adjustment of the economy towards sustainability.

If for example social security contributions are paid for by labour and not capital, labour usage in the economy is reduced. Particularly during the transitional phase it is possible to implement changes to the **labour/capital price relation** towards *a higher contribution of capital towards social security that together with a selection of labour intensive sustainable processes should minimise any loss of emp*loyment opportunities or is even likely to contribute to employment gains.

In the longer term it is however possible that those means are not sufficient and lower growth or no growth is inevitable, regardless of the sustainability considerations because even conventional growth requires conditions that cannot be maintained in the long term.

An advanced society may well move further up Maslow's hierarchy of needs towards higher preference for security and hence savings and less consumption, but it is not certain as the rebound effect mentioned above suggests otherwise. Current trends on heavy advertising suggest that it might well be more difficult in the future to persuade people to consume more. This is however culturally determined - eg Germany's and Japan's fashions for savings are stronger than in UK. Given finite time constraints on consumption, only a certain volume of consumption can be comfortable and sensibly achieved, within that time before even consumption in total suffers from declining or even negative marginal benefits. A good example of this is of too much eating, currently causing a pandemic of obesity as people in advanced economies over consume too much food, too quickly. This actually decreases welfare.

Such scenarios might result in an actual decline in available work in the economy if demand stagnates on a certain level and labour saving technological changes continue to be made. This overall level of work available should then be more evenly distributed among all individuals in society, resulting in a decline in individual working hours, or parts of the society will not be integrated in the formal economy but will still continue to require income none the less.

Some recent studies (Schlyter, Sweden) suggest that the highest hours in longer working hours (e.g. The last 6 hours in a 36 hour week) produce proportionally much more environmental damage, in production and in consumption patterns and less marginal benefit and so therefore shortening working hours would have a direct impact on ecology for example, as consumption rates for luxuries would decline sharply.

The current situation in countries with a high level of unemployment shows that significant parts of society are still willing to believe in growth to rectify this lack of employment, maintain their level of working hours and so the social security system has to deal with the resulting unemployment, despite the fact that this unemployment is paid for out of their income by the people working longer hours.

Existing work arrangements should be gradually transferred into concepts where the overall working time available, (regardless of any additional attempts to increase its volume,) more directly determines the individual's length of working hours. Society as a whole has to start to accept making decent, supporting payments to people who are not integrated in the formal economy.

The transitional period will have to be used to make society more aware of economic realities and to implement policies that collect national insurance contributions which will reflect the overall economic conditions and the behaviour of its participants and their actions.

There does however not appear to be a fundamental necessity for the economy to grow only to create employment for employment's sake.

Company profitability, competitiveness and investments

Profitability, competitiveness and level of investments are very diverse issues related to the level and structure of the economy and its development. There are areas such as renewable energy where investment levels are significantly higher. This is because lower density renewable energy like solar and wind needs to be collected at many diverse places.

Higher labour use in producing high quality goods and repairing items in small units contributes to savings in investment volumes required. The overall level of investments required will be determined by the changes in structure of the economy.

Growth in investments as such may be the interest of the provider of capital who looks for earning opportunities for his capital. However, from an economic perspective the appropriate level of investment is a required quantity derived from the economics aims a society sets itself, not the other way round. If more capital is required for investment into renewable energy, this will create opportunities for capital to be employed. If sustainability can be achieved however by substituting capital for labour to create employment opportunities, then there will be less earning opportunities for capital. For a given structure of the economy, adequate investment needs to be maintained. There is no need to follow the personal interests of any lobby group what so ever.

If a sustainable society requires at least initially higher investments this would normally require higher rates of interest that maintain the level of savings from individuals to supply the funds required.

If it is undesirable that interest rates should rise, then an alternative would be more public funding for the investment projects via tax revenue, or alternatively if savings rates go up due to a change in consumer attitude this will contribute towards the investments for the sustainable future from reduced consumption.

There is no correct level of investment in an economy. There is a required level of investments for a defined purpose of society and as always political feasibility is greatly increased when the general public shares this consensus and acts accordingly.

A stable economy requires savings to be recycled via investments into the economy to maintain output levels. If the society chooses to downgrade, initially higher savings will not be used for further investments as there is no need for new capacity as a consequence earnings will be reduced that reduce the high levels of savings accordingly.

A move towards a sustainable society is likely to require higher levels of investment and as a consequence higher levels of savings which is particularly relevant for societies with traditionally low savings rates. A change in attitude will contribute to this automatically but without such change policies to encourage savings will be required if not then the alternative might be higher taxes and publicly funded investments.

Similarly the profitability of businesses can be maintained in different structural scenarios. Over the life cycle of a product there are significant changes to levels of profitability. However already the Boston Consulting Group matrix suggests that the high growth phase is not the most profitable phase, the maturity phase is suggested contributing mostly to profits.

On the economic level there is no indication that profitability levels and competition are directly related specifically stage of development of a society. Competition and with it the efficiency of production will increase if markets become more saturated and supply remains strong.

Adequate competition levels can be maintained even in a sustainable society as they depend very much on the structure of the economy (number and size of businesses) and the market behaviour, not the overall growth rate of the economy.

High growth rates of an industry are likely to be correlated to innovation, where new products for new markets are made available for the first time. If such innovation helps sustainability it is welcome and the growth effects are desired. Such businesses are likely to be highly profitable. Setting a certain goal for society, that may have a strong effect over how the economy operates and over what is produced, does not change the fundamentals of competition and profitability based on individual price setting by businesses. During the transitional period there should be an opportunity to monitor the structural changes in the economy. Newly emerging businesses that contribute to sustainability should be encouraged to provide compensation or contribute to support for declining industries. In the longer term where growth rates might be low or zero, competition might intensify as there is no space for expansion left in the market and participants compete intensely against each other.

There might be negative effects of such competition in the form of further job losses that can however be mitigated by an adjustment of the factor price relation between labour and capital. Additional labour costs can be paid for in different ways and using different or lower forms of taxation. This results in investment in labour becoming more attractive where it completes with investment in capital. Labour then remains overall reasonably priced and continues to be used in the economy to a high level.

It should be kept in mind that in any case, the conventional economy incurs many changes over time and in the past there have been periods of intense adjustments (beginning with the industrial revolution, post war structural changes, highly saturated markets today) that have not contributed to a loss of profitability of businesses and competition.

The problem is that if one business decides to produce sustainably and other businesses do not, this business will have a disadvantage (prisoner's dilemma) hence the issue of sustainability cannot be left to decentralised market co-ordination in form of the invisible hand.

This creates the misconception among many more business administration focused individuals, that society at large cannot make this transition successfully. As far as international competitiveness is concerned a move towards sustainability triggers the same issues and problems.

The solution must lie with monitoring of unjustified advantages or disadvantages which emerge during the transition. National standard setting must ensure a level playing field for products that are sold into the domestic market. Where higher production standards are required, the situation becomes more complicated if other competitors worldwide are not required to do the same. This problem stems from the fact that public concerns of sustainability result in private costs of production for businesses but only for the businesses that are required to make the changes.

The preferred solution would be international agreements on basic standards that are consecutively made stricter by bodies like the EU that negotiates those standards with other parts of the world.

If such a situation is not feasible, imported goods may require a price adjustment, if selling those goods is deliberately done to undercut domestic competition. There has been a suggestion for a policy of **Preferred Market Access**- where goods are preferred if they can show or carry a standard showing that they have met certain sustainability criteria in order to avoid environmental or social dumping - (Lorenzen)

In comparison to the other issues discussed above that are more based in the political sphere with typical problems involving the difficulty of convincing people to support change and differentiating economic issues and requirements from interest group opinion. These are real problems on the economic level that require careful consideration.

It might be the case that the drive towards more innovative products makes the economy much more competitive, as the supply of sophisticated products, finds strong demand in other countries, (Brown, INSEAD 2008)

It might be the case that the structural changes to the economy result in the country being flooded with products that are produced in an unsustainable way, all depending on the perception of the consumer.

If it is not possible to change people's perception sufficiently during the transitional phase to leave the decision making to the individual, there may be a requirement to develop a particular set of rules, regulations or restrictions rather than protection that set the standards for international trade. Protectionism has been the response so far in favour of sustainability- however it may be that rules and standards and restrictions on quality or impacts have a much more beneficial effect and act as a carrot rather than a stick. This is likely the most important area where almost a complete change in attitude is required, particularly from academic economics that currently still fiercely resist such suggestions.

Public revenue, finance and debt

The main issue in this area is that a sustainable society is likely to require higher public expenditure as the issues of sustainability facing a society are of the 'public goods' nature, and entail protecting the commons, i. e. they require some regulatory activity from a public body or need to be 'supplied' publicly.

It is therefore likely that higher public revenue is required. Alternatively higher public debt might be an option that is equally politically sensitive. In addition the possible lack of growth will not allow for an increase in tax revenue with stagnant tax rates. There might be a small effect of 'cold progression' where, due to inflation people move into different nominally defined higher tax bands, but otherwise there is no further indirectly beneficial effect.

The main problem is that more political honesty is required to tax people in order to ensure for the provision of public goods. This is difficult in practical terms due to political competition but does not raise any specific theoretical questions. If such public goods are not supplied, because the State is not allowed to demand the adequate resources for their provision, those markets will not exist and the growth of the society is likely to be lower.

In the longer term, lower growth in a sustainable society is matched by the increased focus on and design for the end goals, as well as means to obtain them. (Kennet and Heinemann 2006) The appropriate stabilisation policy as indicated in the employment chapter will ensure that those final goals and individual opportunities and duties will be matched. Similarly, in the area of finance and debt, people need to be given time to adjust to such a stable scenario.

In the longer term, levels of private and business debt will need to be matched to income and earning opportunities. Rapidly expanding and growing businesses will require finance and will sustain high levels of debt and declining businesses will need to adjust to their market potential. There is no change to the basics of an ever changing market economy, the only difference is that in a sustainable society final goals are deliberately designed and not left to the automatic outcome of market forces (Smith, Stern). In the long term such a transition requires many individual adjustments that are however theoretically not different to the many adjustments and decentralised co-ordination occurring in the economy anyway. Problems arise if the public is not willing to adjust their behaviour, for example allowing for more differentiated policies regarding unemployment as mentioned above, or if the government is unable to explain or convince the public about the best course of action.

The sustainable economy will have more such requirements as outlined above and its success hinges finally on society being able to accept or understand that these changes are necessary.

The main strategic suggestion to help with such a transition is the split into the transitional period where relatively conventional methods are used to initiate a change in the structure, which is then followed by a change in the overall level of economic activity, as soon as resistance to change has been weakened visibly by the successes of the policies implemented.

This is highlighted by the reference to international problems that indicate that the change only becomes a real problem if some parts of society or if other countries are unwilling to participate. This self fulfilling belief of no one wanting to make the first step and therefore preventing change occurring, is the real problem. (Theoretically this is described in situations like the tragedy of the commons or the prisoner's dilemma).

The variety of individual adjustments required below this higher societal level are politically possible to achieve so long as all parts of society start to share the insights into the issue. The continued avoidance of simplistic competitive solutions is preventing higher level solutions being implemented. This fear may well be unfounded and structural changes needed today, do not actually pose the real theoretical threats that are usually ascribed to them. They changes are not so very different to all the small adjustments the decentralised market economies have coordinated over decades and centuries. We should assist the public in learning to understand and welcome such changes and economic strategy makers to be more innovative and bolder in their economic strategy design and embrace today's requirements and wider economics scope much more fully. The resistance of the inevitable change towards a lower growth economy is now leading to a possible global downturn which could be perhaps avoided if new confidence in wider economics scope and ecology were embraced more fully as an opportunity to evolve a more buoyant economy.

This chapter was originally commissioned by and written for the Sustainable Development Commission as a thinkpiece to form part of research for their report entitled "Prosperity without growth? – The transition to a sustainable economy", published in 2009 forming part of the process of Book Prosperity Without Growth. T. Jackson. Available from: http://www.sd-commission.org.uk/publications/downloads/Miriam_Kennet_thinkpiece.pdf

Picture: The Economics of Housing 2010. Paul Kennet 2010

Picture: The Economics of water 2010. Paul Kennet 2010

Picture: The Economics of Going Shopping for much of the world 2010. Paul Kennet 2010

4.2 What do we mean by "growth", problems with growth and is a return to "growth" possible in the long term?

By Steven Mandel

What do we mean by "Growth"?

Many elected politicians, around the world, are talking of "getting the economy back on a growth path". Or they speak of the need to reduce the size of the state to give room for the private sector, or they might talk of using state expenditure to boost employment and demand in the manner recommended by Keynes.

Most economists and other commentators who talk about growth mean growth of GDP. Gross Domestic Product is measured in three ways, which should all amount to the same:

• The sum of all income earned by individuals, companies and government;
• The sum of all consumption and investment in the country (ie all expenditure), including that by government, less imports plus exports; and
• The sum of all output by firms and government, etc.

(Sometimes people talk of Gross National Income, which is defined by ownership rather than location of production, but the two terms are usually much the same.)

Growth in consumption is closely tied to growth in the use of resources, particularly energy, and up to now growth in energy use has been closely related to output of CO_2. It is true that the energy required for a unit of GDP has been falling and fell quite rapidly between 1980 and 2000, worldwide. This progress seems to have slowed since then. (See BTU per $2000 GDP line.) The carbon density of energy has also been falling but only slowly. (See CO_2 per Quadrillion BTU line.)

Global Efficiency

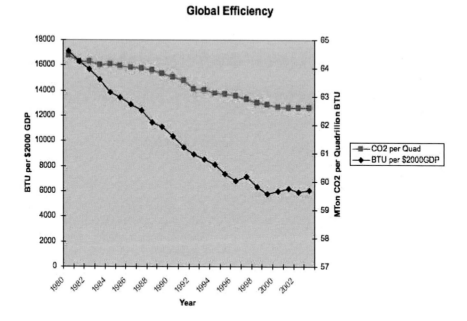

Source:worldchanging
http://www.worldchanging.com/archives/003829.html

These two measures can be combined to give CO_2 per unit of GDP and below are graphs showing the carbon intensity of GDP for a number of countries:

CO2/GDP

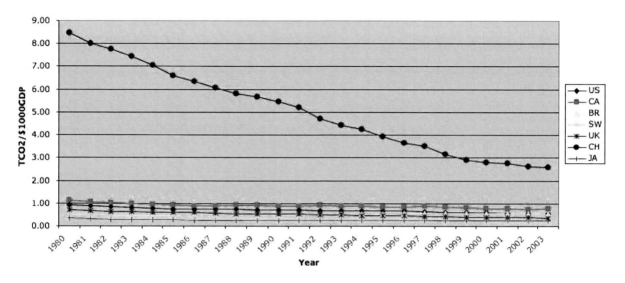

Source: worldchanging.com
http://www.worldchanging.com/archives/003829.html

China starts the period so inefficient in its use of CO_2 that the other countries' performance cannot be easily distinguished. (Despite great progress over the period illustrated, it still uses nearly 3 times the CO_2 of the other countries at the end.) If we eliminate China so that we can change the scale, we get the graph below:

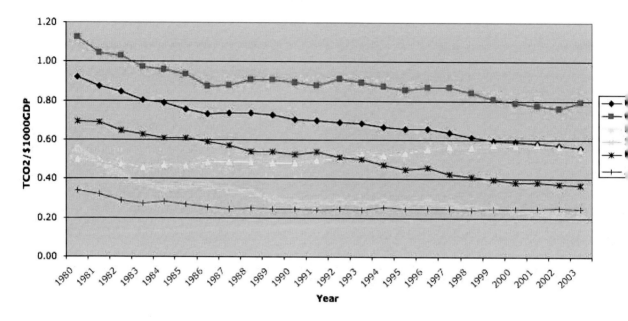

Source: worldchanging.com
http://www.worldchanging.com/archives/003829.html

This reduction in the resource and carbon intensity of GDP is called decoupling. That there is relative decoupling with regard to CO_2 is without doubt. This is shown in the graphs, where tons of CO_2 per unit of GDP are plotted over the period 1980 to 2003. The energy required to produce a unit of output has gone down both in particular countries and globally, from efficiency savings. On top of that the carbon intensity of energy production has gone down, partly from the switch to renewables, but rather more from the switch from coal to gas in electricity generation. (Grubb et al, forthcoming) In addition, individual countries can *seem* to reduce their carbon intensity of GDP by switching from producing carbon-intensive products themselves and importing them instead. This has been happening, to some extent, for example, in Britain and USA as they have moved from being producers of goods to producers of services. However, we have also seen dramatic reductions in carbon intensity of output in China, even as it has increased its production of goods enormously. Naturally the key factor for the atmosphere is the *global* carbon intensity of output.

However, despite this *relative* decoupling, the overall demand for energy has gone up. Reductions in the carbon intensity of a unit of energy have been offset by greater increases in the total energy demanded. What is required for preventing runaway climate change is *absolute* decoupling, and on a massive scale. Is this possible?

If we look at individual countries in the second graph above, we notice that the one that started with the lowest carbon intensity, Japan, has the smallest reduction. In fact it is hard to detect any reduction since 1987. (Japan probably starts in this position because of its high energy prices.) (Grubb et al, forthcoming). The laws of thermodynamics tell us that 100% efficiency is not possible. So we need to decarbonise energy as well as reducing the amount of energy required. Clearly energy can be taken from much lower carbon sources than is the case today, but progress to date has been far too slow to prevent runaway climate change. However, even if nuclear fusion or major advances in concentrated solar heat for electricity generation, carbon sequestration or some other technical advance were to mean we could more or less eliminate carbon from our energy economy, *and* we manage to introduce this worldwide in time to prevent the melting of the icecaps, this would merely delay the inevitable.[1]

This is because we are coming up against not only peak oil, but peak uranium, peak rare earths, peak copper, even peak fishing and so on. Naturally mankind has used the richest seams of minerals first. For a couple of centuries while new continents were being explored new rich sources were being discovered. With the exception of Antarctica, hardly an easy place to work, this option has now disappeared. Most new mines are now exploiting lower grade ores than in the past (or are in inaccessible places), which in turn require higher energy and other inputs to extract. All the earth's resources are finite and if we use them in a way that renders them unrecyclable, we are reducing the resources that are available to future generations. A study by Ugo Bardi and Marco Pagani reported in The Oil Drum: Europe in October 2007 identified 11 minerals out of 57 in the US geological service database of world production which showed clear signs of having peaked already.[2] They identified other minerals that were close to this point. Nor is the problem confined to non-renewable resources. Fish stocks are dangerously depleted and that seemingly endlessly renewable resource, water, is also facing constraints. An interesting analysis of water (which is mainly a renewable resource subject to flow constraints but has a non-renewable component in long-term stored underground supplies) by Dr. Peter H. Gleick et al (The World's Water Peak Water, China's Growing Disaster, and Solutions to the World's Water Crisis) January 2009 Pacific Institute argues that we are already hitting peak ecological water usage rates at least in some parts of the globe.

I was talking to a professor of Economics last year. I said "we live in a finite planet – non-stop growth (in the conventional sense) is therefore a logical impossibility". His response was "Oh surely we can switch to services growth that won't demand extra physical resources."

Can we go on increasing output (in some way) of services without increasing our use of resources? The answer has to be "only to a limited extent" and clearly not for ever.

For our worldwide demand for resources to be in steady state, the world's population has to stop increasing. The supply of labour will eventually, of necessity, therefore be capped. Productivity of labour in services can be improved in some cases but not in all. (Is a doctor seeing more patients in an hour actually an improvement, for example? I'm not sure, if that means the patient does not feel treated with adequate consideration and if it increases the chance that important information is missed, increases in misdiagnosis or mistakes in prescriptions etc.) In any event it is impossible that productivity can continue to improve in perpetuity. (GDP, by the way, measures non-traded services, such as government-provided ones, by the cost of their input. In other words valuing productivity increases, whether improvements in quality or output, are not possible.)

2.   Interim Conclusion

What would be needed for perpetual growth to be possible is that this increase in resource-free productivity carry on for ever, and that all increases in income from this increase in productivity be spent on resource-free services. This seems inherently implausible. Indeed if growth is to be perpetual, we should eventually have to arrive at what Herman Daly calls, "Angelic GDP", where pure spirit takes over from humans. We can therefore conclude that, in reality, growth of GDP is not possible in the long term. So we need to achieve a steady-state economy, not a static one, but one in dynamic equilibrium, which means one that does not increase its use of resources.

Many associate this with a stagnant state and cannot imagine this to be a positive outcome. However, it is not actually the case that increases in GDP are always good.

3.   Problems with GDP as a measure

I hardly need to remind you about the problems with using GDP as a target of policy, but let me quote Robert Kennedy's famous speech: GDP "counts air pollution and cigarette advertising... the destruction of the redwood and the loss of our natural wonder in chaotic sprawl. It does not allow for the health of our children, the quality of their education or the joy of their play....the beauty of our poetry or the strength of our marriages. It measures everything, in short, except that which makes life worthwhile". Nevertheless, that is what they all mean, in spite of the fact that the main architect of GDP as a measure, Simon Kuznets, made no claims for it being a measure of welfare.[4]

In fact, GDP is a measure of consumption (amongst other things) and neo-classical economists seem to assume this is the only goal to be pursued. You can never have too much of a good thing and consumption is good. Or is it?

Since 1970, the UK's GDP has doubled in real terms, but people's satisfaction with life has hardly changed. Similar figures are found in most OECD countries.
The Stiglitz/Sen report to President Sarkozy concluded: What is of "particular concern is when narrow measures of market performance are confused with broader measures of welfare," the authors said in the report. "What we measure affects what we do; and if our measurements are flawed, decisions may be distorted. Policies should be aimed at increasing societal welfare, not G.D.P."[5]

I argue here that the goal of public policy should be to maximise well-being, rather than GDP. The New Economics Foundation report that according to one poll, 81% of Britons believe that the Government should prioritise creating the greatest happiness, not the greatest wealth.[6]

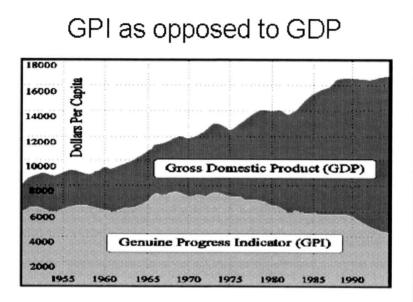

Of course, GDP is relatively easy to measure while well-being is not. A solid attempt to correct for a number of flaws in GDP accounting can be found in the Genuine Progress Indicator (see rprogress.org, Redefining Progress). They start with personal consumption, adjust that by a factor to allow for any change in income distribution, add an estimate of the value of non-traded activity (parenting, volunteering, DIY), deduct economic "bads" such as the cost of defensive expenditures, commuting, crime, deduct a cost for carbon emissions, an allowance for the depletion of non-renewable energy sources, and some environmental costs, deduct investment but add the value of services from man-made capital (for details see their report (2006). Despite the conservatism of some of their assumptions and methodology of the adjustments, the stark difference between GDP and GPI for the US is illustrated by a figure reproduced from Redefining Progress' website:

While this GPI clearly gets much closer to measuring the "goods and positive services" in the economy and to take out the "bads", it is still not a direct measure of well-being. The New Economics Foundation has made an attempt to do just that in its report "National Well-being Accounts" (2009). This is based on a major 2006/2007 European cross-national survey through a detailed module of well-being questions, designed by the University of Cambridge, **nef** and others, that covered 22 countries in Europe. The questions covered a wide range of aspects of well-being, which were grouped into five components of personal well-being and two of social well-being. These were normalised around an average and scored on a scale from 1-10. The results are interesting and by examining the detailed differences between countries, age groups and gender, give a guideline for governments wishing to tailor policies towards improving well-being.

Another problem with GDP is that it totally ignores the consumption of natural capital. (This is apparently shared by the GPI, with the exception of hydrocarbons.) To make the point obvious, let us contemplate the case of Nauru, the island made almost entirely of potash. It was mined for this and a sovereign wealth fund was set up, which at first allowed the citizens of Nauru to enjoy a good standard of education and health care without any taxes and their measured GDP was high. However, their homeland became practically uninhabitable. When a combination of corruption and the Asian Financial crisis of the 1990's destroyed the sovereign wealth fund, GDP collapsed. They had used up their natural capital and then lost their financial capital, which the events of the last two years has shown is often very vulnerable. So they were left with nothing. We are doing the same by failing to take into account the consumption of natural capital when we measure GDP.

All is not doom and gloom, however. As Tim Jackson (2009) suggests, we can have prosperity without growth. Well-being, once material income has reached a certain, quite low, level is dependent far more on non-material matters than on increasing consumption. While there are many factors influencing well-being, life-expectancy captures a fair number of them. The good news is that a decent life-expectancy does not have to "cost the earth", as the BBC programme would put it. The graph below shows that life-expectancy is sharply correlated to national GDP per capita up to possibly $10,000, but that it is almost unrelated thereafter.

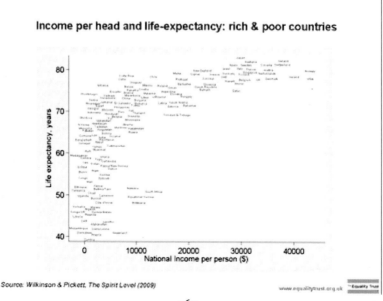

Income per head and life-expectancy: rich & poor countries

Source: Wilkinson & Pickett, The Spirit Level (2009)

www.equalitytrust.org.uk

Given the strong correlation between GDP and carbon emissions, it comes as little surprise that a similar pattern emerges when we display a graph of life-expectancy and carbon emissions (this illustration is also from Wilkinson & Pickett's Equality Trust and carries their title), from which we can reinforce our conclusion that a decent life is possible without high CO_2 emissions, even with existing technology:

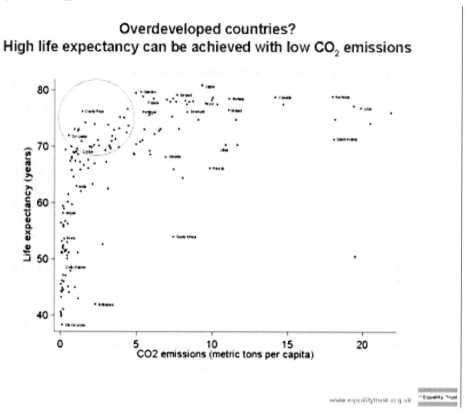

The evidence is now quite strong that well-being is not mainly determined by income once a certain level has been reached. This is discussed in many publications but a recent summary of the debate can be found in **nef**'s "National Well-being Accounts". In fact from the New Economic Foundation's work on well-being we can summarise the main factors influencing well-being (beyond that level) as:

- A sense of inclusion
- A sense of empowerment
- A sense of meaning in life
- A sense of connection with other people, both within our family and in wider society

- Feeling valued – hence an ability to contribute
- Continued learning
- Physical activity
- Adequate health
- Equality and fairness

With the sole exception of health, these factors have almost nothing to do with consumption; but are more to do with the way we organise society, production and consumption, the way we relate to each other, and other non-tangible matters.

Final Conclusion

There is little reason why these factors cannot go on improving as society evolves, without increasing demands on resources. This kind of growth, growth in well-being, that is, could therefore be almost perpetual.

References

M Grubb et al (forthcoming) "CO^{2}NNECT Planetary Economics and the triad solutions to our energy and climate challenges"

Jackson, T (2009) "Prosperity without Growth? - The transition to a sustainable economy", Earthscan, London ISBN 978-1-84407-894-3.

Kuznets S (1934) "National Income 1929–1932". 73rd US Congress, 2nd session, Senate document No. 124, p 7.

Marks, N et al (2009) "National Well-being Accounts" New Economics Foundation, London

Simms A, Johnson, V and Chowla P (2010) "Growth Isn't Possible" New Economics Foundation, London ISBN 9781904882718

Stiglitz, Sen and Fitoussi (2009) "The Measurement of Economic Performance and Social Progress Revisited," Commission for The Measurement of Economic Performance and Social Progress

Wilkinson, R & Pickett, K (05 Mar 2009) "The Spirit Level: Why More Equal Societies Almost Always Do Better" Allen Lane, ISBN: 9781846140396

[1]   Leading NASA climate scientist, James Hansen, recommends a target of 350 ppm CO2 for avoiding dangerous climate change. According to the new analysis, with a growth rate of 3 per cent, this requires an unprecedented and likely impossible change to the carbon intensity of the economy.

- At a growth rate of 3 per cent, in order to stabilise emissions at 350ppm by 2050, carbon intensity of the global economy would need to fall by 95 per cent by 2050 (compared to 2002) or 6.3 per cent per year, an almost five-fold increase in the yearly average between 1965 and 2002.

- However, between 2000 and 2007, the carbon intensity of the economy effectively flat-lined. Given this, in order to achieve a 350ppm target, the annual fall in the carbon intensity of economy would need to improve by more than 200-fold. For each year that the target was missed, the necessary improvements would grow higher still. Growth Isn't Possible **nef** (2010).

[2]   http://www.theoildrum.com/node/3086

[4]   The welfare of a nation can scarcely be inferred from a measurement of national income (Kuznets 1934).

[5]   Stiglitz, Sen & Fitoussi (Sept 2009) "The Measurement of Economic Performance and Social Progress Revisited," Commission for The Measurement of Economic Performance and Social Progress.

[6]   New Economics Foundation National Accounts of Well-being 2009 Data from a poll carried out by GfK NOP in 2006 on behalf of the BBC, reported at http://news.bbc.co.uk/1/hi/programmes/happiness_formula/4771908.stm.

Part 5: How to deal with Climate Change and Energy

**People working to collect mud to use in contruction from the Volta River in Ghana.
Photo: Aase Seeberg**

"We're committed to changing not just light bulbs, but laws. And laws will only change with leadership."

Al Gore

5.1 From carbon markets towards climate social justice

By Maria Delfina Rossi

Social and Climate justice

The current system for using the atmosphere — first come, first served, no limits and no prices — is clearly dysfunctional and unfair. In fact, the climate crisis is a global governance crisis, a multilevel governance crisis: who decides what, securing which objectives, over what period of time? Despite the necessity of tackling this issue from a multidisciplinary perspective, economists provide many instruments to internalize costs such us atmospheric pollution. However, there is a risk of establishing environmental policies without considered other aspects, particularly income distribution repercussions.

There is a huge theoretical debate on how market-based mechanisms are an effective policy, particularly considering strong sustainability. Whether decisions, such as pollution levels, should be left to private agents or ought be taken by a central agent, are at the core of environmental economics. In this sense, green economics has the challenge of re-thinking economics science and providing a new framework from which build up not only green policies but much more besides.

The true is that especially after the Kyoto Protocol, *tradable pollution permits (TPPs)*, also called carbon markets, seem to be the most plausible policy to be accepted and implemented. Although market-based mechanisms have been implemented in recent last years in such a way that polluters and big companies have taken advantage; but these instruments can indeed help to protect the environment and redistribute wealth

The green movement has two options: fight against those mechanisms because they are market-based or decide to specify what the limits should be. From my perspective, there could be a two track strategy: first we need to sensibly argue which kind of carbon markets are we willing to accept and secondly, using a long-term perspective, we can build up a collective vision that accepts a new kind of consumption and production in a way that instruments like carbon tax-and-dividend can be implement.

This chapter argues for the first strategy: what are the tradable pollution permits characteristics and the institutional design, for example how basic principles like polluters pay can be implemented. Thus, TPPs can be powerful mechanisms to reduce pollution; conversely they might have negative effects on low-income families' purchasing power and on international trade, under certain circumstances.

In fact, there are differences in the design and implementation of carbon markets. Currently, the European Union Emission Trading Scheme (EU-ETS) is the biggest cap-and-trade carbon market in the word, while the United States (US) is dealing with a different proposal, named cap-and-dividend. Juxtaposing the EU and US model, I will try to analyze where the frontier between environmental and social welfare lies. In other words, while we are looking for answers to limit atmosphere pollution, we should still consider climate and social justice.

Public good and externalities

An externality, is any impact on any party not involved in a given economic transaction. This occurs when an action causes costs or benefits to third party stakeholder(s), without an intention and with no compensation. Therefore, a market failure appears: the full economic cost of economic activities are not reflected in the private costs, price systems do not reflect all relevant information and they do not lead to a first best allocation.

The atmosphere is a global public good by definition; therefore, in the words of Nicholas Stern, *"Climate change is the biggest market failure the world has ever seen"*. Hence, not adopting environmental policies involves costs, such as welfare losses for society, costs for future generations, overexploitation of natural resources and damage to the environment. The internalization of costs is a crucial goal. To make this happen, there are many economic tools available, for example environmental taxes (pigouvian taxes), environmental standards, sanctions and control, subsides, information and transparency for consumers, or property right markets (tradable pollution permits).

Many of these instruments are built up from partial equilibrium models without considering inter- and intra-generational redistribution. It seems that when talking about environmental economic policies, market efficiency is prioritized over equity. It is true although that none of those instruments alone are enough to stop climate change, a radical change in our consumption and production structure is required. However, we must recognize that TPPs are on the international agenda and are in many cases already being implemented. TPPs in fact pose a new contradiction to the free market theorists by showing that regulation and institutions are necessary to ensure welfare and sustainability.

Carbon markets (or TPPs)

Tradable pollution permits (TPPs) aim to allocate property rights for environmental resources and consequently let the market determine a fair price of those through a cost-minimization problem. Although in reality the implementation process has to deal with lobbies, asymmetric information, global regulation and other problems, the way TPPs function is theoretically simple:

First, the public authority sets out an amount of permits, criteria to identify cover entities under the market (firms that are going to receive the allowances and being able to trade in the market), and a distribution method. Second, entities can take either the allowances by grandfathering or by auction, so that they set their emissions at the point where their marginal cost of abatement equals the allowance price. Third, as a consequence of the process, each firm will have allowances to sell or buy. Fourth, entities go to the market and trade allowances, so that market prices change again until the market clears. Hence, in equilibrium, the permits demand curve crosses the permits supply curve. Meaning that under certain conditions, Pareto optimality is achieved.

There are two main limitations of this explanation. Firstly, pollution is a dynamic externality, and also it remains in the atmosphere after it is produce generating a cost for future generations. Secondly, the concept of a fair price and Pareto optimality does not consider the distributional effect of the cost neither the real impact on the environment. Still, we can reduce pollution with a TPPs but it is clear then that this policy cannot be exclusive of other environment measures nor of a radical change of production, consumption and growth in our societies.

The first big classification of TPPs is between baseline-and-credit and cap regimes. Baseline TPPs are those which expressed the emissions efficiency by setting a benchmark in relation to the activity of the source. There are many of them to regulate air and water pollution. However, given the context of the Kyoto Protocol, cap regimes are more accepted for atmosphere pollution.

Cap regimes set a total target, created by the sum of individual targets over a specific period of time. This total is subsequently allocated in 4 main ways

If the government does *grandfathering* (free allocation), revenue does not go to the government. Instead it goes to some companies' budgets due to the fact that they receive assets that have a market price, but it is a loss for those companies that have to buy permits. This greatly depends on the possibility of creating financial instruments or derivatives from the allowances. It seems that grandfathering can either increase polluters' profits (if the allowances market value rises) or shift the producer benefit from one to others. In this case the cap just acts like a quota, like an entry barrier for new entrepreneurial activity and can induce to create a cartel, increasing the probability of concentration and reducing the welfare of consumers.

On the other hand, a *100% auctions system* can be seen as a carbon tax. Remember that a carbon tax is a tax to be paid by each ton of CO_2 produced. If governments adopt a common cap for all companies, they will set the marginal costs of reduction at the level of the cap. They can also trade the excess of emissions right until they arrive at an equilibrium price.

In "The Problem of Social Cost", Ronald Coase establishes a theoretical statement about efficiency in markets with externalities regulated by property rights. The Coase theorem says that, given two firms, if transaction costs are zero - (meaning any agreement that is in the mutual benefit of the parties concerned gets made)- then any initial distribution of property rights leads to an efficient outcome. So, if there are two firms bargaining, when either one can be polluter and the other affected by pollution, without transaction costs, the market will produce an efficient outcome disregarding how the allowances are initially distributed.

The "Coase Theorem" is an idea that should not be generalized to carbon markets with more than two agents. A TPP can be far from the Coase approach, for example many carbon markets usually have more than two firms and there are two bargaining processes: one between the public authority (representing agents affected by pollution) and the polluters; the second within firms. The approach of this article is based on this theorem, not around Pareto optimality; instead, the main interest here is the income distribution effect of a TPP system.

The theory suggests that TPPs achieve efficient allocation (following Pareto) of resources regardless of the initial allocation system (grandfathering or auctions) under certain assumptions. The assumptions made are that there are no wealth effects on demand, no transactions costs and correct definition of property rights. However, those strong considerations cannot be assumed to be true when we actually apply a policy.

TPP or carbon tax

A cap-and-trade TPP with 100% auction has the same effect as a carbon tax. Both of them allow the internalization of pollution costs and they create a dynamic incentive to adopt new technology so as to reduce pollution.

Environmental taxes based on emissions rather than consumption goods give incentives to the firms to transfer the tax burden through prices, raising consumption prices. TPPs can potentially generate the same effect: depending on the market structure and the demand of each household, it could have negative effects on the income distribution. Of course, this effect will greatly depend on the price elasticity demand of each household with respect to the goods (for instance, we can expect a rural family with a small elasticity with respect to oil prices face a more regressive effect of a carbon market than a urban family that can use public transportation).

In a TPPs (as well as with a carbon or environmental tax), the government can use its revenue to compensate unwanted effects. Particularly, cap regimes can be classified as follows:

> 1.*Cap-and-giveaway*: Free allocation of permits will just raise final product prices but do not generate any extra cost, so the firms and their shareholders will get the money.

> 2. *Cap-and-spend or cap-and-invest*: Permits are auctioned, so the government takes the revenue and uses it to fund public expenditure or specific climate policies.

> 3.*Cap-and-dividend:* Permits are auctioned and the revenue is distributed equally between consumers. (Boyce 2009)

In summary, there are many TPPs and regulations which provoke different impacts on the environment and on the economy: government expenditure, income distribution, competition policy, antitrust agreements, lobbies, etc. From this perspective we can now analyse the EU and US models.

The EU cap-and-trade

The Kyoto Protocol encourages countries to create regional or national carbon markets linked with international trading and flexible mechanisms. To be specific, article 4 sets the possibility to make a burden-sharing agreement between parties of an economic regional area which allows the EU to add up every Member State's target and reallocate them in the best and most cost-efficient way. (Kyoto Protocol 1998: 6)

In 2003, the EU Commission presented a proposal that became the 2003/87/CE Directive of the European Parliament and the EU Council. The EU Emission Trading Scheme (EU ETS) was settled. The EU ETS, which came into power the 1st of January of 2005, is a cap-and-trade market-based mechanism to reduce CO_2 emissions, with the theoretical advantage of setting a certain environmental outcome for a concrete period of time.

It is the biggest multinational carbon market in the world and one of the EU Climate Change policy pillars. Currently, it covers more than 10.000 installations from the energy sector and industry, which represent almost half of EU CO_2 emissions and 40% of greenhouse gases.

The EU ETS is a regime based on decentralized decision-making processes and a strong control by the European Commission. Each Member State proposes a national plan that includes the total number of permits and the procedure of distributions, considering that each allowance equals 1 ton of CO_2 and covering at least entities related with energy sector, metal production and transformation, mining industry and pulp manufacturing.

The market has experienced two periods of trading. In the period 2005 2008, 95% of permits have been distributed under grandfathering. In the second one, from 2009 to 2012, free distribution was reduced until 90%. The remaining 10% are distributed by auctions.

The ETS has a Fine and Sanction Mechanism for those who are not presenting their allowances by the end of April. This mechanism previews not only money penalties but also the obligation of carrying out the CO_2 emission reduction afterwards. Furthermore, the ETS allows the compatibility of permits coming from the Kyoto Protocol flexible mechanism such as Joint Implementation and Clean Development Mechanism and the indeterminate instrument of carbon capture and storage.

A new directive in 2009 revised the EU ETS to achieve greater emission reductions in energy-intensive sectors and to regulate the third trading period, which starts on 1st of January 2013. Thus, the EU ETS is moving from a cap-and-giveaway to a cap-and-invest model. It is moving from grandfathering to a progressive process of auctioning.

There are particular concrete aspects of the new directive: heavy industry will have to cut its GHG emissions by one-fifth compared to 1990 levels by 2020, Member States will progressively auction permits from 2013 onwards until arriving at a 100% auction allocation by 2027, the estimated 6 to 9 billion euro revenue will be used for the financing of clean technologies, and projects in carbon capture and storage and those countries with higher needs (more dependence on fossil fuels or insufficient connection with the European electricity network) will receive more allowances so as to create higher revenues.

However, up to now, the combination of grandfathering and auctioning systems generates an asymmetrical outcome. Different companies are affected by different allowance costs. This not only creates disequilibrium inside the market, but also acts as an entry barrier and discriminatory policy. Insider companies have an incentive to form a cartel, lowering the consumer benefit and to lobby in order to maintain their market power.

Private companies have being trying to maximize the number of free allowances that they receive, instead of minimizing their pollution. Some industrial lobbies use their influence to slow down the process of auctioning and to increase the differences between insiders and outsiders of the ETS. For example, the iron and steel sector has managed to remain out of the carbon market until 2012. Although there is a clear limit for pollution, offsetting can dilute the effect of the cap in a specific geographic area. In any case, companies do have an incentive to reduce their emissions and become more environmentally friendly.

It is expected that a future cap-and-investment system will cover the expenditure of the market function and (depending on how the investment is done) have a positive effect on low-income families and in creating incentives for environmental-friendly industries.

The US Cap-and-Dividend

The United States never ratified the Kyoto protocol. However, given its dimension and its impact on the global economy it is important to follow their different environmental policies. Currently in the US congress there are three main projects related with carbon emission. Besides of their limits, one of them for example has a huge bias towards nuclear power and carbon capture and storage technology and all of them use the 2005 year-base for calculate emission reduction.

One particular project S. 2877, the Carbon Limits and Energy for America's Renewal (CLEAR) Act was presented by Senators Cantwell and Collins on December 11, 2009. In general it is a cap-and-dividend and investment that would cover 80% of U.S. Greenhouse gasses emissions, requiring fossil fuel producers (e.g., coal mines, gas wellheads) and importers for the CO_2 emissions related to the fossil fuels they produce or import.

This particular project has a clear link with the one presented by van Hollen, a Democrat in the US House of Representatives. The "Cap and Dividend Act of 2009", that would generate a market starting 2012 with 2005 as base year. The text is divided into three main parts: the carbon market, the consumer dividends and the international trade implications (House of Representatives 2009: 1).

Therefore, we can read the CLEAR Act as a modification of the Cap-and-dividend idea. CLEAR adds a particular aspect on renewable energy investment. This system would have an impact not only in the redistribution of wealth throw different social sectors but also throw states. To understand the aspect of re-distribution we will focus on the first idea of a cap-and-dividend.

In the "Cap and Dividend Act of 2009" proposal, the Environmental Protection Agency (EPA) will be the authority in charge of distributing the permits and verifying compliance. Any US company selling fuel, fossil or not, will have to participate in the market (regardless of whether they actually produce in the US or import the sources). These carbon permits do not constitute a property right since by considering the atmosphere state property the government holds the right to take and re-distribute the permits at it wishes.

The distribution of allowances will be done through at least 4 auctions per year. In the proposal, there is a maximum limit of the amount permits per single entity in the auction and there is a minimum price. The permits can be sold, exchanged or transferred to another entity. If a company pollutes more than the permits it has, it should pay a penalty equal to three times the last year price of the emissions rights.

The project incorporates a tax on carbon-intensive goods for imports and a subsidy for exports of carbon-intensive goods that have to compete with products manufactured in other countries without an equivalent measure. This leaves the door open to future conventions or international agreements, where the US could be able to enter with its own market-based instrument.

A "Healthy Climate Trust Fund" is the main difference with the EU ETS. The fund is established to re-distribute the auctions revenue among the US citizens.

The Congressional Budget Office (CBO), a US institution that analyses the ex-ante effect of any federal policy on the income distribution and revenue and expenses of the government, estimated that the system would cost 175 American dollars per household, with an aggregate cost for the economy of 22 billion American dollars by 2020 (CBO 2009: 3). The analysis includes the cost of restructuring the production and use of energy, but it does not include the economic benefits of the reduction in greenhouse gases emissions.

Furthermore, the EPA has recently published a study where it estimates the allowance prices at $13 in 2015 and $16 in 2020 (EPA 2010: 2), where each allowance represent one metric ton of CO_2. Considering the current EU ETS allowance price and the high quality level of the agency, the approximation seems accurate.

The next figure shows the positive relationship between carbon emissions and expenditure per capita (Boyce & Riddle 2009: 08). Metric tons of CO_2 per capita is a proxy variable of households footprint, an environmental impact measure. There is a positive relation between income and pollution. Thus, if pollution increases with income but the redistribution is linear, this will generate a progressive impact, since those who pollute more will pay more

The cap-and-dividend model considers an auction system to distribute permits followed by a lump-sum payment to each person, disregarding her real income. Through auctions, producers will face the immediate cost and since the atmosphere is a public good, revenue will be equally redistributed. *"Carbon emission-reduction policies have a regressive impact on income distribution – unless coupled with revenue-recycling policies that protect the real in-comes of the poor and middle classes."* (Boyce & Riddle 2009: 08)

Recently, Charles D. Kolstad and Corbett A. Grainger used 2003 consumption data and emissions factors from 1997 US economy. To simplify, they assume a carbon market with 100% auctioned permits (which is the same as a carbon tax) and that cost are all passed to consumers. They make a first-order estimation to test whether a cap-and-trade market is regressive. Under the assumptions a cap regime will be regressive in the US and thus a dividend should be implemented. Hence, considering a $15 tax or permit price, we can see the lowest quintile households will pay 21.70 tons per $15, that is, $325 per year, while the wealthiest quintile will pay 75.99 CO_2 tons per $15, which is $1140 annually. Obviously, the regression must be seen as a percentage over income of each quintile; the table at the end shows its effect:

Conclusion

These pages were an examination and comparison of the recent US cap-and-dividend proposal compared to the EU cap-and-trade. Although in the US there is no concrete measure apply yet and there are many under debate, we can take the cap-and-dividend proposal as a benchmark to understand the relevance of environment policies and wealth distribution. Thus, the dividend is the main difference of the US cap regime and the EU ETS. In Europe there was no public discussion regarding these consequences of the carbon market. It is true that the impact expected was not really relevant since most of the allowances are distributed by grandfathering, however, US studies show that even a 15$ or 13€ per ton of CO_2 allowance might have a regressive effect over income. This means that a current study of European households' consumption and carbon-intensive product prices must be done to determinate distribution effect of the EU ETS.

We could ask ourselves now if the US proposal is more efficient or fairer than the EU model, but there is no straight answer. First, we can expect the US proposal to suffer many changes before it even gets the approval of the chambers. Second, since nothing like the CBO exists at a European level and we do not have any information about the EU ETS repercussions for consumption prices and over households' welfare. Yet we can conclude that the design of the policy can have very different effects not only on efficiency, but also on income redistribution and market functioning.

The US cap-and-dividend makes no distinction between companies and guarantees the maximum for those who are willing to pay more in order to get the allowances so that the distribution is efficient. The EU ETS is a mixed system of auctions and grandfathering that leads to an asymmetric outcome between companies and encourages lobbies

The new CLEAR Act proposal in the US which not only proposes a dividend but also a percentage of investment in renewable energies also raises one question: can the application of a cap-and-dividend-and-investment also influence the distribution between countries in the EU? In other words, could an environmental measure with transfer to low income families and green investment contribute to create a true economic convergence in the process of the European Union Integration? Again seems that climate, the principle of polluters pay and social justice cannot be understand separately

Carbon markets (TPPs) generate a cost that might be passed on to consumer prices, stock returns, wages and other stakeholders, changing the national income distribution. Indeed, the distribution of costs and benefits determines the winners and losers from environmental policy. CBO papers should warn us about the regressive effects that cap regimes may have on the income distribution. They also put on the table the existence of a trade-off between environmental protection and equality. The principal idea here is that under the assumption that permits costs are passed on to final prices, there is no substitution effect and the demand is almost inelastic, then cap-and-trade regimes are a regressive policy that increase income inequality.

Distribution can be strongly affected by the consequences of international trade agreements and barriers. Thus, the implication of environmental policies in global trading is especially relevant for developing countries that highly depend on their exports. Europe and the US should reach further agreements if they do not want to damage their own firms. The climate crisis is a multilevel global governance crisis. The possible effects of any TPPs on international trade and country competitiveness stress this fact and the possible risk of applying uncoordinated policies in different regions (US, EU) without any clear international framework. International cooperation, especially inside WTO and UNFCC, is fundamental in order to avoid inaction promoted by the short-minded desire of countries to help their own firms and retain the status-quo.

Lastly, there is an open question regarding the future implementation of the EU ETS and possible negotiations under the UNFCCC. Given the fact that TPPs cap regimes can be regressive and can harm international trade, complementary policies should be implemented to compensate for this. Indeed, the question is how to ensure that the principle of "polluters pay" is achieved in the final instance and how can we design policies that aim for both environmental protection and social justice?

Main differences between

EU ETS and US Cap & Dividend

	EU-ETS	US Cap & Dividend
UNFCCC	Inside Kyoto Protocol	Outside Kyoto but in the UNFCCC Convention
Target baseline	1990	2005
Targets	Legally binding by Kyoto agreements	Depends on the political final decision of the US Congress
Price/ expected price	€13-15	$15
Distribution	Grandfathering moving progressively to auction	100% auction
Entities	Final producers of energy and others industries located in the EU.	Entities that are first fuel seller in the US, where fuel means oil, natural gas, coal or any other combustible fuel.
Offsetting	Yes (CDM, JI, International Trading Emissions)	No clearly specified yet
Carbon Capture and Store	Yes	Yes
Revenue	Environmental projects (not clearly specified)	Equal/Flat dividend to households and administrative costs.
Taxation over importers	No	Yes, fuels importers are covered

5.2 An Introduction to Climate Change

By Alan Bouquet

The Greenhouse Effect

The greenhouse effect is a relatively simple, dynamic atmospheric effect. Various greenhouse gases in the atmosphere, particularly carbon dioxide, nitrous oxide and methane act like the glass of a greenhouse. Heat enters the system via solar energy, some is absorbed by the Earth's surface, the rest is reflected back into the atmosphere. Depending on the quantity of greenhouse gasses and various other 'forcing' elements, a certain amount of that energy is reflected back towards the Earth. This effectively warms the planet more than would be the case were we not to have an atmosphere. The moon for example, is the same distance from the sun, but is considerably colder.

Research has spent much time working out just how much the greenhouse effect impacts us and what the sensitivity of the Earth is to changes in these gasses.

The Drivers of Climate Change

Compared to pre industrial levels, the quantity of carbon dioxide, nitrous oxide and methane in the atmosphere has increased markedly (Table 7). Carbon Dioxide is the most important of these due to the vast quantities produced by man. While the other two are many times more potent greenhouse gasses, their quantities are more limited. This is due to their source; The latter are produced mainly through agriculture, whereas carbon dioxide is produced in startling quantities by fossil fuel burning and land use changes. As shown in the table below, these changes are marked and completely attributable to anthropogenic factors. The IPPC considers the rate of increase of these gases to be unprecedented in the last 10,000 years.

Table 7: Greenhouse gas concentrations (Source: IPCC)

Gas	Pre Industrial	Current (2005)
Carbon Dioxide	280ppm	379ppm
Nitrous Oxide	270ppb	319ppb
Methane	715ppb	1732ppb

What Causes Radiative Forcing?

Radiative forcing or 'forcing' is the effect of greenhouse components on the temperature of the planet. The IPCC recognises the following to be forcing components:

- Long Lived Greenhouse Gases – These are CO_2 and other halocarbons such as methane, which remain in the atmosphere for years. Currently they are almost completely due to anthropogenic sources. They impact on a global scale.

- Ozone – This is likely to cause a warming of the troposphere (lower atmosphere) due to emissions of ozone forming chemicals like carbon monoxide and nitrous oxides.

- Surface Albedo – Changes in land use and black carbon on snow change the reflectivity of the ground. Darker surfaces absorb more heat. In some places this can cause a feedback effect, such as in the Arctic, where melting causes darker surfaces which causes more melting.

- Aerosols – Aerosols such as sulphur emissions from power plants have a considerable impact on global climate. Although it can cause a net cooling, it can produce acid rain and pollute the air. Measures to 'clean up' industries emitting these particulates could cause a sharp increase in temperatures.

- Linear Contrails and Water Vapour

- Natural Factors – Solar irradience can be an important factor in temperatures. However the small changes in solar activity in recent times do not account for the recent warming. In fact, these changes are an order of magnitude smaller than the current warming trends. Volcanic ash can also have a cooling effect. As was seen when mount Pinatubo erupted in 1992 causing cooler temperatures and increased precipitation.

Direct Observation of Climate Change

As we have said, warming of the system is completely unequivocal. The globe has warmed on average around 1 degree celcius since the pre-industrial, but how has it changed? How do we observe climate change?

The oldest record of temperature comes from the central England temperature record, stretching back into the 17th century. Records from all over the world, including ships records for ocean temperatures are used to compile a massive network of records. This has been built up over the last several decades.

Temperature data is 'homogenised' by comparing station data and taking into account site changes, changes to the surrounding area around the station and the method of recording the data. Where it is applicable, the data are corrected to account for this, where they cannot be, such as when a station has a town or city grow up around it causing an urban heat island effect, the station is discounted.

Other methods of recorded data are also included, specifically satellite data, glacier information and sea level data. This all goes toward building an excellent record of world temperature, especially for the last century. The records show that:

- A massive majority of the warmest years have come in the last decade.

- The rate of warming is increasing.

- The oceans are absorbing much of the heat (about 80%) caused through global warming, which has various disastrous impacts on them.

- Glacier and snow cover have declined dramatically. Arctic temperatures are increasing at about twice the global rate and permafrost temperatures are rising considerably quicker than global temperatures.

- Losses from ice sheets have very likely contributed to sea level rise

- Sea levels are rising at 1.8mm per year.

- Extremes of temperature and precipitation are changing as well. Cold days, nights and frost are less frequent and tropical cyclones appear to have become more intense and active.

- Droughts have become more intense and more widespread.

Palaeoclimatology

All these changes we can be very sure of. The next question to ask is how important are these changes on a longer time scale. How do we go back further than the instrumental record? This is where palaeoclimatology comes in. Palaeoclimatology 'studies use changes in climatically sensitive indicators to infer past changes in global climate' over periods of decades to millions of years. This is called proxy data. Various proxies can be used to produce excellent indicators of past climate; Tree ring data, ice core data, corals, bore holes and even various species such as beetles which are highly temperature sensitive.

What does all these data tell us? Northern hemisphere temperatures are very likely (90% confidence) warmer in the last 50 years than they have been in the last 500 years over a 50 year period and likely (66% confidence) warmer than the last 1500 years. This is a highly useful extension of the climate record.

Attribution of Climate Change

Having determined what is happening to the planet, we need to understand why it is happening. Attributing climate change is essential in understanding whether climate change is natural or anthropogenic. Various models are run using natural forcing only (solar and volcanic activity) and with both anthropogenic and natural forcing. All these models show that natural forcing on it's own cannot explain the warming trend of approximately the last 50 years in the surface, atmosphere or the oceans. In fact, volcanic and anthropogenic aerosols have likely offset some of the warming due to greenhouse gasses. At smaller scales, the reliability decreases, but on a global and continental level we can be very sure that anthropogenic climate change is happening.

The Future

One of the problems we face in interpreting climate change is that various feedbacks are present. The world is a huge, integrated system that is very difficult to understand. The 'sensitivity' of the planet to various stimulators is key. The IPCC says that it is probably in the region of 1.5 to 4.5 degrees Celsius. Which means that for a doubling of CO_2 in the atmosphere, temperatures will increase by this amount. We cannot be certain of this figure however and there is a possibility the sensitivity is well above this figure; in fact, recent trends suggest it is at the upper limit of that estimate. So while we can be sure that change is happening, it is difficult to determine how some of these changes will develop and the rate of this change.

Models are used to try to determine what the future holds and in order to cover all the possibilities, the IPCC uses a range of 'emission scenarios'. These include a fossil fuel intensive path, a business as usual path, as well as a range of different future economies based around moderate or severe emissions reductions. Our current emissions suggest we are looking at a 3-5 degree warming by the end of the century, which would prove catastrophic. We have already warmed the planet by over a degree and two degrees, the recommended target from the EU is looking to be extremely unlikely to be met unless immediate and extreme measures are taken. Precipitation changes can also be modelled in a similar way and show some severe changes in the quantity and intensity of rainfall.

Emissions Targets

Based on the impacts that have already occurred and will occur in the future, as well as the various modelled scenarios, targets are set by various world bodies and in particular the

UNFCC. The EU has adopted the 2 degree target as the point at which 'dangerous' climate change occurs. In fact, it is very difficult to determine exactly where dangerous change occurs. At 2 degrees most corals will have been bleached and many island states will be at risk of higher sea levels. Is this not dangerous?

The IPCC have various emissions reduction pathways which are used to demonstrate exactly how we should act and at what stages we should be reaching certain reduction targets. This is how the EU has come to adopt the 80% by 2050 reduction target. The IPCC report speaks of 'tolerance windows'. These are effectively pathways that demonstrate the pace of reduction required to reach each target.

Whatever target we use one thing is clear. The sooner we act and cut emissions drastically, the lower the temperature change and the less severe the climate change.

Part 6: Sustainable Development

Iguassu Falls, Brazil. Photo By Martina Falck

**"Only when the last tree has been cut down,
Only when the last river has been poisoned,
Only when the last fish has been caught,
Only then will you find that money cannot be eaten."**

(Cree Indian Prophecy)

6.1 Creating a sustainable future: transformational learning, ethical inquiry and social enterprise

By Bronwen Rees

Director of Centre for Transformational Management Practice, Anglia Ruskin University) and Ed Bentham (Founder trustee AWF)

BACKGROUND

The World Economic Forum 2009 Report raised the following call for action: "It is time to rethink the old systems and have a fundamental rebooting of the educational process." Some radical institutionalist economists argue that these problems can only be solved through the transformation of the deeper structural relationship of institutions and culture. According to Joel Magnuson, this can only happen when a deeper, evolutionary transformation of human consciousness takes place.. For some writers the time is running out (Orr, 1998, Robinson and Tinkler, 1997, O'Sullivan, 1999, Reardon, 2009).

It was against the background of ongoing economic and environmental crises that the AWF gained European funding for an EU-funded youth-in-action workshop for European youngsters over a three-week period. These workshops have to be understood within the context of, firstly, the operational framework for action provided through the AWF and, secondly, the dynamic support and project development structures that were made available to workshop participants, again, through the AWF. There were two main strands to the workshops: the first was the creation, identification and implementation of projects within the AWF framework, and the second was a programme of ethical inquiry that supported the project work through a processes of inner reflection and outer ritual.

Ethical inquiry

Ethical inquiry is a method of working that has emerged from the Centre for Transformational Management Practice, and has been developed over a period of 6 years trial. It began as a simple attempt to introduce meditation into businesses. It developed into a process for inquiring into personal and organisational conditions in order to help the creation and unfolding of ethical and sustainable communities and businesses (Rees, 2012, forthcoming). It embraces a view of life that understands that life is systemic and interconnected. These systems exist at different levels: organismic, family, social, eco, and cosmic.

Social enterprise and the AWF

The AWF is a UK registered charity, charged with the mission to provide opportunities for young people around the world to work together for the common good, particularly as regards communities under threat, endangered species and habitats. The AWF's operating base is running the volunteer programme on the whale watching boats of Tenerife in the Canaries from where it coordinates a range of projects in countries as diverse as Ghana, Sierra Leone, Vietnam, Bolivia, Sri Lanka and Cape Verde Islands, all inspired by working towards the UN's Millennium Development goals. Over the years the AWF has developed effective processes for inspiring and motivating its volunteers. Volunteers arrive for different periods of time, and are immediately thrown into the volunteer community. Once there, they may carry out research projects as part of their university internship, or they may begin to work on the AWF project bases. Every night, they will report back, share their work, and plan the next day. Volunteers will learn on the job, but the evenings are a time for collaborative discussion and planning. In the last year, and particularly during the workshop many of the AWF projects have taken on the structure of social enterprises, thus providing educational opportunities for the volunteers, opportunities for the different communities in which AWF operates and a financial ground for the AWF further to grow.

THE 'TRANSFORMATIONAL' PROCESS

Creating the learning environment

Two days before the workshops AWF volunteers and the workshop leaders created the learning space in which the event would take place. This involved erecting a multiple tent, buying silks for the tent, and also a large Buddha form as a ritual space., and building some of the multi-bedded accommodation. The tent was erected on a rocky outcrop, and within it was also a cave. The communal living areas were transformed into learning spaces, and the AWF media volunteers set up the technology necessary – bringing together both old and new, the mythological and the technological. Participants were 6 in a bedroom, and had a long terrace with wonderful views over the island and a swimming pool. From the outset, participants were immersed in group activities including working with AWF volunteers on whale-watching boats and organising cooking and cleaning rotas.

Content of workshops

The practical work was supported by the workshops we put the group through. This guided their thinking, and helped them take ownership of their projects, developing both awareness of the bigger picture and a sense of individual and group responsibility as well as ideas for developing their own contributions. Workshops covered:

Global Issues in the context of the UN's Millennium Development Goals – Our work at each of our project bases is framed within the context of achieving these goals. Individuals/ small groups can select projects which help achieve an element(s) from one or more of these goals. UN development goals cover: Poverty and Hunger,;Universal Education; Gender Equality; Child and Material Health; Combating HIV/Aids; The Environment, and Global Partnership; Access to Technology; and Fair Trade. These workshops look in detail at the complexities in the underlying issues and use case study materials to learn from the experience of others trying, to achieve different goals. They examined the complexities at each project base in relation to each of these issues.

Project Management – This workshop covered core skills needed in achieving targeted project goals, ranging from team building, critical path analysis, decision making, task allocation. Each group had to develop a business plan for its own project and present it to the whole group, and the latter was critically appraising from both the logic and schedule on an ongoing level throughout the programme.

Fund Raising – The groups had to finance themselves and participants passing developed different fundraising strategies to be presented to, and argued through, by the whole group.

Risk Evaluation – Each group had to identify all potential risks and develop strategies to minimise these. This workshop helped them through this process, which had to be specific to each group and its project, by outlining the various types of risks to be covered and ways in which they can be mitigated.

The focus in these workshops was on self learning with discussions, presentations, internet research, case study materials. The aim was to create a learning environment, as opposed to providing information on a plate, and to then critically examine ideas and strategies generated by individuals at the level of the group. The experiential learning approach means that individuals take responsibility and ownership both for their learning and for the ideas they develop

Creating the 'bigger picture' though the above workshops was quite simple. The statistics on what is happening to communities, species, habitats, languages etc spoke for themselves, and are quite shocking. It is easy to demonstrate the scale and nature of the problem, and it was easy to identify causes and delve into the complexities underlying those causes through appropriate case study materials.

Once the individual/ group has a sense of responsibility then the issue becomes one of motivation to actually do something. The workshops in project management and marketing and fundraising were critical in providing the necessary skills but the main issue is in convincing people that they have the capacity to actually pull something off (as opposed to making them feel they should try and do something). Building self confidence was critical. Key aspects of the development process were the way in which individuals work, learn and think in a collective space whilst being encouraged to reflect on an individual level in order to develop their personal contribution. Every evening the entire group had to discuss and critically examine elements of each group's thinking, and individuals had to learn how to harness the value of this activity for their own work.

Decision making was devolved from day one to individuals and groups,; they had to decide what they wanted to do and evolve objectives, strategies and time lines, identifying critical issues, imperatives that they need to consider and work out . Daily, they had to present and defend their ideas to the larger group, learning that critical examination is more valuable than polite claps of approval; that it is important their ideas and strategies have absolute integrity.

Team-building skills were vital as teams had to learn how to identify skills required and how the complex of individual talents can mesh together to provide everything that is required to achieve results. Where skills sets were not adequate they had to demonstrate an awareness of the deficiencies and suggest actions to make the necessary compensations. Taking responsibility for self-learning and project development was critical. In this process they started to take ownership of their work and actions, the fundamental basis of all inspired action.

The ethical inquiry element

The ethical inquiry element of the programme took place alongside the more concrete project work. It consisted of talks, discussion, meditation and ritual. In the opening ceremony, on the first night of arrival, participants walked down a candle lit path, and were introduced to the idea of 'spirit' in its widest possible sense, supporting the work. On the first day, participants were introduced to the idea of 'scientific method' and its role its place in the bigger context of knowledge and wisdom both East and West. This was set up to challenge existent frames of reference, and open up minds to new ways of looking at the world. This created the reflective ground. Participants were initially introduced to some basic meditation practice, which then ran daily throughout the programme.

Ethical inquiry exercises

On the first day, each participant was asked to reflect and share one moment in their lives when they had been really moved. This began to deepen the communication from the outset, so that participants were engaging with one another beyond the level of the rational, and moving into feeling states and tones. On another day, participants were asked to examine their own personal, mental, spiritual and emotional resources. The idea of this was to provide a solid ground of positive experience that could support participants as they entered into a process of transformation. At the same time as this was happening, the participants were being introduced to the different elements of the millennium goals – which meant having to take on board some disturbing aspects of human existences – the ethical inquiry workshops provided a space for participants to reflect on their responses to such experiences. Another day was spent in an exercise where participants were asked to respond to an exercise of ranking behaviour in terms of its ethical nature, and to agree to this amongst their groups Participants were from different cultures, genders, educational backgrounds and this prompted some fierce discussion. The objectives of these exercises were to help participants reflect on how their own views and belief systems were formed, and to challenge these in the light of others' experiences. This was to offset the ethnocentric domination of Western (particularly English and UK) educational and value systems. On another day, they were asked to reflect on their own actions in the world in the light of the consequences of their actions, and to prepare their own action plans about bringing more awareness into the intention and nature of their actions.

Ritual and myth

A final important element of this element of the programme was that of ritual and myth. This provided the 'frame' of the workshop experience, with a ritualistic opening of the space, thus creating the idea of a 'sacred' ground in which the work was to be done. This was the creation of the 'reflective ground'. This was completed by a 'stone ceremony' where participants were invited to take three stones – one red, one white, and one black. In a ritual, participants took the black stone, and buried this at El Desierte, where the workshop took place, the white was ritualistically deposited at the AWF project base, and the red was taken home by the participants to serve as a memory of their experience. Optional group work was organised such as a 'cave meditation' or 'incubation practice' which took place in the actual cave! Participants lie down and are led on a visualisation to ancient Greece, where they may connect with an inner guide. This practice is derived from the ancient 'incubation' healing practices.

Finally, each participant was offered individual mentoring on their own individual future.

EVALUATION
Whilst the process that has been set in motion is still on-going we are presenting here the first results of the workshops.
Social

After the first sessions on UN Goals, the group broke into twelve teams and worked on developing projects within the context of the AWF framework.

The following projects were identified, a project plan drawn up, and ideas for funding and action researched .

> *Creation of centre's for women* became **The Dragonfly Project A Place for Women**
> *Creation of arts cultural centres* became **the Heart Project**
> *Preservation of sharks* became **Utila Island Marine Project**
> *Preservation of bats* became **the Bat Action Trust**

Tree planting/ education became **Plant a Tree, Fund a Dream Project**
Restoring a Romanian castle became **Re-counaste Romania**
Preservation of Herbal remedies became **Spiritual Cleansing in Peru**
Micro financing became **Eunomia**
Preservation of elephants became the **MEF- AWF Collaboration**

The workshops were a great success as evidenced by the work that was produced, the work and energy that was put in to getting everything done and the follow up subsequently. The real test will be how things develop over the coming year.

Each team's presentation of their strategy and goals for the coming year was exceptionally well thought through, focused and enthusiastic.

For each of these projects there are various levels of work that is already in place – for example the MEF-AWF collaboration was already in place, and this project built on how this would work. For the creation of the women's centre, there is already a project base in Sierra Leone that has taken two years to build so a community is already building around this. Other projects were not quite so developed – for example the shark project began here, but a place for this has already been identified, and at the time of writing bookings have already been taken.

Each team's ideas have been integrated onto the AWF's website and each team has active forum and fundraising pages linked to their web pages.

On the ethical inquiry side, we are still in the process of eliciting responses, and following up the participants' progress. However an AWF video consisting of interviews with participants, clearly shows the transformation processes that the young people were beginning to make with their lives. Longer-term transformations will be followed up later.

To the future

The unfolding consequences of the workshop are only just beginning, but we believe that we have laid the seeds for young people to have the confidence to inquire into themselves and the world in which they are living, have the tools and infrastructure to make an ethical living for themselves in the world, and to begin to build their own communities. Participants on the programmes now have a supportive living community, aided by the AWF forums, skills and networks to begin to make a difference in the world. The whole programme took immense energy, experience and commitment to making it work, and this would be difficult to translate into a university environment which is more attuned to education for the global marketplace, and its powerful stakeholders.

References

Magnuson, (2008)'Mindful Economy and Ecology', *Interconnections*, Issue 2 pp 10-20)

Orr, D, W (1998) Transformation or Irrelevance: The Challenge of Academic Planning for Environmental Education in the 21st Century. In Blaze Corcoran, J.L.Elder&R. Tchen, (Eds.) *Academic Planning in College and University Programs: Proceedings of the 1998 Sanibel Symposium* (pp1-2) Rock Spring, GA:North American Association for Environmental Education

Reardon, J (2008) 'Sustainability:Why Should we Care?' *Interconnections,* Issue 2 pp.2-10

Rees, B (2012, forthcoming) 'East meets West: The Development and Methods of Crucible Research' in K. Schuyler (ed) *Inner Peace and Global Vision* – in *The Influence of Tibetan Buddhism on Leadership and Organizations* ed. Kathryn Goldman Schuyler, Information Age Publishing

Robinson, J and Tinkler J (1997) Reconciling Ecological, Economic and Social Imperatives: A New Conceptual Framework in T.Schrecker (Ed), *Surviving Globalism: The Social and Environmental Challenges* (pp. 71-94). New York:St Martin's

World Economic Forum "Educating the Next Wave of Entrepreneurs " Global Education Initiative Report of the World Economic Forum Report (2009)

6.2 A Thought Experiment

A cultural approach to achieving sustainability

Clive Lord

Rapanui (Easter Island) is a classic 'Tragedy of the Commons'1 case study, as revealed by archæological excavations. This should be taken extremely seriously, because the 'Tragedy' is in danger of being played out on a global scale. Imagine an island which will support 10,000 sheep As long as there are 9,999 sheep or fewer it is in everyone's interest to increase numbers, but at 10,000 or more the interests of each shepherd and the community as a whole are suddenly, diametrically opposed. But the difference is so subtle that no one notices, so flocks continue to increase. The island is over- grazed, and the society collapses.

On Rapanui, around AD 900 a small group of Polynesians arrived on what was a lush but isolated sub-tropical island half the size of the Isle of Wight. By 1500 there were at least 7,000, and possibly many more, but the trees used for fishing canoes, statue transport and which supported soil fertility were fast disappearing. Weapons first appeared then, followed shortly after by human bones instead of fish in rubbish heaps. In 1722 a Dutch ship discovered 3,000 survivors on a barren island.2

Professor Jared Diamond offers evidence that similar incomprehensibly self-destructive behaviour seems to have been typical of human groups as they colonized new territories3. Why? I believe the explanation lies in their cultural patterns. According to a recent television documentary presented by Dr. Alice Roberts, the entire human population outside Africa is descended from a single family group similar in size to the one which colonized Rapanui. That group crossed the southern tip of the Red Sea a mere 70,000 years ago. Ever since then human groups have been expanding. The generally overlooked significance of that is that each and every human group outside Africa developed a *culture* suited to expansion.

Expansion must sooner or later meet limits. But instead of the foresight with which humans are credited leading to rational preparation for this foreseeable eventuality, a culture which evolved to take maximum advantage of the potential to expand reacts very differently. It will normally be individualistic, and highly competitive. As competition for ever scarcer resources becomes intense, the reaction is not co-operation or restraint, but aggression, and then warfare. Arguably a globalised world is now following a similar course for exactly the same reasons. Unlike climate change, on Rapanui there could be no scepticism on either the cause or consequence of felling all the trees, yet the islanders could not change their behaviour *before* a catastrophe.

However, whether or not the 'Tragedy' is the norm, most societies clearly recovered. Even on Rapanui, by the time Captain Cook was able to converse with the islanders in 1774, the descendants of the survivors were beginning to evolve a sustainable way of life within the meagre resources not destroyed4. In contrast to Rapanui, the Siane, a tribe in New Guinea, had a culture which distinguished between necessities, which were shared unconditionally, and luxuries which could be traded in a kind of 'free market', so that everyone had an identity of interest when dealing with ecological limits.5 Despite their minimal technology and resources, the Siane perceived themselves to have a comfortable margin to spare above necessities. The reason so-called 'primitive' tribes did not develop advanced technology was not necessarily because they were less intelligent than Europeans, but because they did not need to.

If Professor Diamond is right, the ancestors of the Siane must have gone through at least one 'Tragedy', and possibly more. But the difference is that they had arrived at their present home several millennia ago, whereas it was Rapanui's first experience of dealing with resource constraints. If humankind is truly intelligent, then it should be possible for the world community to adopt the Siane culture without first going through the 'Tragedy'. We do not have to return to their way of life, just to adopt their strategy for sharing wealth. But somehow we have to overcome the current culture which dominates the world. If its inertia was formidable on Easter Island, how much more so is it globally? Naturally the central imperative is for growth, but whilst agreements to limit economic activity require unanimity (or effective control), a competitive culture is more likely to intensify into aggression, warfare, and at worst genocide7. The answer to the biblical question "Why do the nations so furiously rage together" (incidentally in contrast to other animals) suddenly becomes obvious.

So how can we adopt the 'Siane' strategy – or something which achieves its purpose? My suggestion is a thought experiment in which the central idea will be a Citizens' Income (CI). This is an adaptation of the system which enabled the Siane to live sustainably, in a form appropriate to a developed monetised western state. Every man, woman and child will receive a weekly sum sufficient to cover food, fuel, clothing and accommodation. The CI will be tax free, paid to individuals and unconditional. Everyone will keep it, working or not, or whether they need it or not. It will replace all existing social security benefits and tax allowances for the able bodied. It will be paid for out of taxation, so those on higher incomes will pay more in tax than the CI is worth to them. (In passing, this includes me).

Green Economics Methodology : An Introduction

The primary purpose is 'an identity of interest when dealing with ecological limits'. But indispensable to that aim is a communal approach to wealth sharing. Many who have addressed this problem hitherto have asserted that this meant socialism. It does entail a considerable reduction in inequality, but I advocate the CI in preference to socialism because it allows the better off, including entrepreneurs, to keep at least some of their differentials. This widening of potential support – the fusion, not just compromise between old enemies - is crucial. Unfortunately old tribal attitudes still hamper this rapprochement. Doorstepping during elections indicates that support for measures necessary to achieve sustainability has never been higher than 28%, and it has slipped during the economic downturn. There have been suggestions that democracy may have to be sacrificed if the planet is to be saved for human habitation6. It is to head off this risk that the CI - as a thought experiment - is vital.

Crucially the CI abolishes means testing. So far as low paid recipients are concerned, means testing amounts to a massive tax on their earnings. Actually *everyone* who does not receive means tested benefits pays this disguised tax on the first part of their income, but that is irrelevant for all but the lowest paid. This unorthodox view of the poverty trap is corroborated by a surprising source - *Dynamic Benefits8,* a policy report in a series edited by Ian Duncan Smith, now Minister for Work and Pensions, whilst he was still in opposition. The graph on page 88 shows benefit withdrawal rates as if they were taxes. Marginal tax rates vary between 100% and 70% on incomes from 0 to £11,000 per annum, falling to 30% above that rate, eventually rising to 50% on very high incomes. *Dynamic Benefits* explicitly admits that withdrawal of benefits is exactly the same as a tax so far as the person losing a benefit is concerned. Those who avoid entering the labour market are not 'scroungers' but are acting rationally.

The Citizens' Income merely shifts this real but hidden tax burden on to the shoulders of those who should bear it. If critics object that the CI means workers paying for shirkers, this has been so ever since means testing was introduced in 1603, but the workers who pay are those who narrowly fail to qualify for benefits. On the contrary, the CI, although it does allow people not to work, actually re-instates a work *incentive*. The point to keep clearly in mind in this complex area is that the CI is simply an application of the 'Siane' strategy to a Western democracy.

Green philosophy starts from the proposition that the biosphere - the space within which life is possible - is a thin shell around a little ball. For some it is irrelevant whether we are approaching its limits to cope, because they believe a technical solution will *always* be found to any problems. Their confidence seems justified because we have repeatedly won this gamble in the past, though not always without a heavy cost so some sections of humanity. But how will we recognize when the gamble does become foolhardy, and how will our competitive culture respond? Innovations may well make further expansion possible, but clinging to this hope is dangerous. Even the more obvious Green policies, recycling, public transport, renewable energy, reducing air travel, more efficient engines etc. etc. are worse than useless if used as desperate attempts to avoid challenging the assumption of perpetual growth. We must get away from a *dependence* on growth. The normal expectation should be a steady state economy. But that means restricting options we have grown used to taking for granted. A steady state economy will look like a recession in terms of conventional economics. When I first knocked on doors 37 years ago using the Green Party as my pretext to test public response, less than 1% agreed with me, 9% took my concerns seriously, 80% were not interested and 10% thought somebody would always outwit what I said was inevitable. The 10% who listened has grown to about 25%. That is enough for some lip service to climate change, but it leaves 75% who might reject a party – even a Green Party - which spelled out what avoiding action might mean in practice. Hence the need for a thought experiment.

A Citizens' Income can become a fusion - not just a compromise - of core ideas from the now outdated 'left' and 'right'. In itself the CI is radically redistributive from the well off to those in the poverty trap, but it allows some ideas to make sense which are rightly condemned as oppressive in its absence. A minimum wage (MW) becomes unnecessary. Studies claiming that a MW does not destroy jobs may be valid in in an expanding economy, but this cannot be true in a steady state economy. Reminders that the ecological footprint of the world in general, and Britain in particular are already too large raise implications which are not congenial to those who welcome the redistributive effect of a Citizens' Income.

Notions of personal responsibility for one's actions can seem unfair in a patently unjust society, but where security is guaranteed they will become important. For example, the CI must not encourage large families, as that would be contrary to Green principles. I would envisage a generous CI for a first child,9 an adequate CI for a second child, but tapering amounts for subsequent children. Responsibility for childrens' welfare will rest with the parents. In the modern context this scheme might look 'right wing', yet prior to 1911 it would have seemed radically socialist in the extreme.

The Tragedy of the Commons dictates that any measures to bring about sustainability will be ineffective as long as anyone can act independently. Sustainability in one country will not work. So how do we bring the USA, China and all the others who are globalizing and industrializing with varying degrees of willingness into a steady state consensus? There is an admittedly conjectural possibility bound up with the 'Siane' strategy. The trick is to moderate consumption internally whilst maintaining the ability to supply the unabated demands of others. China's advantage relies on the fact that her workforce still has lower expectations than ours. If the Citizens' Income has the hoped for effect of reducing consumerism internally, Britain would temporarily find itself in a stronger trading position! This is not the final object of the exercise, but it would prompt others to adopt the CI with the same internal effect. That would allow the first rays of hope for effective international agreement. Rather than smashing capitalism, the only way to stop Earth-threatening expansion is for consumers – world wide - to stop buying the extra products.

To share necessities unconditionally, but to have whatever rules you like, subject only to their sustainability for anything else, is a strategy which needs to be adopted as between nations internationally, as well as between individuals within each nation. 'Contraction and Convergence' is one proposal which begins this process:

> *A policy in which all nations seek to reduce their levels of green house gas emissions, and converge levels towards a point where all citizens of the world are entitled to emit equal amounts of pollutants.10*

Viewed from the perspective of finite resources, conventional 'wisdom' that prosperity depends on everyone buying as much as possible seems fatuous. But there are legitimate concerns to be addressed. For example, if goods are to be made to last, manufacturing must contract. Some form of management will be needed. But a regrettable aspect is that if the Citizens' Income principle had been in people's minds before the current economic downturn, the transition to a steady state economy could have seemed a natural outcome, in place of the fear and insecurity which has hitherto been associated with recessions. The Citizens' Income, purely as an idea, can *allow,* but not automatically bring about attitudes consistent with a sustainable environment, just as the underlying principle has done in less sophisticated cultures. The point of this approach is to gain publicity. Green policies cannot be implemented until a majority accept them, however reluctantly, but to gain 20% of the vote in an election would make them the prominent talking point they need to be if this is to happen in time.

References and notes

1 Hardin, Garrett (1968) 'The Tragedy of the Commons' *Science* 162 (1968) pp1243-48

2 Diamond, Jared (2005) *Collapse: how Societies choose to fail or survive* Penguin/Allen Lane

3 Diamond, Jared (1991) *The Rise and Fall of the Third Chimpanzee* Vintage UK Random House

4 According to a *Horizon* documentary on BBC1 on 9th January 2003, strategies to live within their depleted environment had begun to emerge even on Easter Island

5 Wilkinson, Richard G. (1973) *Poverty and Progress* Methuen, London p48

6 Ophuls, W, *Ecology and the Politics of Scarcity* 1977 San Francisco: Freeman; Hardin, G *The Limits to Altruism* 1977 Indianapolis: Indiana University Press; Heilbroner R, *An Inquiry into the Human Prospect* 1980 (2nd Ed) New York: Norton.

7 In *The Rise and Fall of the Third Chimpanzee* Professor Diamond identifies 37 instances of genocide between 1492 and 1990

8 *Dynamic Benefits: Towards Welfare that Works* (2009) Economic Dependency Working Group, of the Centre for Social Justice 9 Westminster Palace Gardens, Artillery Row London SW1P 1RL www.centreforsocialjustice.org.uk

9 There will have to be a definition of 'family' which I do not address here

10 Early Day Motion 538, placed before Parliament on 18.01.05

(Presented at a Green Economics Institute seminar at Oxford 18th-19th November 2011)

6.3 The South African Millennium Dilemma: Sustainable Development

By Mzoxolo Elliot Mbiko

Introduction

This chapter looks at the issue of sustainable development in the context of the South African millennium dilemma. The country is faced with many development challenges and to address economic growth, whilst considering climate change, calls for immediate global action. In the struggle to alleviate poverty through provision of basic services such as electricity amongst others, carbon footprints are rising to higher levels. The South African government and other relevant institutions are challenged with the task of reconciling the fundamentals that seem to contradict the notion of development, economic growth and issues of climate change. The integrated public policy, at all government levels especially local level, the process of working together with business and civil society, is regarded as the best option to address sustainable development. Integrating climate change into development goals is set to mitigate the South African millennium dilemma.

Introduction

It is no secret that the world is faced with different challenges emanating from different angles. Currently, these challenges range from climate change (which impacts strongly on the poor) the global economic down turn and health pandemics such as HIV/AIDS and the recent outbreak of swine flue (H1N1). The solution lies with the global consensus on ways to deal with the world-wide complexity, as it affects every nation.

It is estimated that more than 1.6 million people in the developing world lack access to electricity, more than 2 billion rely on traditional fuels for cooking and energy demand is expected to increase by more than 50% by 2020 (United States Agency for International Development (USAID):2009). As energy consumption grows, greenhouse emissions (GHG) are set to grow as well. USAID states that climate change and development are inextricably linked. USAID recommends a holistic approach; focusing on the policy and regulatory framework, public-private partnerships, training and institutional development, amongst others.

Energy-related carbon emissions compose the largest share of South Africa's green house gas emissions. Coal is the primary fuel produced and consumed in South Africa and contributes to the increasing concentrations of greenhouse gases in the atmosphere (Ramakrishna et al 2003). South Africa has an abundance of coal, however, in the face of climate change, fossil- fuel based development pathways are losing credibility.

However, its dependency on coal as a source of energy has raised major environmental concerns not only within the country, but within the global community as well (Winkler 2006).

It is categorised as the Non Annex 1 country in the United Nations Framework Convention on Climate Change (UNFCCC) by an Intergovernmental Panel on Climate Change. This means that South Africa (SA) is not obliged to make commitments to reduce GHG emissions. SA has recognised the importance of international agreements on climate change and its position as the 14th highest emitter of greenhouse gases worldwide and has acknowledged its role as a developing country with rapidly increasing greenhouse gas emissions.   However, the development goals such as provision of health care, electricity, housing the poor remain key issues to the government in the midst of the climate change difficulty.

The South African post-apartheid government places access to affordable energy among its national top priorities, especially to previously disadvantaged groups. Energy production is one of the main contributing factors to the social and economic development of South Africa, hence free electricity programmes have been introduced. Ramakrishna et al, 2003, articulates that despite various improvements, much of the population lacks access to the basic securities of employment, safety and health care.   It is still deep in the struggle for development and improvement of quality of life for its citizens.

1. South African Three Dimension Contradiction

The South African government has development goals to meet within the context of the climate change challenge. The country faces a dilemma to realign and integrate its policies in light of the situaiton. Some of the economic development goals and climate change mitigations contradict. These development goals include, provisions of basic needs such as electricity, health services, development of human capital and water and sanitation. The contradiction of economic growth and development and climate change discourse, means that South Africa is caught up in a dilemma.

"The challenge for government, business and civil society is to outline how these different, clashing imperatives, may be reconciled to create pro-poor and climate-resilient development" (Earthlife Africa, 2009:9). In the approach to lessen poverty, develop the economy, and include climate change, South Africa is heading towards a disaster and development will not meet the needs of the poorest.

South Africa's programme of action, in terms of achieving its development goals, can be traced from its Reconstruction and Development Programme RDP (1994), Growth, Employment and Redistribution strategy GEAR (1996) and Accelerated and Shared Growth Initiative for South Africa ASGISA (2006). Through these programmes the government is committed to poverty eradication and achieving universal access to electricity by 2012. However, the government is aware of its international obligations to mitigate climate change, which includes reducing its reliance on coal as a main source of the countries energy.

The South African economy is highly dependent on energy extraction, combustion and consumption. Climate change has set in on the global stage and this poses significant challenges for South Africa and its energy development. Not only does South Africa have an extremely energy-intensive economy based primarily on coal (and thus leading to relatively high emissions), but it simultaneously faces a host of daunting development challenges, exacerbated by the legacy of apartheid. Challenges for development include a dramatic gap between the rich and the poor, a heritage of racial oppression and inequality, a lack of infrastructure, high levels of unemployment and urbanisation, an economy adjusting to globalisation and the new challenge of AIDS (UNDP 2007/2008).

South Africa is faced with a dilemma to handle three imperatives – development (conventionally based on fossil fuels), poverty eradication and climate change. The country is under severe pressure to fast track provision of adequate transport, power, sanitation, water and other infrastructure services. The developments are set to increase South Africa's GHG emissions. The recent protest for provision of basic services and Eskom (a company generating electricity in SA) load shedding give some indication of the dissatisfaction felt.

The country needs to be careful as some of the conventional developments may lead to poverty and ill-health.

The challenge is how South Africa presents itself on a global stage as a model of development in the region, addressing inequalities, poverty and its development needs, while at the same time mitigating climate change.

It is widely known that economic development does not necessarily mean economic growth; the type of economic activity can change without increasing the quantity of goods and services. But many argue that not only is economic growth compatible with sustainable development, as long as it is the right kind of economic growth, it is in fact greatly needed to relieve poverty and generate the resources for development and hence prevent further environmental degradation. The issue is the quality of the growth and how its benefits are distributed equally, not mere expansion.

The South African National Treasury acknowledges that "As the South African economy continues to develop, it is increasingly important to ensure that it does so in a sustainable manner and that, at the same time, issues of poverty and inequality are effectively addressed. It is therefore important to appreciate that it's not just the quantity of growth that matters, but also its quality"

Climate change is used interchangeably with global warming. The concept refers to changes in the average weather conditions for any given season lasting an extended period of time.

However, there is no consensus among scientists as to the exact causes of climate change. Developing countries are the most affected by global warming whilst contributing less to the causes of global warming compared to developed countries. Thus climate change is expected to exacerbate poverty in developing countries. The source of energy is the main challenge presented by global warming. The primary energy comes from coal and it is believed to contribute to 90% of global warming.

Climate change has become a worldwide reality and should not be overlooked as it presents many challenges. Climate change has implications which extend beyond purely environmental concerns, including deep questions of economic growth, sustainability, intergenerational equity, and national security. Therefore combating climate change should be exercised at all levels, including individual, households, firms, governments and multilateral organisations.

The Intergovernmental Panel on Climate Change (IPCC)'s report 2007: 387 states 'that oceans are warming and ice is decreasing at alarming proportions'. Over the period 1961 to 2003, global ocean temperature has risen by 0.10 C from the surface to a depth of 700 m. Evidence points out that much of the increase of greenhouse gases has been the result of human activity. Global warming posits detrimental health effects on all humanity and possible extinction of all living species.

It is believed that South Africa has a huge task ahead to respond to the impacts of climate change by reducing emissions, as well as to ensure that the programmes to help the poor adapt to the changing climate are implemented.

The National Climate Change Response Strategy for South Africa, led by the Department of Environmental Affairs and Tourism, highlights some socio-economic implications of climate change in South Africa; strategic objectives, principles which encompass mitigations to climate change, and adaptation are key issues and challenges, amongst others. The document states that climate change challenges must not be addressed at the expense of economic growth and development as climate change is the crux of the strategy.

The Government has also to develop a Long Term Mitigation Scenarios document, released in 2008, which primarily focused on the how part to reduce GHG emissions in South Africa. The challenge at the moment is the integrated implementation of programmes highlighted in these documents. Although there are great developments, in so far as climate change and development goals are concerned and South Africa being a Non Annex 1 country, more work is required at government level with reference to coordination in partnership with relevant institutions.

The last crucial document that has ever been developed by DEAT is the National Framework for Sustainable Development in South Africa. It is a very important document as it acknowledges all dimensions such as social, economic as well as environmental ones which need to be addressed in a coherent matter. Although the framework provides a basis for a long term process of integrating sustainability as a key component of the development discourse, it is still not substantially sufficient as it lacks action plans and programmes.

In an attempt to make the concept of sustainable development more specific, some authors have given a narrow definition focused on the physical aspects of sustainable development. They stress using renewable natural resources in a manner that does not eliminate or degrade them or otherwise diminish their "renewable" usefulness for future generations whilst maintaining effectively constant or non declining stocks of natural resources such as soil and groundwater etc. Some economic definitions of sustainable development have also focused on optimal resource management, by concentrating on "maximizing the net benefits of economic development, subject to maintaining the services and quality of natural resources".

Increasingly, definitions of sustainable development attempt to cut across or encompass several aspects or dimensions. The new strategy outlined by the World Conservation Union, *Caring for the Earth,* defines sustainable development as "improving the quality of human life while living within the carrying capacity of supporting ecosystems"

Sustainable development, as the World Commission defined it, is development that "meets the needs of the present without compromising the ability of future generations to meet their own needs"

Sustainable development as a process requires simultaneous global progress in a variety of dimensions. According to South Africa's National Climate Change Response Strategy sustainable development encompasses the social, environmental and economic dimensions for development. One tends to slightly differ to the model as the model seems to be exhaustive and exclude information and communications technology and institutional (ICT). It is believed that IT contributes about 0.2% GHG emissions on climate change. It is largely contributing to climate change - drawing back to mineral requirements and still holds the key to tackle it.

Therefore the dimensions include society, economic, environmental, institutional and information technology factors. It is believed that a holistic approach should be adopted and in a dynamic context.

2.1 Society

Development could only be considered sustainable, if and only if, social justice through certain mechanisms such as equitable resource allocation, eradication of poverty and provision of basic needs i.e. education, health services are equally accessible.

It is believed that the social dimension of sustainable development is based on the idea that people play a crucial role in development. The main objective should be to achieve needs for both present and future generations.

2.2 Economic

At an economic level, economic welfare must be provided at present and for the future. Plants, soil, bio-environmental system are also regarded as important in this category.

2.3 Environmental

Environmentalists tend to focus on what is known as "environment borders". The concept means that natural environment systems have certain limits that should not be exceeded by excessive consumption.

Limits should be set with regard to consumption, population growth and pollution as well as the faulty effects or by products of production which include wasting water, cutting forests and soil erosion.

Natural resources are not infinite, therefore must be used sustainably. Ecological preservation should be encouraged otherwise economic goals will not be achieved and environmental degradation is set to defeat economic development goals.

2.4 Institutional

The participation of all relevant parties in the decision-making process is imperative. This dimension could be mainly concerned with the organisations responsible for direct and indirect implementation of strategies and policies. Partnership is the key as the government cannot deal with the concept of sustainability alone.

2.5 Information Technology & Communications (ITC)

This last dimension is inclusive due to its relation to other dimensions, the enhancing importance of information and communication technologies and the important role in development. The inclusion of ITC has been supported by MDG summit of November 2003 where sustainable development was a crucial element of the summit.

Multinational corporations are regarded as sources of technology transfer by most developing countries through foreign direct investment. However, the absorptive capacity of developing countries should be in good state in terms of infrastructure, energy, financial structures, institutional factors and required skills for technology transfer purposes. Technology transfer should match with internal research and development of sectors, companies and the economy at large.

3. Action Plan

It is commonly noted that the world needs a new economics to deal with 21st century challenges, which are dynamic and mixed in nature. The solution which one proposes lies with Green Economics that go beyond mainstream economics. Cato (1987) asserts that this branch of economics should view society and ecosystems as subsets of wide approach and unbounded global economy.

Another aspect is to change the way the economy is viewed to present a paradigm for the 21st century. Participants from areas such as industry, government and academic institutions would need to come to the fore and cooperate with one another. However, an integrated approach by government is necessary but not sufficient.

It is in agreement with Annie Leonard on her video (www.storyofstuff.com) that the world cannot run a linear system type of economics forever on a finite planet, a circular system type of economics coupled with Green Economics is recommended.

South Africa's climate change strategy and mitigation scenarios are necessary however, but not sufficient to address the development needs of the country. The department of economic development seems to be an institution that could integrate development goals into climate change.

South Africa is still yet to effectively implement its climate change strategy as well as long term mitigation scenarios. The execution will need to be forceful at a local level. Citizens are uninformed of green work and now is the time to ensure that South African people become green citizens. Green Economics should be taught at early learning stages in schools.

Green Economics institutions need to nurture young people to be green citizens. Moreover green schools should be established to teach children and people about environmental responsibility and foster environmental awareness and sustainability. This will assist with the lessening of the primary footprint (direct emissions of CO_2 from the burning of fossil fuels including domestic energy consumption and transportation (e.g. car and plane). Let's foster sustainable production and consumption together to concurrently address development and reduce our carbon footprint.

Picture: The economics of childhood. Photo by Paul Kennet

References

Accelerated and Shared Growth – South Africa (ASGISA) (2006) www.info.gov.za

Cato, M.A, 2008, Green Economics: An introduction to theory, Policy and Practice

Growth, Employment and Redistribution Programme (GEAR) (1996) www.info.gov.za

http://www.moneoman.gov.om/book/sdi/English/1/1-2.pdf accessed 16 July 2009

Intergovernmental Panel on Climate Change (IPCC)'s report 2007: 387

Ramakrishna, K. and L. Jacobsen, eds. 2003. Action versus Words: Implementation of the UNFCCC by Select Developing Countries-Argentina, Brazil, China, India, Korea, Senegal, South Africa. Woods Hole, MA: Woods Hole Research Center.

Reconstruction and Development Programme (1994), www.info.gov.za

UNDP 2007/2008 http://hdr.undp.org/en/reports/global/hdr2007-2008/ assessed 16 July 2009

World Commission on Environment and Development (1987) Our Common Future, Oxford University Press, Oxford, p. 37.

(UNFCCC: 2009) http://unfccc.int/2860.php

US Agency for International Development www.usaid.gov – keyword: climate change

Tristen Taylor: 2009. Climate Change, Development and Energy Problems in South Africa: Another World is Possible. Earthlife Africa, Johannesburg.

6.4 What is possible.

Precedents for a sustainable world

Clive Lord

Chapter 6 in my book Green Economics and the Citizen's Income closed with a warning from Professor Jared Diamond on the parallels between the history of Easter Island and the present world economy, despite which he sees grounds for optimism. Oddly enough, even on Easter Island a sustainable way of life was beginning to emerge, but not until *after* the islanders had comprehensively trashed their Garden of Eden. By the time of Captain Cook's 4 day visit in 1774, accompanied by a Tahitian able to converse with the islanders, a competition had emerged whereby each clan chose a young man to race across the shark-infested waters to one of the islets where birds still nested. The clan of the first to bring back an egg had sole right to that source of food for a year, on the clear understanding that they did not endanger this precious resource.

In his book *Gaviotas: A village to reinvent the World,* Alan Weisman describes the ecological community of Gaviotas, in of all places, Colombia2. The cover text explains:

In 1971, a group of visionaries and technicians led by Paolo Lugari decided to prove they could thrive in one of the most brutal environments imaginable: Colombia's *llanos,* the barren eastern savannas. Despite the constant threat of political turbulence, this is now the setting for one of the most hopeful environmental success stories ever told. For more than three decades scientists, artisans, peasants, ex-Bogotá street kids and Guahibo Indians have elevated phrases like *sustainable development* and *appropriate technology* from cliché to reality. Sixteen hours from the nearest major city, they invented wind turbines that convert mild tropical breezes into energy, solar collectors that work in the rain, soil-free systems to raise edible and medicinal crops and ultra-efficient pumps so easy to operate they're hooked up to children's see-saws. The United Nations has named the village a model for the developing world. An unexpected marvel has also occurred: the regeneration of an ancient native rainforest in the shelter of millions of Caribbean pines which the Gaviotans planted as a renewable crop (the resin from which provides a substantial income). As Paolo Lugari himself said

"They always put social experiments in the easiest, most fertile places. We wanted the hardest place. We figured if we could do it here, we could do it anywhere."

Gaviotas has developed a highly communal ethos. Many of the basics of life are free, including housing, health care, food, and schooling, so that it does not matter that payment of salaries is often intermittent. A visiting Chinese diplomat described Gaviotas as 'a socialist paradise', to Paolo Lugari's alarm lest the Colombian Government might assume that they were sympathetic and therefore giving assistance to the FARC (Communist) guerrilla insurgents. It did not help that there might be a grain of truth in the visitor's description. In fact, before it was closed by a law which made sense in the cities, but not in the desolate *llanos,* the magnificent and ecologically self-sufficient Gaviotas hospital treated casualties from both sides of the interminable strife which eddies round their oasis of peace.

Weisman summarizes the net result of the Gaviotans' efforts as follows:

Surrounded by a land seen either as empty or plagued with misery, they had forged a way and a peace they believed could prosper long after the last drop of the earth's petroleum was burned away. They were so small, but their hope was great enough to brighten the planet turning beneath them no matter how much their fellow humans seemed bent on wrecking it. Against all skeptics and odds, Gaviotas had lighted a path through a magnificent but darkened land, whose sorrows mirrored a beautiful, embattled world.

Too good to be true? Whilst it is reassuring to have a working example, Gaviotas is not my preferred blueprint for a sustainable world. There is an immediately obvious problem in that the Gaviotans started from scratch, and the participants were self- selected, and therefore unanimously committed to the project from the outset. The majority of the world's population cannot start afresh in a semi-desert, and most of us don't want to. I just want to stay where I am, but with the rules and aims of society geared towards sustainability. As I hope to make clear shortly, I even believe that such an ambition could become widespread, unlikely as that may seem at the moment. What we need is a way of getting to grips with the dynamics of the Tragedy of the Commons before the conflict based default setting takes over, and the fascist strategies of the far right are the only options which can resolve resource issues.

Fortunately the precedents are not uniformly pessimistic. One can even assert that the history of Easter Island is no more typical than that of Gaviotas. Although I suspect that all human groups other than hunter-gatherers must have experienced at least one 'Tragedy', many so-called primitive societies had reached something close to ecological equilibrium prior to disturbance by Europeans. The danger arises from the fact that Easter Island was as a special case which unfortunately bears more resemblance to recent and current global developments than do any of the more optimistic examples. How did the others do it? What can we learn from them?

One especially heartening precedent is Tikopia. As Professor Jared Diamond explains:

Tikopia is another success story of bottom-up management. With an area of 1.8 square miles, it supports 1,200 people, a population density of 800 people per square mile of farmable land, without modern agricultural techniques. The island has been occupied continuously for almost 3,000 years. . . .As you approach from the sea, Tikopia appears to be covered with rainforest, but when you land you realize that true rainforest is confined to a few patches on the steepest cliffs, and the rest of the island is devoted to food production. . . .This whole multi-storey orchard is unique in the Pacific in its structured mimicry of a rainforest, except that its plants are all edible whereas most rainforest trees are not.3

Again, although Tikopia could have given Rapanui some valuable advice, it would not be easily transferable outside the tropics. Monastery and kitchen gardens and allotments have followed a similar principle in temperate latitudes, but in most urbanized areas the population is far too dense for this to support everyone. Moreover although Tikopia had undoubtedly achieved long term sustainability, there is evidence that it was only the arrival of developed world contraception which allowed the islanders to stop using warfare as a last resort means of population stabilization.4 Nevertheless, Tikopia does have a lesson of global significance as to possibilities *provided that population and economic activity are strictly limited.*

Along with *The Tragedy of the Commons,* another seminal influence at a time when my personal paradigm was undergoing a drastic shift was a book called *Poverty and Progress* by Richard G. Wilkinson.5 His thesis, as described on the back cover, was as follows:

Richard Wilkinson demonstrates that the pursuit of progress is not the real driving force behind change. He argues that economic development is simply the escape route of societies caught in the ecological pincers of population growth and scarce resources. The things we think of as the fruits of man's search for progress ... such as ... increasingly sophisticated technology ... are part of the struggle to keep up with the growing productive task created by ecological pressures. In this light, primitive societies appear less poor than we imagine, and advanced ones less rich.

Wilkinson outlines the norm of ecological equilibrium. He first explains mechanisms by which animals achieve this, and goes on to give examples of pre-industrial human societies whose cultural patterns perform this function. A major point which he makes is that starvation - or even shortages other than as isolated, exceptional features - are unknown in either animal or human populations *except where they are in the course of transition,* normally following some disturbance in their environment. The implications of the last sentence are quite staggering, so I repeat: poverty is extremely rare in undisturbed populations. Malthus' theory that starvation was the effective check on the size of populations is now generally thought of as unduly alarmist because it is assumed technology will continue to come to the rescue. In fact, Malthus did *not* predict the apocalypse of which he is generally accused. He actually predicted something quite close to what has happened: a permanent race between food production and population increase, leaving large swathes of people under-nourished for long periods. Wilkinson accepts that this is indeed the case *in changing or disturbed societies.6* All undisturbed populations have somehow found a limiting mechanism which normally allows a standard of living comfortably above the minimum for *all* their members.

If dumb animals and supposedly ignorant savages with minimal resources and technology can ensure that no individual suffers hardship, something must be seriously wrong with an advanced, technologically sophisticated society which does not. However, I personally believe that there is an inability rather than a refusal to eradicate poverty. This is not a simple matter of greed, or of those with wealth not caring about the rest. Many 'haves' do indeed rationalize the poverty of others as 'their own fault', but even if this never happened, I believe that the paradox of poverty in a world of plenty would still exist. It is the sharing *strategy* which is at the root of the problem. A society can consciously choose a sharing strategy, indeed it is the theme of this book that our society must do just that - globally. I shall explore what that strategy should be in the course of this and the next chapter. But for most of the time in most societies that choice is effectively unconscious and driven by inertia, i.e. tradition. The sharing (more accurately *not* sharing) strategy current in Britain (for example) is patently malfunctioning. The circumstances in which it developed and suited our ancestors - gradual expansion into pastures new - can no longer be taken for granted. Greed and selfishness are as much symptoms of the insecurity endemic in Western society as causes of it.

Wilkinson sets out certain core features commonly found in societies in or near ecological equilibrium:

Some societies limit their populations *consciously* to prevent food shortages. Others however limit them in relation to a scarcity of other goods associated with prestige and status which have nothing to do with subsistence. Competition for essential resources is replaced by competition for socially valued goods. If social order and stability are to be maintained, people should not have to deny each other the basic necessities of life.

In many societies there is a sharp distinction between the way food and other goods are exchanged. If a society uses a form of money, it can often only be exchanged for socially valued 'wealth objects'. Frequently food cannot be bought or sold within the village or tribe: sometimes it is distributed equally between people and sometimes it is subject to some sort of gift exchange.

Among the Siane of New Guinea there are three distinct groups of goods: The notion underlying the basis of distribution of food is that of equal shares, a balanced reciprocity. Luxury goods are exchanged according to self-interest in a nearly free market situation, and the exchange of ceremonial goods is a political affair accompanied by 'strict accounting'.,7,8

An important by-product of such systems concerns the homogeneity of societies. The more equitable the system for the distribution of food and other necessities, *the greater the identity of interest within the society when faced with ecological problems* [my italics].9

Wilkinson then contrasts these stable systems with the ecological imbalance of complex societies. However, it is not necessarily the complexity which is responsible for imbalance.10 Human groups have been slowly expanding into new areas ever since they first left Africa less than 100,000 years ago. As the anthropological evidence drawn on by Wilkinson shows, some managed to return to an ecological equilibrium without destroying their environment. It would be useful for us to know how. As explained in the passage just quoted, we know that they eventually found a way of regulating their affairs sustainably, but not how they got back to that state after the luxury of not needing to.11 Pending such information, my own suspicion is that this process involved much trial and possibly ghastly Easter Island style error.

For most of the human race however, that process of slow expansion was still proceeding at the time of the Industrial Revolution in Europe. All those groups had spent millennia ignoring ecological constraints. They had not prevented their populations from slowly expanding, and even more important in highly developed societies, the development ethic was, and still is, deeply ingrained culturally as an alternative to population limitation. Wilkinson details the response of Europeans as they came up against the limits of their land to supply their needs. Expansion into colonies was a part of that response, but he points out that each of the innovations which constituted the Industrial Revolution had been just as feasible for several hundred years. If they were such a good idea, why did these changes not happen until they were unavoidable?

The Polynesians were another group who had been able to continue expanding due to their seafaring ability. In most Polynesian societies population was traditionally stabilised by infanticide, abortion and *coitus interruptus* as well as colonizing expeditions, though periodic inter-clan warfare reminiscent of chimpanzee communities was not unknown.4 These avoided the much worse fate which befell the Easter Islanders. The overall pattern among Polynesian societies seems consistent with their having begun the transition back to sustainability, but not having had enough time to develop the comparatively conflict-free strategies described by Wilkinson in New Guinea. Like Europeans, they were still prone to fall back on the aggressive 'default setting'. Many groups must have simply perished at sea engaged in the same gamble as the original Easter Island settlers. The hazardous practice of sailing off into the blue yonder may have been a cultural choice, as space exploration may be in the future, even in a sustainable world, but it could equally be a clue that true sustainability had not been a feature of the ancestral society. However, Easter Island was large enough to let the group which discovered it go on ignoring ecological limits for several hundred years, but too small to allow time to impose restraints when the exponential principle took them by surprise.

I have suggested that the world as a whole is on a similar course to ecological disaster. Fortunately, we have something the Easter Islanders lacked: not only their example, but also a model of societies which did make a successful transition back to stability. Most if not all have been changed out of recognition and incorporated into the global economy by now, but at least we know that there have been societies able to live within their means indefinitely. As the above quotation from *Poverty and Progress* makes clear, the Siane are only one example of many such societies.

Just as it would be a mistake to dismiss the Easter Islanders as more stupid than western global mankind, I am equally loath to assume that the Siane were more intelligent. No doubt they made a mess of *their* first attempt to stop expanding beyond the limits of their environment. With the advantage of the infrastructure and technology at our disposal which was not available to them, we should have no difficulty in instituting corresponding arrangements to abolish poverty *even as a possibility* at both a national and international level - once there is the recognition of the need, the political will, and a plan of how to do it.

Notes and References

1 *Horizon* documentary, first broadcast on BBC1 on 9th January 2003

2 Weisman, Alan (1998) *A Village to reinvent the World* Chelsea Green Publishing Company 205 Gates-Briggs Building, PO Box 428 White River Junction Vermont 05001 www.chelseagreen.com

3 Diamond, Jared (2005) *Collapse: How societies choose to fail or survive* Allen Lane

4 Firth, Raymond (1936) *We, the Tikopia* Stanford U.P. Chapter XI, p374

5 Wilkinson, Richard G (1973) *Poverty and Progress* Methuen & Co

6 *Poverty and Progress* p51.

7 Nash, Manning (1966) *Primitive and Peasant Economic*

Systems pp. 48-51 San Fransisco Quoted in *Poverty and Progress,* p49.

8 Sahlins, Marshal D (1965) *On the sociology of primitive exchange,* in association of Social Anthropologists Monographs No 1, *The Relevance of Models in social Anthropology* (London), pp139-236. Quoted in *Poverty and Progress,* p49

9 *Poverty and Progress* pp47-50.

10 I shall make clear in later chapters that I am *not* advocating a

'deep Green' return to a primitive life-style.

11 See Descola, Philippe (1993) *The Spears of Twilight* English translation 1996 Harper Collins London for an account of life among the Jivaro in western Amazonia which was sustainable and free from inter-tribal warfare, but with a high level of vendetta-related homicide. Bearing in mind that human colonization is believed to have been more recent in South America than in New Guinea, it is possible that this is an intermediate 'post-Tragedy' phase, before a more satisfactory sustainable culture has developed

6.5 Green Economics Model and Sustainable Development: Challenges and Opportunities for the Initiation of Realistic Policy Responses

By Chidi Magnus Onuoha

Introduction

When in the 1970s it became evidently clear that despite the fairly good records of growth in gross national product(GNP) of Less Developed Countries (LDCs), economists and other social scientists began to think of a more meaningful understanding of economic development. They argue that if poverty, inequality, and unemployment have all worsened for a given society over a period of time, then it would be absurd to label the result development even if per capita income had doubled during the period.

Economic growth thus was not sufficient in the struggle against poverty. It was complemented with a set of social and related policies, which not only target the most impoverished but also empower the poor through productive employment, access to resources and delivery of basic social services, education, health and water supply.

In the 1980s, development theory was broadened to embrace sustainable development - reflecting increasing concern about the environment. The state of the environment is the major determinant of the growth and development objectives of any nation and has a pervasive effect on the safety and standard of living of the populace.

Unfortunately, after nearly three decades of sustainable development, we have become complacent with the notion of sustainability. The concept needs to be managed, planned, and administered, in the line of resource allocation, management, and conservation. All these will require significant institutional and cultural changes in order to achieve a sustainable society.

This paper argues that it is only the introduction of a holistic multi-disciplinary and enabling model, as provided by green economics, and reflected in the four thematic areas-economic/ecological, intellectual/reality, political/Structural, and morality/poverty issues, which will deliver changes which sustainability requires. Effective and realistic sustainable development policies could be initiated through innovations of individuals, special groups, industry, government and the international community. Such initiatives and innovations include Green GDP Initiative (GGDPI), Small Group Tree Planting Initiative(SGTPI), Briquettes- Alternative to Fire Wood Initiative(B-TFWI), Green Wall Sahara Vulnerability Initiative(GWSVI), Green Oil and Gas Mandate(GOGAM), Campus Project Greening Initiatives(CPGI) and Climate Science Development Studies Agenda(CSDSA). Government, trade regimes and Multinational Corporation have a responsibility in strengthening partnerships, promoting technological innovation and facilitating global programmes in environment, employment, human health and freedom.

INTRODUCTION

Past growth patterns adopted world-wide were highly dependent on an excessive use of natural resources with very little consideration for its replenishment. These patterns have created serious environmental problems such as persistent degradation of the environment and increasing loss of natural resources. Decreasing natural habitat and fragile ecosystem are precipitating diminishing biodiversity, exploitation of natural resources is accelerating at an unsustainable rate which is higher than the rate of replenishment and /or replacement, land degradation, as well as human induced environmental disasters. In a bid to find solution to these problems, the development theory was broadened to embrace sustainable development- reflecting increasing concern about the environment. The credit goes to the World Conservation Strategy of 1980 for stressing the importance of integrating environmental protection and conservation values into the developmental process.

SUSTAINABL DEVELOPMENT

The term 'sustainable development was brought into common use by the World Commission on environmental development (The Brundtland Commission) in 1987, calling for the development that "meets the need of the present generation without compromising the needs of the future generations". This definition emphasizes a focus on both equity (meeting people's needs) and long term impacts of current behavior and decisions on future generations. The Brundtland Commission report also highlighted the need to simultaneously address developmental and environmental imperatives.

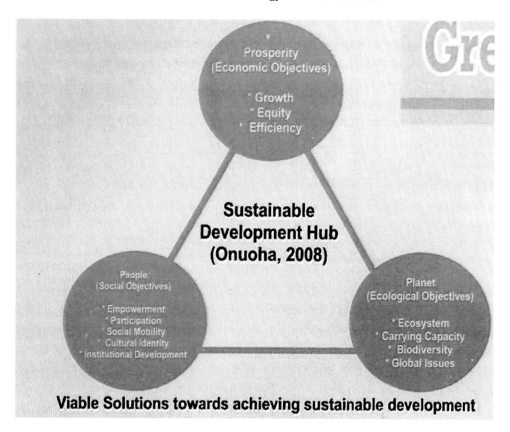

Sustainable development has varying definitions. But for purposes of this paper, it is the strategy of managing all natural, human, financial and physical assets to achieve long-term wealth and well-being. This definition entails control over the mobilization and utilization of resources to ensure that benefits accrued are used to maintain and improve the asset base, and for its effectiveness, local control must be central. Hence, countries and regions world-wide must be prepared to take control over the depletion of their resources and distribution of benefits accrued to ensure sustainable development.

Sustainable development is further premised on the fact that over half of the world's populations live in countries that are struggling to develop adequate mechanisms for income and employment generation. In effect, practices in those countries are suffering from environmental stress as they increase their dependency on natural systems. Changing the situation in these countries presents a major challenge because some of the past development strategies cannot be repeated. They will continue to widen the gap between the rich and the poor and worsen environmental problems. Current practices have led to major differences in the world regions and equity problems. As a result industrialized countries enjoy economic affluence but have weaknesses such as over-consumptive habits, excessive waste production and emission of adverse gases. Relatively few have benefited in poor developing countries, the majority continue to suffer from poverty and human misery along with a degraded local environment. Hence new equitable development paths are required.

GREEN ECONOMICS: BUILDING BLOCK FOR A SUSTAINABLE AND EQUITABLE DEVELOPMENT PATH

Sustainable development introduced to the international community over two decades ago is still in its infancy in terms of practical application. We have become apathetic with the notion of sustainability over the years that we forget that it is a concept that needs to be managed, planned and administered, in the line of resource allocation, management and conservation. This will inevitably require institutional and cultural changes. A holistic (multi-disciplinary) and enabling model as provided by green economics is a major building block that will deliver the changes that sustainability requires. A cursory look at the justification of the model and its attendant thematic areas will suffice.

GREEN ECONOMICS: JUSTIFICATION

Green economics as a holistic, multi-disciplinary study is an understanding that the economy operated by human beings is dependent on the natural world and could not exist without it. It pre-supposes an interaction between human economic activities and the natural world such as land, water, minerals, seeds, animals, and the atmosphere. It also entails that the pre-conditions for economic activity inherent in the discipline reveals a far richer picture than the conventional economics which tends to take all these human pre-conditions for granted and begin to study the economy. The economy would be impossible without the following pre-conditions-'preparation' of human beings through birth, looking after babies and children, education system, health services and existence of basic features of life such as language, sufficient degree of trust and cooperation among people. These pre-conditions could be investigated within the ambience of sociology, history, anthropology and religious studies.

Green economics study would also have both psychological and philosophical dimensions. From the psychological prism, rather than making simplistic assumption about a rational man seeking his utility, it posits that it would be more realistic to actually look at evidence about human behavior and the factors which influence people in deciding what to buy, what jobs to do etc. Psychological perspective is not purely an individual matter, it also considers whole cultures and the influence they have. The philosophical assumptions basic to the culture entails we look at the key concepts of economics such as production, consumptions and investment by asking what they mean, what they exclude and where they have come from. These assumptions should not be taken for granted as givens.

Green economics is also synonymous with rapid technological change. Technology is not another black box (input) taken as given. Technology is not a short term phenomenon but a long term one. Green economics is concerned with long term change. Green economics also posits that economic life cannot be value-free. It is not sensible to let our values in economics thinking to be subjected to the whims and caprices of wishful thinking and jumping into abstract conclusions.

GREEN ECONOMICS AND SUSTAINABLE POLICY DIALOGUE: UNVEILING THE THEMATIC AREAS.

From my knowledge and understanding of green economics over the years, and for effective research capacity building and sustainable policy dialogue programs, four thematic groups have emerged: Ecological and Economic Issues(EEI), Intellectual and Reality Issues(IRI), Political and Structural Issues(PSI) and Morality and Poverty Issues(MPI). The thematic groups are the building blocks of the research programme. They constitute the research hubs for producing frontier knowledge based on teamwork, international research networking, scientific validation and quality assurance.

a)   ECOLOGICAL AND ECONOMIC ISSUES(EEI):

Here we shall engage in the discussion of the fact that there is an overwhelming evidence that the resources of the planet are being annihilated, plundered and disturbed(Goldman 2005), putting paid to the argument by mainstream economics that these resources are in abundance and available to be raided are indeed becoming scarce (Broswimmer,2002). Such topical issues to be discussed here include, but are not limited, to the following: Limits of growth, ecology and nature, emphasizing the appropriate size and scale of production, management of consumption downwards-reuse, reduce, recycle, repairs and transparency of the supply chain. Population issues and the concepts of 'browning' and 'greening' will also be engaged here as well.

b)   INTELLECTUAL AND REALITY ISSUES(IRI):

Here green economists will justify their much longer terms than the short term business cycle found in the neoclassical and business school of economics. It will take a long term view, back through anthropology, archeology, and environmental science and use this knowledge to filter its analysis of economic decision-making. The holistic and multi-disciplinary nature of green economics will be amplified here. It is the very economics of interconnectedness as there is no human activity, and no part of the planet that is not of interest to the subject. Issues to be engaged here include, but are not limited, to the following: reformulation of demand, supply and growth, longtermism, holism, new relationship to science/natural sciences and technology (Green Technology) and specific in the examination of issues temporally and spatially.

c)   POLITICAL AND STRUCTURAL ISSUES(PSI):

Here we shall engage in research that seeks to reconnect the values of and costs of transaction with the natural world with social structures. This will seek to enhance the local economy, support bioregional development, democracy and access to all and seek global governance through new institutions designed for this purpose. Accordingly such issues as progress made in the economy measured by new indicators(Green GDP), wellbeing, quality of life, sustainability, longtermism, examination of power structures, reformulation of global institution to provide global governance, among others will be discussed here.

d)   MORALITY AND POVERTY ISSUES(MPI):

Here earlier moral concerns of economics are reincorporated taking cognizance of one-fifth of the earth's 6.3 billion people still trapped by life-threatening poverty. These are in the form of social and environmental justice, inclusiveness, equity and accessibility. We shall explore how the 'invisible hand' (Smith, 1776) will be assisted by the use of data from natural sciences on resource potential and from social science about needs, right, requirement and local conditions. Hence appropriate decisions will be taken which will allow access and transparency for everyone. Issues to be engaged here, include among others, regional, locally diverse and democratic solutions, using analysis of power relations and institutions, feminist analysis of patriarchy and accumulation, critique of tickle down theories and wealth creation with local power decisions.

CHALLENGES AND OPPORTUNITIES FOR THE INITIATION OF REALISTIC SUSTAINABLE DEVELOPMENT POLICY RESPONSE IN A GREEN ECONOMY:

1) The Green GDP Initiative (GDPI):

The major challenge of a green economy is to change how the wealth of the earth is measured not just in terms of money (GDP), but indicators that reflects its true value by providing a home for humans and other species (Green GDP). Ecosystem services such as protection from floods, maintenance of clean water supplies and carbon storage are linked to biodiversity and are vital for human survival as they help to regulate the climate of the earth. Unfortunately, they are being degraded as habitats are destroyed and biodiversity lost mainly as a result of human activities. But there are costs associated with ecosystems services in terms of their intrinsic value. There are also major value costs associated with loss of biodiversity. Currently, ecosystems services are mostly public good. They are not included in current markets and have not been attached with any economic value and thus not included in the current economic system. Therefore, the economic costs of ecosystems degradation and biodiversity loss have not been included in economic policy. Estimating both the value of ecosystem services and the costs of biodiversity loss, provides a sound argument for biodiversity protection. Thus repairing societies' defective economic compass and providing decision makers with the information to create new policies, modify old ones, and create new markets.

However, effective and realistic sustainable development policies could be initiated through the innovation of individuals, special groups, industry, government and international community.

Some of these initiatives and innovations are detailed below and they form part of the long term programmes of Green Economics Nigeria:

2) Small Group Tree Planting Initiatives (SGTPI):

Through the NMA baseline methodology (simplified methodology for small holder AIR in areas undergoing continued deforestation), the tree planting work of small groups of 6-12 participants can be established in various communities.

The program would involve thousands of individual groves (units) planted by thousands of small groups. Threes will be planted around their homes, gardens, fields and villages. Unlike the monoculture plantations, most of the groves would be less than 1 hectare in size. Each grove would be identified with a unique number and geographic coordinate. The total collective number of a grove would be the boundary of the project. By growing enough trees, participants would be able to sequester carbon and take advantage of the natural mortality of the trees and get fuel from their own groves. Furthermore, a successful program should attract additional income for participants from carbon payments by the United Nations which can serve as alternatives to investments in this period of economic meltdown which has made investments in shares less attractive.

3) Briquettes-Alternative to Firewood Initiatives (B-ATFWI):

A briquette can simply be defined as a compressed carbonized charcoal dust, or biomass, used for fuel and kindling. Over the years, large quantities of wood wastes (residues) like saw dust and other residues, such as rice husks, groundnut shells etc have been produced as a result of forestry activities, timber production, and agro-industrial processes.

Being regarded as waste and valueless, these wood residues are often left to rot away, or burnt indiscriminately, thereby causing more environmental and health hazards to the citizenry by releasing GHGs such as carbon dioxide, hydrogen sulphide, and sulphur dioxide. Carbonized briquettes from briquette plants do not release carbon dioxide into the atmosphere, thereby making it an environmentally friendly energy sources. Briquetting projects could be eligible under the market based mechanisms of the Kyoto Protocol for certified carbon emission credit earnings for sustainable development.

4) Green Wall Sahara Vulnerability Initiatives (GWSVI):

The Green Wall Sahara Program is a programme aimed at checking the advancement of the Sahara Desert into the hinterland through massive afforestation and reforestation and industrialization initiatives. In order to ensure a sustainable realization of the African program, the GWSVI as a proposal is set to address the vulnerability of countries affected by drought and desertification. The Nigerian model- the Green Wall Sahara Nigeria Program (GWSNP), a strategy of greening the desert prone and desert infested eleven(11) states of Northern Nigeria will be used as case study.

5) Green Oil and Gas Mandate (GOGAM):

With fossil fuel expected to continue in a foreseeable future, to play a dominant role in the energy mix, it is important to promote the development and dissemination of clean fossil fuel technologies. These technologies if developed and applied will significantly reduce $Co2$ emissions from oil and gas to the benefit of both producers and consumers.

For instance, the Carbon dioxide Capture and Sequestration (CCS) technology, if developed along with other mitigation measures, could significantly reduce the cost of stabilizing GHG concentration and increase the flexibility to achieve our objective in the context of sustainable development, by helping to increase the Clean Development Mechanism(CDM) projects in the oil producing developing countries.

6) Campus Project Greening Initiatives (CPGI):

It is a project initiated by Green Economics Nigeria, in collaboration with the University of Nigeria Nsukka located in the South East of Nigeria.Here a dynamic Campus Verde Innovation Club (Green Economics Club), with over 60 members under the guidance of Center for Entrepreneurship Development (CEDR) University of Nigeria Nsukka, is promoting the awareness about the importance of living in harmony with our environment in a sustainable way, as well as adopting the attitude of saving culture in our tertiary institutions.

The focus is on green transportation, recycling, nature (tree planting and tagging), energy and water conservation and other outreach programs. The programs are designed to offer an excellent means of business and mindset amongst students, with a focus on the practical application of technology in today's business. Getting students involved in carbon offsetting programs by reducing emissions is, no doubt, a strategic measure to mitigate climate change.

7) Climate Science Development Studies Agenda (CSDSA):

CSDSA program is aimed at influencing curriculum development and knowledge of climate change in tertiary institutions. The proposed curriculum challenges students to seek integrated approaches to the study of health sciences, social sciences, natural sciences, and management. Integrating these core disciplines will provide students with substantive knowledge required to analyze and diagnose multi-dimensional problems of malnutrition, extreme poverty, climate change and infectious disease control. Likewise, tackling hunger requires an understanding of agriculture, which in turn requires an understanding of the water systems, which in turn requires an understanding of the climate patterns, which in turn requires an understanding of global energy systems.

CONCLUSION

As earlier stated past economic growth patterns adopted world-wide were highly dependent on an excessive use of natural resources with very little consideration for its replenishment and these created environmental problems. In finding solutions, sustainable development came into the development theory lexicon, stressing the importance of integrating environmental protection and conservation values in the developmental process. Over the years there have been some challenges in terms of complacency with respect to the practical implementation of sustainable development policies and practices. These challenges could to a reasonable extent be addressed if the aforementioned initiatives discussed here are implemented. It is high time development practitioners, and indeed developed countries, realize that there is an alternative to the rampant economic growth and developing countries to invest in capacity building in order to increase their self-reliance. Finally, in order to ensure realistic sustainable development policies and practices, governments, trade regimes and multinational corporation have a greater responsibility in strengthening partnerships, promoting technological innovations and facilitating cooperation in global programmes on environment, employment, human health and freedom.

REFERENCES:

1- Anderson V. (1999) Can there a Sensible Economics? In: Green Economics, Beyond Demand and Supply to Meeting the Peoples Needs. Green Audit. Aberystwth.

2- Anderson V. (2006): Turning Economics Inside Out. IJGE, Vol. 1, Nos ½ Inderscience Ent. Ltd. UK

3- The Green Economy (2010) A Publication of Green Economics Nigeria.

4- Lunn, C.E.(2006): The Role of Green Economics in Achieving Realistic Policies and Programs for Sustainability. IJGE. Vol. Nos.1/2, Inderscience Ent. Ltd. UK.

5- International Commission on Education for Sustainable Development Practice (2008) Masters in Development Practice Programs. Macarthur Foundation. Earth Institute, Columbia University.(Oct. 30)

6- Onuoha C.M.(2009) A New Deal on Environment, Employment and Sustainable Development (Unpublished)

7- Kennet M., et al. The Handbook of Green Economics:A Practitioner's Guide. (2011) Published by The Green Economics Institute.

6.6 Towards the new understanding of sustainable development

By Igor A. Makarov

Lecturer, National Research University – Higher School of Economics
Moscow, Russia

I. INTRODUCTION

Sustainable development is one of the major concepts in conventional environmental economics and pretends to become the major principle of environmentalism as a whole. Nevertheless the conventional sustainable development concept is unable to respond to current environmental crises. Some new ideas concerning the content of sustainable development studies are necessary to make the concept relevant to current environmental and resource challenges.

The short introduction of this paper is followed by the second section which reveals the main drawbacks of conventional approaches to sustainable development. The third section examines the concept of critical capital which is the most successful attempt so far to make conventional theory more robust. The fourth section proposes the new approach to sustainable development based on the recognition of institutions' roles in coping with environmental problems. The last section provides some conclusions .

II. CONVENTIONAL APPROACHES TO SUSTAINABLE DEVELOPMENT

Though sustainability is one of the vaguest categories in conventional environmental and natural resource economics it is often considered to be one of the aims of economic development and one of the guiding principles of any long-term economic strategy. According to the classical definition given by the World Commission on Environment and Development sustainable development is that one which "implies meeting the needs of the present without compromising the ability of future generations to meet their own needs" (1). This extremely broad definition can have various interpretations and despite its moral attractiveness has nearly no practical importance.

There are two conventional approaches to the interpretation of this definition, which were named 'strong' and 'weak' sustainability.

The example of strong sustainability is given in the guiding principle proposed by UNESCO "Each generation should leave water, air, and soil resources as pure and unpolluted as when it came on earth... Each generation should leave undiminished all the species of animals it found existing on earth" (2). In other words, the 'strong' sustainability concept supposes that within the life of one generation the amount of natural capital should not be decreased. Natural capital is defined as the stocks of ecosystems which are capable to generate the flow of services in the future (3). According to the strong sustainability concept natural capital shouldn't be substituted by any other form of capital, so the decline of natural capital shouldn't be offset by the increase of physical one. Substitution across different types of natural capital (e.g. across oil and natural gas) may however be possible.

Strong sustainability can be measured by means of an "ecological footprint" which is defined as "the corresponding area of productive land and aquatic ecosystems needed to produce the resources used and assimilate the wastes produced by a defined population at a specified material standard of living, wherever on earth that land may be located" (4). Compared with existing Earth biocapacity, an ecological footprint is a simple measure to identify whether the demand for environmental goods and services exceeds their supply. Analysis of data (5, 6) shows that it does exceed.

Though the concept of strong sustainability and especially the footprint approach are of great academic interest they don't bear scrutiny as a relevant indicator of sustainability. Any consumption of non-renewable resources even if it is necessary for human development conflicts with this concept, as it results in the decline of the amount of natural resources at the disposal of future generations.

In response to the critics of this kind the concept of 'weak' sustainability has appeared. It supposes the possibility of substitution across major forms of capital. The proponents of 'weak' sustainability approach argue that substitution of the part of natural capital is not only inevitable but even reasonable from the perspective of human development. Economic development is considered to be sustainable if there is no decline in the possibility of capital to generate flows of service. The aim of sustainable development is the increase (at least non-diminution) of total welfare which is comprised of natural, physical and human capital (2). The decline of natural capital may hence be offset by the increase of physical or human capital.

The World Bank uses the concept of 'weak' sustainability while proposing the genuine net savings indicator involves the measures of positive and negative investments in physical (net saving), human (education expenditures) and natural (depletion of natural resources and pollution damage) capital (7).

World Bank statistics show that about 30 countries in the world developed unsustainably and the others succeeded in reaching 'weak' sustainability. It is at variance with the intuitive assumption according to which the current intensity of environment degradation and natural resources depletion are unlikely to be associated with sustainable development. Kenneth Boulding greatly illustrated this conflict of conventional economics and common sense in 1966:

"Anyone who believes in exponential growth that can go on forever in a finite world is either mad or an economist" (8).

One of the most remarkable examples of irrelevance of the conventional 'weak' sustainability concept is the 'Nauru tragedy'. Nauru government depleted the huge stocks of phosphates – the main natural treasure of the island – substituting them with physical and human capital that resulted in one of the highest living standards in the world (9). Thus economic development of Nauru remained sustainable for at least a decade until the natural capital became absolutely depleted and ceased to generate flows of benefits.

These contradictions put a great challenge to the concept of sustainable development. W. Beckerman states: "Strong' sustainability, overriding all other considerations, is morally unacceptable as well as totally impractical; and 'weak' sustainability, in which compensation is made for resources consumed, offers nothing beyond traditional economic welfare maximization" (10). The concept of sustainable development doesn't meet the requirements of the postindustrial world which faces the severe environmental crisis. Though it pretends to be the guiding principle of development it can't provide any stimuli to turn economy to the green direction. Green economics which should become the ideological and instrumental base of future development needs something new.

III. CRITICAL CAPITAL

The drawbacks of 'strong' sustainability are caused by non-substitutability of different forms of capital while the drawbacks of 'weak' sustainability, on the contrary, result from the lack of constraints on substitutability across them. Ways out of the trap can consist in the concept of critical natural capital – the part of natural capital which has vitally important functions and can't be substituted by any other forms of capital or even other types of natural capital (11).

Critical capital concept seems to be intuitively very attractive. It is senseless for human civilization to decrease emissions of greenhouse gases to zero, as well as it is unjustifiably costly to eliminate any water pollution or land degradation (though 'strong' sustainability requires it). At the same time development according to traditional 'weak' sustainability concept is also unacceptable as it leads to the depletion of critical capital. Critical capital is the intermediate one that allows substitutability across different forms of capital but defines some part of capital which in no circumstances can be substituted.

Adding the critical capital concept into sustainability studies doesn't however completely eliminate its various contradictions.

Firstly, it is not clear what components should be involved in critical capital. Should it include only those types of natural capital which are necessary for survival of humanity; or those which are sufficient for the restoration of natural capital in initial form and volume; or should any other limits be established? Finally, how to measure the volume and specify the forms of capital considered to be critical?

Secondly, critical capital is measured in total values and fails to take into account distributional aspects. It is easy to imagine that critical capital is provided but a large part of the population has no access to it. This is the story of contemporary water scarcity – fresh water supply exceeds demand, nevertheless the uneven distribution of water resources leads to severe water stress in some regions.

Thirdly, the conventional sustainable development concept proceeds from the prerequisite that the larger amounts of physical, human and natural capital generation possessed the better it is able to respond to challenges it faces, including natural resource and environmental ones. This prerequisites is however not always relevant. As E. Ostrom concluded in her comprehensive analysis of local commons the general welfare of the country (i.e. the amounts of physical, human and natural capital its citizens possess) has no direct influence on the ability of local groups to create robust institutions for ensuring the sustainable development of local resource systems (12). Either there is no statistically significant correlation found between the welfare of a country and the state of its environment. For example the top ten greenest countries according to the Environmental Performance Index developed by Yale University include such relatively poor countries as Costa-Rica, Cuba and Columbia (13). So, maybe the level of welfare of the country matters but it definitely doesn't play the key role. There should be something else that matters more, and this "something" should be involved in the concept of sustainable development.

IV. RETHINKING SUSTAINABLE DEVELOPMENT

Nearly all environmental problems can be interpreted as different types of G. Hardin's "tragedy of the commons" (14). Their solving depends on the society's ability to respond to social dilemmas which appear in situations of conflict between individual and common interests. This ability is determined to a great extent by the state of formal and informal institutions. They form institutional capital –the fourth dimension equal to physical, human and natural capital that should be added to the conventional concept of sustainable development.

Institutional capital is important for responding to environmental challenges for several reasons.

Firstly, better institutions result in lower transaction costs which have significant importance while solving social dilemmas. Institution of trust plays the principal role here. F. Fukuyama compares the deficit of trust with the additional tax imposed on transactions (15). Trust is especially important on the local level, where actors stay in direct contact, but on a national level it also matters contributing to the formation of civil society which has a positive impact on solving environmental problems. In international relations trust has been ignored by the mainstream realist paradigm of international relations theory, but nowadays it attracts the growing attention of both officials and academics (16). Cooperation which is considered to be necessary to respond to global challenges is impossible without trust while the conventional sustainable development concept doesn't take it into consideration.

Secondly, robust institutions decrease the vulnerability of society to environmental challenges. It can be illustrated by an argument proposed by A. Sen that democratic countries never face hunger (17). Formal state institutions based on the priority of state of law and civil society can better defend more vulnerable parts of its population.

Thirdly, transparency and the free distribution of information on environmental problems allows them to combat them more efficiently. Civil society is able to unite the whole society in green initiatives. "Green" becomes up-to-date, and this green fashion is quickly distributed by market mechanism. In 2007 "green" became the most trademarked term in the USA (18). Firms engage with their competitors in a real green race for consumers, try to "overgreen" one another (18), minimizing the ecological footprint of the production. Consumers simultaneously become more economical in consuming resources. Economic benefits encourage the ecological culture and the latter provides new economic benefits. Such positive feedbacks are not provided by physical or human capital but are provided by institutional capital.

Substitution of the part of physical, human of natural capital by institutional capital is reasonable as it will increase the welfare of future generation. Decrease in three major forms of capital can be offset by the increase of social goodwill (macro-level analogue of goodwill of a firm) – intangible asset, reflecting the role of institutions in overall welfare. Such offsets fully correspond to sustainable development goals. It is necessary to add some indicators of social goodwill (for example, World Government Indicator (19) and Trust Index (20)) in value terms to the methodology of the genuine net savings calculation and to develop a new index of sustainability, involving the physical, human, natural and institutional dimensions.

CONCLUSION

This paper provides the idea of rethinking the conventional sustainable development concept. Both 'strong' and 'weak' sustainability approaches are irrelevant to the changes taking place within the interrelations between economy-society and environment. Introducing critical capital concept can contribute to eliminate some drawbacks of 'strong' sustainability but can't significantly improve the 'weak' one. Most of the drawbacks of conventional 'weak' sustainability are caused by ignoring institutional capital as one of dimensions of sustainable development. However it is institutional capital that ensures the ability of society to respond to global environmental challenges. It is an underestimated treasure which should be kept and expanded. The first steps should be done within the academic sphere.

REFERENCES

1.   World Commission on Environment and Development (1987) Our Common Future, Report of the World Commission on Environment and Development
2.   Solow R. (1993) Sustainability: An Economist's Perspective // In Dorfman, R. and Dorfman, N. S. Eds. Economics of the Environment. – New York.
3.   Constanza R. et al. (1997) The value of the world's ecosystem services and natural capital // Nature, Vol. 387, pp. 253-260.
4.   Moldan D., Dahl A.L. (2007) Challenges to Sustainability Indicators / in: Hak T. et al. (eds.) Sustainability Indicators: A Scientific Assessment. Washington, Covelo, London, Island Press, 2007.
5.   The Worldwatch Institute. (2010) Vital Signs 2010: The Trends That Are Shaping Our Future.
6.   Wackernagel M. et al. (2002) Tracking the Ecological Overshoot of the Human Economy // Proceedings of the National Academy of Sciences, July 9.
7.   Bolt K. et al. (2002) Manual for Calculating Adjusted Net Savings. World Bank, September 2002.
8.   Kula E. (2003) History of Environmental Economic Thought. – Routledge.
9.   Gowdy J.M. et al. (1999) The Physical Destruction of Nauru: An Example of Weak Sustainability // Land Economics, Vol. 75, No. 2.
10. Beckerman W. (1994) 'Sustainable Development': Is it a Useful Concept? // Environmental Values, Vol.3, No. 3.
11. Ekins P. et al. (2003) Identifying Critical Natural Capital // Ecological Economics, Vol. 44, No. 3
12. Ostrom E. (1990) Governing the Commons. The Evolution of Institutions for Collective Action. – Cambridge.
13. EPI Indicator: http://epi.yale.edu/Countries
14. Hardin G. (1968) The Tragedy of the Commons // Science, No. 162, 1968.
15. Fukuyama F. (1995) Trust: The Social Virtues and the Creation of Prosperity. – New York
16. Vogler J. (2010) The Institutionalisation of Trust in the International Climate Regime // Energy Policy, Vol. 38, No. 6.
17. Sen A. (1999) Development as Freedom. – Oxford.
18. Friedman T. (2008) Hot, Flat, and Crowded. – New York City.
19. Kaufmann D. et al. (2009) Governance Matters VII: Aggregate and Individual Governance Indicators for 1996-2008. – World Bank, Washington, D.C., June 2009.
20. Medrano J. P. Interpersonal Trust: http://www.jdsurvey.net/jds/jdsurveyActualidad.jsp?Idioma=I&SeccionTexto=0404&NOID=104

Part 7: How to avoid further catastrophic runaway climate change

"Cooperation between human and nature"
Photo By Martina Falck

"Only when I saw the Earth from space, in all its ineffable beauty and fragility, did I realize that humankind's most urgent task is to cherish and preserve it for future generations."

Sigmund Jahn
German Cosmonaut

7.1 Ten Key Points for Reversing the Trend of Climate Change

By Davide Bottos

One of the goals that drive us is to imagine a sustainable future. Global warming is perhaps the most dangerous threat, and must be stopped if we want to build a future. Most of the actions that we know are effective in this regard, must certainly be taken by governments. The International conferences on climate, however, show that the path is not easy. With the hope that China and the U.S. finally move the important step in the fight against global warming, while we can identify some key points that describe climate change. Most of these are related with our daily lives, so that we have the opportunity, with our behaviour, to act in a sustainable manner.

1. Reducing CO2 emissions

People can act by using public transport, car sharing, bike sharing, etc. and governments should promote them. But the majority of the Co2 emissions in the world (approximately 80%) comes from industrial activities. For that reason we have to try to eradicate the problem at its root, for example by increasing the supply of electricity from renewable sources for industries.

2.Stopping deforestation and overbuilding of natural territory

Everyone knows that the only living being capable of capturing CO_2 is the plant. In the idea that we have of sustainable future, the plants are a key element, to preserve and, it would be desirable, to increase. For that reason is necessary to stop the actual trends of deforestation and overbuilding. This last point is also the main cause of many recent floods in Europe, in the U.S. and Indonesia.

3. Recycling

Even today, when a product runs out of its life cycle, it is often discarded and replaced with a new one. In most countries, even advanced, is no longer treated and ends up in dump. Here we have devoted a lot of scarce natural resources (eg, iron, plastic, etc.) so that they can not be reused. By the time it is easy to imagine that they will run out, so it is essential to reverse the trend by recycling as much as possible. Nobody throws a gold ring just they don't use it anymore. We should begin to have the same perception of the preciousness that we have for the gold, for all the other scarce materials.

4. Reusing

One of the failure of the free market is that it allows each one to transform natural resources into products which, once exhausted their life cycle, become unusable and are destined to dump. In order not to transform our world into a big dump, we must ensure that the products we use in everyday life do not run out once their cycle of life, but can continue to maintain their usefulness over time. Regulating productive activities and placing particular restrictions on products are necessary to stop the loss of utility of materials, such as iron and copper, but especially plastic products.

5. Promoting research
The man has always discovered new innovations and many of these have proved incredible in the past. It started with the fire, passing through the wheel and the language, up to the DNA. Each generation has the feeling that it can not go over the level of knowledge acquired. This impression, however, is significantly wrong and we must be confident that many current problems will be solved by future discoveries.

6. Promoting freedom of information
Some developing countries may not be aware of the trend of global warming and therefore not to adopt all the behaviors to prevent it. For this reason is fundamental, and this is one of the main goal of Green Economics Institute, promulgate the knowledge of these topics around the world. Nowadays we have internet, a powerful instrument that gives to everyone the opportunity to get in touch with anyone around the world. Therefore, each of us may contribute inquiring first, and then informing.

7. Banning and regulating economic activities that pollute and destroy natural resources
There are products for which the packaging needs more materials (paper, plastic, etc.) than the products themself. By reducing the amount of packaging products, where they are not strictly necessary, we could preserve a significant amount of materials and natural resources (eg plants). Today we see that in the Mediterranean Sea the presence of fish products has been steadily declining. This is mainly due to unregulated exploitation and destruction of the seabed by boats. Without a law that preserves the marine ecosystem, it is threatened in its natural play.

8. Promoting renewable energy and energy efficiency
This point regards both states that people: governments can provide incentives to the production of electricity from renewable sources. They can also reduce energy inefficiency, for example by controlling the level of heating of the public locals. Nowadays anyone can install a solar panel on his roof (of course this has to be convenient). Moreover, in everyday life we can significantly reduce energy consumption (for example by using energy-saving bulbs, completely turning off appliances when not in use, etc.).

9.Promoting investments in green economy
This point regards both states that people: governments can act creating laws to promote investment in «green» activities (for example by reducing taxes on green banks) and people can

act in this way as well, such as choosing where to allocate their personal investments.

10. Controlling the growth of world population

In 1798, Thomas Robert Malthus assumed that «food production would increase in arithmetic progression against population's geometric progression, keeping us on the brink of insufficiency». This theory has been much discussed and it still is today. What we can be sure of, is that the earth is a finished place, so that the production of natural resources could grow up in the future, thanks to scientific discoveries, but can never reach infinity.

All these points are interrelated and should be considered together. They (or their absence) represent the current reasons of climate change and, at the same time, they suggest us how to act to stop global warming, biodiversity loss, waste of natural resources, pollution and all the other threats that make up the «climate change». For this reason we think that this historical period is both a period of serious crisis for our planet and a great opportunity to build for the first time a sustainable future.

Photo: The Green Economics of Biodiversity. (Photo by Miriam Kennet 2011)

" "If the bee disappeared off the surface of the globe then man would only have four years of life left. No more bees, no more pollination, no more plants, no more animals, no more man"

Albert Einstein

7.2 The Financial Crisis and New Welfare Approaches
-Better Perspectives to Create Green Economics

By Rosita Bujokaite

Introduction

The aim of this paper is to indicate the possibilities and perspectives of creating green economics after the recent financial-economic crisis. The author argues that the last worldwide crisis is a good opportunity to reassess the economic approaches towards welfare, resources, wealth and other economic categories. This is a theoretical analysis of the changes made by the crisis which could be the best precondition in order to change the endogenous variables of the economic system. The author will conclude that, due to the redistribution of preferences of consumers, there are several possibilities to reconstruct the global or local economic systems into green economics.

Introduction

The last worldwide crisis was devastating in terms of production downturns and the loss of profits for companies and revenue reduction for consumers. The causes of the crisis have been explained in various ways, but the most important task, indeed, is not to indicate the "guiltiest criminals" and "causers" of this crisis; the target should be to discover ways of benefiting from this economic collapse or indicating the positive points, if any, which it creates.

The methodology used in this paper is mainly theoretical analysis - the assumptions and conclusions are made according to economic and logical rules. The main idea is to prove that the crisis period is the optimal moment to introduce and promote essential changes in the economic system, particularly those referred to in the field of green economics.

The paper is divided into four parts. The first section is dedicated to the main concepts of the paper: the economic crisis, green economics and the theoretical aspects of these concepts and phenomena. The second section returns again to the crisis and analyzes it through illustrative statistics. The third section is dedicated to the newest green and welfare approach developments. The fourth section is the systematic reassessment of the concepts discussed before. It links the last economic worldwide crisis and green economics through discussion about new opportunities for the efficient changes. The main conclusions are exposed in the last separate section.

1. Main concepts: economic crisis and green economics

The latest economic crisis was caused by the chaos made by modern financial instruments and the misleading management of risk in the financial sector. This was just the beginning though. Afterwards came the need to cope with the macroeconomic effects which followed (revenue and production downturns, the effects on national balances etc.). Naturally the reform of financial systems and markets was needed as a consequence of the crisis, which was complemented by political, social and security policies all over the world (D.K. Nanto, 2009). Also the "green packages" of investments were introduced in certain countries (OECD, 2009). It is not inevitable for the financial-economic crisis to be followed by green reforms, but we are going to discuss that some of them coincided. Moreover the crisis is the best moment to promote green changes.

1.1 Economic crisis

As we have already mentioned, the last financial crisis turned into an economic crisis after some time, and forced politicians to take urgent and unpopular decisions into account. This section is dedicated to discussing the crisis concept and outcomes in order to indicate the possibilities of green economics to be enforced due to the crisis.

First of all, the origin of the crisis concept is to be discussed for understanding why the crisis is not only a tragedy, but also an opportunity.

The definition of crisis given by dictionaries includes such key words as 'sudden decisive change', 'tension' or 'conflict', which requires a reaction in order to be overcome. In economic terms, the crisis is the situation of a sudden downturn, which is accompanied by falling GDP, drying up liquidity, changing price level and similar negative economic effects.

So it is obvious that the 'economic crisis', regarding its origins and essence, is in need of reform or is the reform of the system itself. Progress is being made through crisis, which requires a decisive change. It is a case to quote the study of the Congressional Research service on the reforms needed in order to overcome the consequences of the economic crisis:

> *"In making policy changes, Congress faces several fundamental issues. First is whether any long-term policies should be designed to restore confidence and induce return to the normal functioning of a self-correcting system or whether the policies should be directed at changing a system that may have become inherently unstable, a system that every decade or so creates bubbles and then lurches into crisis."*
> *Source: D. K. Nanto (2009)*

Practically, an economic crisis is an opportunity to introduce fundamental changes due to the character of its essence. First of all, the situation requires changes and the policy maker chooses which changes they are going realize. Agents facing those changes are changing themselves and their behaviour, for instance, people tend to adapt themselves and to consume less during the crisis.

Table 1 shows economic changes in the world and the main economies during the last crisis. The economies are divided into advanced and emerging or developing economies.

Table 1
World Economic Outlook Projections

	2008	2009	Projections	
			2010	*2011*
World Output	**3.0**	**-0.6**	*4.2*	*4.3*
Advanced economies	**0.5**	**-3.2**	*2.3*	*2.4*
USA	0.4	-2.4	*3.1*	*2.6*
Euro area	0.6	-4.1	*1.0*	*1.5*
Emerging and developing economies	**6.1**	**2.4**	*6.3*	*6.5*
Russia	5.6	-7.9	*4.0*	*3.3*
China	9.6	8.7	*10.0*	*9.9*

Source: IMF World Economic Outlook, April 2010

As we are able to see, the downturn of GDP in advanced economies was larger compared to emerging or developing economies when we observe their respective average outputs. Less production, however, means not only lower revenues, but also less pollution and less resource waste.

Such a decline of production needed to be given a response, and the quotation above emphasizes the necessity of choosing either to recreate confidence into an old system or to remake it. Here, the possibility to enforce green economics appears. Only strong incentives are needed, which would permit the global changes to favour green economics.

1.2 Green economics

Green economics is a new concept to be promoted. According UNEP (United Nations Environmental Program):

> *"green economy" can be defined as a system of economic activities related to production, distribution and consumption of goods and services that result in improved human well-being over the long term, while not exposing future generations to significant environmental or ecological scarcities. (UNEP, 2009)*

Green economics can be characterized by substantially increased investment in green sectors, both public and private; sustainable consumption and production processes; the assurance of more green and decent jobs; reduced energy and material intensities in production processes; less waste and pollution; as well as reduced greenhouse-gas emissions. (UNEP, 2009).

Experience over recent decades has shown the inefficiencies related to monetary based evaluation for the well being of humanity. "Green economics" is regarded as a wider concept than one which regards only ecology. The green economists are concerned about well-being of future generations and concepts of sustainability (see: Figure 1), and it is fundamental to have a broader green economics' concept in mind.

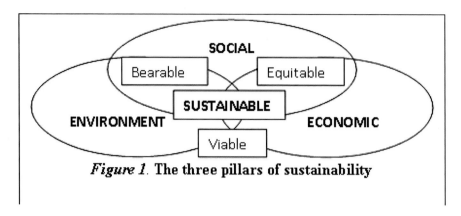

Figure 1. The three pillars of sustainability

Source: D. Meadows (2007)

To be more conceptual, green economics is defined as follows:

> *"Green economics" is the ideology of economic science which supports the sustainable economic growth in terms of duration and persistence (long-term), assuring social and psychological well-being of humans, seeking for equality and elimination of disparities between poor and rich, eliminating waste and overconsumption in order to save energetic resources and looking after the environment.*

This kind of definition involves all three pillars of sustainability. It must consider the responsibility for the Earth's limited resources and environmental issues, as well as the responsibility for the social security and parity. The ideology makes sense, only if it is complex and includes as many aspects of reality as possible. Parity is the psychological environment of humans and could be linked to physical environment by giving reasons to look after physical environment and assure the ecology.

Green thinking is supposed to be regarded not only as the way of thinking, but also as the moral system of conceptualizing economic thought. Only by changing the nature of economic approaches, it is possible to change the system itself. Taking into account responsible consumption, educating the producers and consumers to seek utility of psychological origin, rather than monetary, one could initiate a great step forward to enforce the responsible use of resources and enforce ecological economics, as well as social ecology.

The current conditions are those of the radically changing world outlook due to the economic crisis. This kind of situation could be regarded as including both negative and positive impacts. Also, if there are more negative factors lately acting upon the richness and revenue of humanity (theoretically less possibility for investment, including green investment), we can deduct some of the possible positive changes, in case those particular conditions had been fulfilled. But first of all let us look at what exactly has changed in the world due to the economic crisis.

2. Economic crisis and global changes

As far as it was discussed, it is clear that the crisis itself is a change. Moreover, it requires the reforms for the system to be changed. The external shocks change the reality and the economic agents change according to the changed reality. The policy makers have a chance to change the economic environment, for it is a need felt by anybody. So due to these factors, the global changing process is currently unavoidable. In this section we are going to dig deeper and consider the real changes due to the last economic crisis: external shocks and the nature of the crisis.

2.1 Economic loss due to the economic crisis

First of all, the crisis brought the downturn of liquidity in financial markets and then the productive sector was depressed. This had an effect on international trade, production, employment, retail revenue volumes and significantly reduced the producers' and consumers' confidence and expectations (see: Figure 2).

Figure 2 shows graphs related to the indicators mentioned above and their dynamics before and during the crisis. We can see that given indicators show that the advanced economies (Europe, United States) were worse off compared with the emerging economies (China, Russia and similar). The countries experienced worsening in production sizes and naturally employment decreased due to this effect, combined with lower retail sales.

Figure 2. **Current and forward looking indicators** *(percentage change of 3- month moving average)*

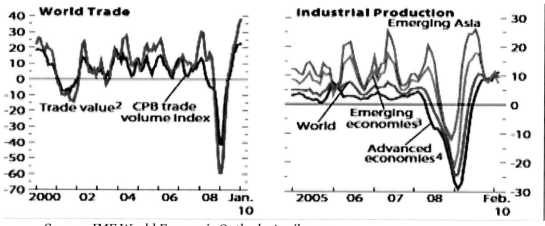

Source: IMF World Economic Outlook, April 2010

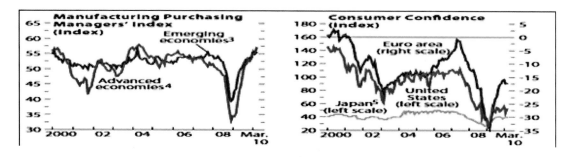

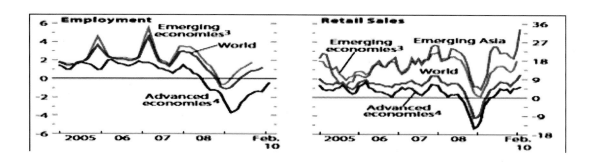

It is a negative consequence that workers lose jobs, but it also provides a stimulus to adapt better, to gain new qualifications or change their lifestyle, possibly into a better one after the crisis. The preconditions for promoting green jobs began to form. Moreover, the reduction of production means not only a loss of revenues, but also in certain terms it could result in less waste and less consumption of energy and non-renewable resources.

So firstly, we must link the changing situation to the rationale and conviction that decreasing possibilities to consume is not only unavoidable, but also a good way to save the planet from excessive use of natural resources and environmental damage. The next section discusses the positive side effects of a crisis.

2.2 Gaining from an economic crisis?
An economic crisis creates pressure on the revenues and monetary capacity of a vast majority of the economics participants. They have to adjust their behaviour and consumption habits according to their changed budget. This is a necessity and should be treated in the correct way.
First of all, policy makers could benefit from the changing situation by re-educating consumers and implementing policies of green economics, based on solutions of social and environmental issues. This would be possible to achieve after the welfare approach has been changed.
B. Vis, K. van Kersbergen and T. Hylands (2010) have completed a theoretical analysis of the welfare state, related to changes made by the financial-economic crisis. They did not find the

empirical evidence that those fundamental changes will be realized, but they theoretically stated that all the preconditions exist for the welfare approach to be changed from the background and that this background is best for the essential reforms:

> *"In fact, the current financial crisis offers a strong spur for welfare state reform: all theories of welfare state change predict reform under this circumstance. Following an institutional line of argumentation, for example, the crisis offers a critical juncture at which it is possible to divert from the original path of development and embark on radical reform, including serious retrenchment and major restructuring...*
>
> *Given the high strains brought forth by the financial crisis, such as rising levels of unemployment and budget deficits, this perspective predicts reform to follow. An ideational account expects ideas to have a transformative capacity at this time, because a crisis causes uncertainty that fosters the take-up of groundbreaking ideas to transform the welfare state radically... "*
>
> *Source: B. Vis, K. van Kersbergen, T. Hylands (2010)*

The crisis demanded and justified making huge inflows of state money in many economies. Different social and economic programs have also been introduced within the state investment packages. For instance in the EU, 3.3 % of European GDP was assigned to the various economic stimulus programmes, and this accumulated to be over 400 billion Euros (Euro stat, 2009). The next question is how efficient and rational is this spending and could it have been directed more towards green economics?

The crisis released the tight limits of the public deficits, which have increased dramatically. There is no need for justification of why governments are spending so much money during the crisis, because the crisis is an explanation itself.

Giving a chance to reassess the limits and the possibilities of improvement in the economic system, the crisis also provided the chance to invest in green economics. It has already occurred in many advanced economies and several institutions have benefited from promoting the green philosophy due to crisis chaos. It is more than only positive development; it is crucial for changing the way of thinking at all and directing economies towards sustainability.

3. Latest green economics developments

In order to build up a system grounded by sustainable norms, a strong ideological influence is needed. It is necessary to follow the trends of economic thought and scientific achievements, which indicate the sustainable progress supposed to be promoted and advertised. In this section we are going to review the possible sustainable welfare approaches and the latest trends of diffusion of green economic achievements.

3.1 New welfare economics

Evaluating economics after the traditional concept of GDP, means thinking about the wealth linked to the produced value. The economies' capacity tended to be estimated according to the value of output produced, but this is no longer the case.

About three decades ago, scientists took into account that it is not constructive to base concepts of wealth and well-being solely on the monetary aspect of happiness, which is practically evaluated in GDP. A series of new indicators appeared in order to estimate the well-being or welfare of nation states. Further welfare approaches have also been created.

One of the new well-being approaches is the capability approach:

> *The capability approach stresses that we have to make a clear distinction between the means or inputs and the ends of the quality of life. Income can be an important means for some aspects of well-being (e.g. for the health care sector, for education, etc.), but not for all capabilities (e.g. long-term unemployed are more often socially isolated and depressed, for which there are no simple monetary solutions). Similarly, economic growth is important as it provides the means for some important capabilities, but it does not tell us anything about other capabilities.*
> *Source: I. Robeyns (2005). The capability approach and welfare policies*

Under other capabilities, environmental conditions are also met. If we are capable of maintaining our planet as clean and undamaged, it will be hugely beneficial for the capabilities and well-being potential of current and future generations.

New welfare economics (NWE) also analyses the sustainable consumption (on the broader analysis of NWE approaches see: Gowdy, 2004). The main difference that was brought to attention by NWE is that the sustainability of the welfare state can be analysed in terms of three sustainability pillars. It is also important to mention the emphasis on the environmental issues used in NWE.

The changing way of thinking is the first precondition for the system to be changed. So trends in NWE tend to show the concerns towards sustainable and green growth of the economy and it will definitely allow us to improve the economic functioning from the inside, if realized.

3.2 Latest trends of diffusion of green economics

The diffusion of green economics is determined by essential and significant evidence. There is a lot of evidence, in terms of high emissions and energy consumption. Fast growth of economies all over the world has had negative impacts on the environment, but this does not assure poverty reduction:

> *"The impressively high economic growth rates over the past 20 years, resulting in the doubling of Asia Pacific regional GDP, was unfortunately driven by production processes which have generated high emissions and high levels of energy consumption. Though the overall poverty level in the region has reduced over the*

recent years, the characteristically high levels of poverty in the region makes it more vulnerable to climate change effects; the potential is there to break this vicious cycle through sustainable growth strategies that are based on good practices from other parts of the world."
Source: Fernando and Okuda (2009)

Although there are some critics of green actions who believe that there is no real evidence of our impact on the planet (see: Krugman (2010), Atkinson and Hackler (2010)), governments take actions against these global effects of economic growth together with its side effects. They are introducing green stimulus packages as well as encouraging green technologies:

"Governments in OECD and major non-OECD countries are launching economic stimulus packages to address the recession. Governments are also using their economic stimulus packages to help the greening of the economy and promote investment in green technologies. In most stimulus packages, investment in green technologies is an important part (after infrastructure investments, education, and R&D). Germany, for example, has dedicated EUR 5.7 billion to green technologies, Australia AUD 5.7 billion, and Canada CAD 2.8 billion."
Source: C. R. Kounatze (2009)

Green economics is needed and is diffusing quickly. It is implemented by governments and consumers are beginning to reflect on this concept. The best scenario would be to influence the vast majority of politicians, producers and consumers into understanding the issues and behaving responsibly towards the physical environment. This is achievable through various educating programs and supportive projects, as well as the green stimulus which has already been introduced.

4. Green economics perspectives after economic crisis

Green economics has good perspectives and is a developing quickly. The current crisis gave an incentive to take into account the green stimulus as a measure to cope with the crisis. The World Bank analysis carried out by Strand and Toman (2010) revealed the positive effects as well as the possible inefficient aspects of a green stimulus. Their conclusion about the positive influence of stimulus is described below:

Environmental cleanup, energy efficiency retrofits, and at least some natural resource maintenance and safeguarding measures are likely to have reasonably strong stimulus effects as well as significant positive effects on environmental and natural resources. Local environmental effects of bio-energy expansion and carbon sequestration will depend on the specific impacts on land and other natural resources and on the environmental characteristics of the fuel use.
Source: Strand and Toman (2010)

Green investments are likely to bring positive effects on the environment which will become evident in the medium to long term. The most important point, is to continue to have the same green direction in economic thinking and doing.

UNEP (2008) gives the definition to "green jobs" and discusses the range of benefices as well as measures to achieve them. Furthermore, the ILO (International Labor Organization) (2009) emphasizes the importance of the "Green jobs" program for overcoming the current crisis:

> *Green jobs are crucial to overcoming the economic crisis. They are a practicable and effective option for reviving economies and can contribute to creating large numbers of jobs quickly. This is also true for the major investments needed to adapt to climate change. If invested wisely, the resources to overcome the economic crisis could leave a legacy of energy-efficient infrastructure, rehabilitated ecosystems, renewable energy sources, and enterprises and workplaces that are more resilient to climate change. They could lay the foundations for a greener economic future which is environmentally sound, economically productive and socially sustainable.*
> *Source: The green jobs program of ILO (2009)*

Green jobs include direct employment in the manufacture, installation and operation of low-emission renewable energy, but also indirect jobs in making steel for gearboxes and windmill towers, composite chemicals for blades and concrete for the foundations of a windmill. A socially just transition for enterprises, workers and communities is part of the ILO agenda on green jobs (ILO, 2009).

In Figure 3 the potential to reduce emissions is estimated (ILO, 2009). Within the rational policy, this potential is supposed to become a physical reduction of waste. The incentives in order to achieve this are already being practised.

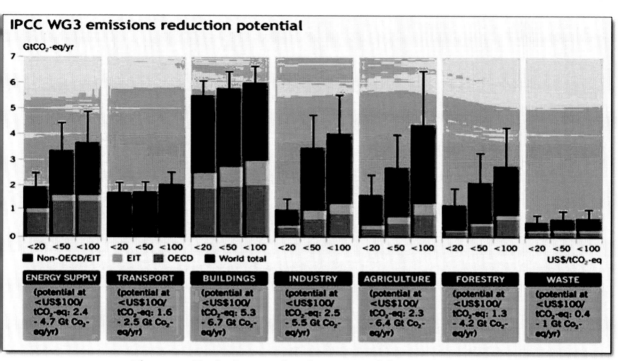

Figure 3. Emissions reduction potential
Source: The green jobs program of ILO (2009)

Green economics is a new and successful line of thinking. However there are analysts who emphasize that uncertainty is the crucial consideration, if green thinking and doing is going to give the expected results. Araghi (2009) gives such notes linking the green thinking to the overcoming of the crisis:

> *"There are, however, two problems with this line of thinking: (1) "Green production" in the rich countries is likely to be compensated by externalizing costs at the expense of poor areas in the world economy, and (2) "green consumption" in the rich countries is likely to be compensated by "forced under consumption" and poisonous consumption elsewhere in the world. The long-term alternative to the current crisis would therefore have to go beyond reformist (green) capitalist solutions."*
> Source: F. Araghi (2009). Political economy of financial crisis: a world-historical perspective

It is true that the world economy is not yet functioning as it is supposed to. There are a series of problems related to poverty and unsustainable growth. This does not mean, however, that no changes could be made.

The field of green economics has achieved more attention and significance during the current economic crisis. Furthermore, green thinking is the best way to proceed in directing the world economy towards sustainable development. The perspectives are likely to be positive and promising.

Conclusions

The worldwide economic crisis brought a need for change in the economic system. The current situation can be used in order to promote green economics, which could also provide some solutions for coping with the crisis.

The global production and consumption decline also has positive aspects. Less production means less pollution and fewer resources are wasted. The decomposition of consumption trends and consumers' natural adaptation to the crisis situation should be used for re-educating participants of economies and directing them towards sustainable consumption.

Indeed the green packages have been introduced in certain countries and this is a positive change. Green packages help to create green economics and to build up the new line of thinking. The new welfare approaches are still developing. They emphasize the need of re-evaluating economic growth and support for sustainable development, regarding environmental issues, as far as facts show the reasons to concern about the ecological state of the planet.

So the crisis could be regarded, in some instances, as beneficial, as it has created an opportunity to promote green economics: at ideological as well as practical levels. Programmes that are being run by different institutions and policymakers are great support for the green philosophy and are going to lead the world economy into better conditions if they persist and are realized.

References:

Araghi, F. (2009) "Political economy of financial crisis: a world-historical perspective", Economic and Political weekly, Vol. 43. No. 45. 2008

Atkinson, R. D., Hackler, D (2010) "Ten Myths of Addressing Global Warming and the Green Economy", The information technology and innovation foundation, http://www.itif.org/files/2010-green-economy-myths.pdf

Fernando, P., Okuda, A. (2009) "Green ICT: A "Cool" Factor in the Wake of Multiple Meltdowns", ESCAP technical paper, http://www.unescap.org/idd/working%20papers/IDD_TP_09_10_of_WP_7_2_907.pdf

Gowdy, J. (2004) "Toward a new welfare economics for sustainability", Analysis, Ecological economics 53 (2005) 211-212, Elsevier

ILO (2009) "The green jobs program", Turin, Italy

Kounatze, C. R. (2009) "Towards Green ICT Strategies: Assessing Policies and Programs on ICT and the Environment", OECD, http://www.oecd.org/dataoecd/47/12/42825130.pdf

Krugman, P. (2010) "Building a Green Economy", New York Times, 5 April, 2010 http://www.nytimes.com/2010/04/11/magazine/11Economy-t.html?_r=1

Meadows D. (2007) "ASTM Standard Breaks Barriers to Global Sustainable Development", http://www.astm.org/SNEWS/NOVEMBER_2007/meadows_nov07.html

ODI (2009) "The global financial crisis: poverty and social protection", Briefing paper, August 2009

Robeyns, I. (2005) "The capability approach and welfare policies", Conference in Bologna

Strand, T., Toman, M. (2010) "Green stimulus, economic recovery and long term sustainable development", World bank

UNEP (2008) "Green jobs: towards decent work in a sustainable and low-carbon world", New York

Vis B., van Kersbergen K., Hylands T. (2010). „Did the Financial Crisis Open Up Opportunities for Welfare State Reform?", Amsterdam, Netherlands

7.3 Global Green Human Being: concepts and main issues

By Kristina Jociute

Introduction

The world faces such global problems as climate change, poverty and income inequality. Though major efforts and a lot of discussions are taking place, 25.19 % of the population (according to 2005 data) still lives in households with consumption or income per person below the poverty line (World Bank, 2005). Only 20 per cent of the world's population has adequate social security coverage and more than half lack any coverage at all (ILO). Overall warming since the mid-19th century totals ~0.8°C (almost 1.5°F), with most of the increase occurring since 1970 (MacCracken, M.C., 2009). These striking pieces of data force us to give pause to the thought that something is wrong with the way we are living. This work will try to examine where we are going wrong, what the consequences are and what should be done if we wish not to ruin the Planet but to solve the problems which the World faces.

Misguided economics management concentration

Local and global government authorities take responsibility of their own states economic management. As the world becomes more global and economies more open, countries are faced with global as well as national issues such as unemployment, inflation, downturns, etc. Both for local as well as for global authorities relevant indicators are GDP, unemployment and price indexes. Considering those indicators and their prognosis authorities take relevant decisions which influence the population, its welfare and such essential issues as climate change. The prevailing macroeconomic indicator is Gross Domestic Product (GDP), which is derived from Keynes.

"In a series of three articles published in The Times of London, Nov. 1939, economist John Maynard Keynes noted that in World War I, excessive money creation stemming from defense spending led to inflation, which greatly hurt the working classes. Can we avoid this in World War II? asked Keynes. We can. But how? First by calculating "the maximum current output we are capable of organizing from our resources" (i.e. GDP). Next, "by estimating how fast we can safely draw on our foreign reserves by importing more than we export" (i.e. Imports minus Exports). Next, by estimating the minimum necessary capital formation needed to maintain plant and buildings (Gross Capital Formation). Next, by estimating how much will be required by our war effort" (Public Defense Consumption). What is left is "the size of the cake which will be left for civilian consumption" [i.e. both personal and public]. Keynes recommended using taxation and compulsory saving to ensure that consumption spending did not exceed that 'cake,' so that demand-pull inflation should not emerge."
(Maital, Sh., 2009).

Green Economics Methodology : An Introduction

In macroeconomics, science and global economies GDP, and more specifically its growth, is a central feature. GDP information influences all agents in the economy: consumers, savers, investors, banks, stock and option markets, private companies, the government, central banks and international organizations (Bergh, J.C.J.M., 2007).

The main GDP calculation is: $GDP = C + G + I + NEX$, where C – consumption, G – government expenditures, I – private and public investment and NEX – net export (export – import). In the past as well as now, governments make announcements that X economy is experiencing a downturn as its GDP has declined by Z % or Y economy is expected to revive as its GDP is now stabilizing and not declining. As well as this fixation with GDP at a macro level the same is also true at a micro level with companies, as the main indicator used is profit rate. However, we must not lose sight of the fact that all of this, both at a micro and macro level, is based purely on calculations.

Therefore GDP used as an indicator to measure countries wealth level has been created for robots existing in a mechanical planet. The purpose of GDP according to Keynes was to calculate and manage countries' wealth. However, it ignores each person as an individual / personality, and all the Earth as the whole of those individuals interacting between each other and the entire surrounding environment. It also ignores the quality of all these interaction processes as well as damage done to the environment, including the ineffective and reckless exploitation of natural and non renewable resources.

For more than half a century discussions have centered on the notion that GDP is not the most suitable indicator in terms of identifying the real state of a country and its society's welfare situation. Furthermore, GDP doesn't indicate sustainable development processes: i.e. to what extent a country's development is environmentally friendly and takes account of future generations as well as equally for all the Earth's population without any exceptions.

It should be clearly possible to focus on the true final goals of the economy and to incorporate all ecological issues simultaneously. This means an end to tweaking growth into ever different purposes which are not in line with the most important objective of the economy of providing people with a higher quality of life (Heinemann, V. and Kennet, M., 2008). While analyzing and seeking well-being and equality for society and all the planet, opportunities to act for ALL the planet's people, accessibility to those opportunities and protection from external negative factors should be taken into account as well as care about environmentally friendly processes. Economic growth at any price is dangerous for every individual, as well as the whole of society and the entire Planet.

Negative consequences of unlimited human needs satisfaction and inequality

Mainstream economics is still too bound up with concerns of price, profit, economic growth and the perspective of the owners of production versus the workers (Kennet, M. and Heinemann, V., 2006). Mainstream economics deals with how to satisfy unlimited human needs with limited resources. It is concerned mainly with human needs. However, this is quite dangerous as humans, after they reach a certain level of income and consumption level (the one that they had targeted to reach), start to want to achieve higher and higer levels. This has created a consumer society with over-consumption, over-exploitation and profit seeking issues.

Maslow posited a hierarchy of human needs based on two groupings: deficiency needs and growth needs. Within the deficiency needs, each lower need must be met before moving to the next higher level. Once each of these needs has been satisfied, if at some future time a deficiency is detected, the individual will act to remove the deficiency. The first four levels are (Huitt, W. , 2007):

1. Physiological: hunger, thirst, bodily comforts, etc.;

2. Safety/security: out of danger;

3. Belongingness and Love: affiliate with others, be accepted; and

4. Esteem: to achieve, be competent, gain approval and recognition.

According to Maslow, an individual is ready to act upon the growth needs if and only if the deficiency needs are met. The growth needs are as below:

1. Cognitive: to know, to understand, and explore;

2. Aesthetic: symmetry, order, and beauty;

3. Self-actualization: to find self-fulfilment and realize one's potential; and

4. Self-transcendence: to connect to something beyond the ego or to help others find self-fulfilment and realize their potential.

A significant proportion of the world's population is not able to satisfy the first of these (physiological needs) so they can hardly try to satisfy the fifth need, which is mostly related with the education level of that society. Ideologies offer different ways to live, and hence different ways to use resources. As the effects of globalization are creating further disparities and inequalities, around the world we are seeing an increase in violence and human rights abuses as disputes about territories, food and water are spilling into wars and internal conflicts. People are fighting for basic needs (Shah, A., 2001).

Mainstream economics seeks GDP growth, i.e. seeks growth in consumption - often without any concern about consumption quality and responsibility. Consumption was specifically encouraged in order to stimulate markets, rather than to meet people's needs, and this ignored the limits or requirements of other species or the planet (Heinemann, V. and Kennet, M., 2008). In addition, concern just about GDP growth means we overlook the need for consumption equality among all the global population. In "super-size-me" land, Americans gobble up more than 120 kilograms of meat a year per person, compared to just 6 kilos in India, for instance (Pearce, F., 2009). Figures 9 and 10 below reveal the true facts about global consumption inequality, which is mainly due to income inequality. In Figure 9 it can be seen that the poorest 20% of the population consume just 1.5 % of the world's private consumption, whereas the richest 20% of the population consume 76.6 % of the world's private consumption (in 2005). Meanwhile, Figure 10 reveals the huge private consumption gap that exists between the poorest 10% of the population and the richest 10%.

This shocking situation is based mainly on income inequality consequences.

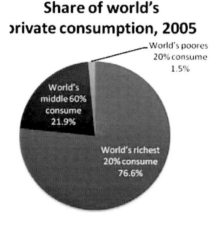

Share of world's
ɔrivate consumption, 2005

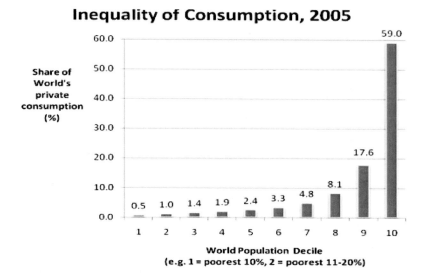

Figure 9 and Figure 10 (Shah, 2008)

In order to demonstrate real facts, the weekly food expenditure of families from different countries is now displayed (Halberg, T. and Halberg, Ch., 2007):

1. Italy: The Manzo family of Sicily: Food expenditure for one week: 214.36 Euros or **$260.11**

2. Germany: The Melander family of Bargteheide: Food expenditure for one week: 375.39 Euros or **$500.07**

3. United States: The Revis family of North Carolina: Food expenditure for one week **$341.98**

4. Mexico: The Casales family of Cuernavaca: Food expenditure for one week: 1,862.78 Mexican Pesos or **$189.09**

5. Poland: The Sobczynscy family of Konstancin-Jeziorna: Food expenditure for one week: 582.48 Zlotys or **$151.27**

6. Ecuador: The Ayme family of Tingo: Food expenditure for one week: **$31.55**

7. Bhutan: The Namgay family of Shingkhey Village: Food expenditure for one week: 224.93 ngultrum or **$5.03**

8. Chad: The Aboubakar family of Breidjing Camp: Food expenditure for one week: 685 CFA Francs or **$1.23**

Such an outcome happens not because of different human needs. Mainly it occurs, as has been mentioned previously, because of income inequality and created consumerism as the authorities seek GDP growth, which is possible by consumption encouragement. The major problem occurs as GDP is not concerned about basis consumption in order to satisfy basic needs as well as environmentally friendly consumption. Such consumption inequality reveals tender global issues such as poverty.

"Eradicating extreme poverty continues to be one of the main challenges of our time, and is a major concern of the international community."

United Nations Secretary-General BAN Ki-moon

The fact that people in employment still suffer from poverty is further proof of failing mainstream economic processes. The share of the extreme working poor in total employment was 21.2 per cent in 2008, representing a total of 633 million workers living with their families on less than USD 1.25 a day. In the case of the USD 2 a day working poor, 39.7 per cent of all workers were in this category, equal to 1,183 million workers around the world (ILO).

According to macroeconomics' schemas, possibly used by authorities, GDP growth influences unemployment reduction in the sense that as production volume grows employers demand more labour to satisfy increased demand for goods and services. However the main global issues still remain unsolved and it is a most relevant fact that GDP does not care about damage done to the environment. Despite strong economic growth that produced millions of new jobs since the early 1990s, income inequality grew dramatically in most regions of the world and is expected to increase due to the current global financial crisis. Global employment rose by 30 per cent between the early 1990s and 2007, but the income gap between richer and poorer households widened significantly at the same time (ILO).

Under existing poverty a major part of the population is starving and suffers from undernourishment, which is defined by the Food and Agriculture Organization (FAO) as the status of persons whose food intake regulary provides less than their minimum energy requirements. Hunger has increased not as a result of poor harvests but because of high domestic food prices, lower incomes and increasing unemployment due to the current global economic crisis. Many poor people cannot afford to buy the food they need. Most hungry people live in Asia and the Pacific (642 millions) and Sub-Saharan Africa (265 millions), with not such high volumes in Latin America and the Caribbean (53 million), Near East and North Africa (42 million) and in developed countries (15 millions) (FAO).

Figure 6 provides information about the world's undernourished population volumes in total and as a percentage of the total world population. It can be seen that over the timeframe in question the percentage of undernourished persons has decreased but the total volume of undernourished persons has varied and during 2004-2006 was almost the same as in 1969–1971. The FAO estimates that 1.02 billion people were undernourished worldwide in 2009. Thus there are now more hungry people that at any time since 1970, the earliest year for which comparable statistics are available. It is most interesting that GDP during the same period has notably increased.

These facts provide further evidence that mainstream economic counting and management processes do not work. The FAO claims that the world currently produces enough food for everybody, but many people do not have access to it. During 1979-1981, 1989-1991 and 2000-2003 daily consumed calories per capita were respectively 2549, 2704 and 2738, while the average minimum energy requirement per person is about 1800 kcal per day. Taking into account the fact that 13-19% of the world population do not consume even 1800 kcal daily per capita it gives us a striking conclusion that the remaining part of the population has been over-consuming food.

Under overconsumerism a major part of the world's population consumes more food than it needs, taking those used natural and non-renewable resources from future generations, whilst leaving one part of the population to starve.

If humans could be rational (unfortunately they are often not) then there would be enough food for ALL the Earth's population and even food production and consumption could be lower. Unfortunately, by chasing GDP growth and consumption growth this problem is left unsolved.

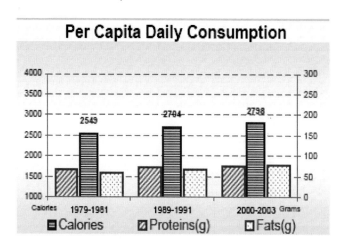

Figure 11. (Food and Agriculture Organization of The UnitedNations)

For as long as GDP, profit and consumption growth indicators remain central to our way of thinking, the Earth will continue to be damaged and poverty and inequality issues will remain unsolved.

Human overconsumption shows that we are an unconscious species. Most people are aware and take account just about seeable threats which directly impact them, such as illness, financial problems, the death of a sibling-, theft from them etc. Still they are not thinking about the subsequences of those threats and disasters. So most humans don't think about how their every action influences others and nature, and are not aware about climate change problems.

Before humans emerged on the Earth, the ecosystem circulated and acted in its own way. After humans evolved there was a period - in which they lived in harmony with the entire ecosystem. However, later we started to intervene in the ecosystem and brought chaos which influenced climate change processes and harmed the Earth through a rise in global sea levels, a change in vegetation zones, an increase in disease levels, and a change in ecosystems (UKECN).

Some factors such as distance from the sea, Ocean currents, direction of prevailing winds, relief, proximity to the Equator and the El Nino phenomenon, affect the climate naturally. However, it is human activity that has mostly influenced climate change processes. Global temperatures have risen by 0.6 degrees Celsius during 1860 – 1990 (UKECN). Often humans don't take account of the fact that their actions affect climate change, various cataclysms and biodiversity loss. Biodiversity provides many benefits for humans including fresh air, clean water, rich soils, medicines, natural beauty, and more. However biodiversity is diminishing in the face of several threats, including climate change, pollution, overpopulation, environmental degradation overexploitation and consumption, and invasive species (Earth Council Geneva).

Inequality exists not just in terms of social and income issues, but also from an environmental perspective. First of all humans tend to think of themselves as superior to nature, even if it is vice-versa in reality as humans are not able to manage environmental process such as hurricanes, rains, etc. Secondly, poor people damage Earth less than rich ones. However, the effects of climate change, which will have dramatic consequences in many cases, will more rapidly and intensely impact the poor and indigenous peoples because they have fewer resources for proactive adaptation (MacCracken, M.C., 2009).

Stephen Pacala, director of the Princeton Environment Institute, calculates that the world's richest half-billion people - that's about 7 percent of the global population - are responsible for 50 percent of the world's carbon dioxide emissions. Meanwhile the poorest 50 percent are responsible for just 7 percent of emissions. The carbon emissions of one American today are equivalent to those of around four Chinese, 20 Indians, 30 Pakistanis, 40 Nigerians, or 250 Ethiopians" (Pearce, F., 2009).

Such figures are really quite astonishing. It is possible here to notice that some countries do not care about human equality and keep overconsuming and overpolluting. The result is that they are indirectly destroying ecosystem balances and overexploiting resources, which negatively impacts other countries' citizens as well as their own.

Green being schema concept

It is desperately necessary to analyse economics not through a "quantitative prism" but rather by taking into account environmental issues, the health of individuals and other qualitative indicators. Though considering qualitative economic development an important role goes to human consciousness and effective consumption of resources without any overconsumption. All of this should be done for both us and future generations.

There are two alternative ways of humans acting and managing the economy:

> 1. Concentrate on needs satisfaction at any price. Take account just on GDP growth as well as production, consumption and profits growth.

> 2. Concentrate on quality and "green" relations between economic agents (government, human, companies, NGOs) as well as "green" ways of acting, i.e. think about green economics. Green Economics and its development is in fact one of the most holistic and multidisciplinary economics the world has ever seen. The aim of Green Economics is to create a new discipline that works for the benefit of all people eveywhere, for the planet, the biosphere, non-human species, nature, and other life forms (Kennet, M. and Heinemann, V. 2006).

It should be realized that the Earth consists of renewable and non-renewable resources as well as a wide spectrum of biodiversity which provides humans with many benefits. Humans should think in a mainstream economic way, i.e. how to use all the resources in a better way in order to produce more. It is not the way to over-exploit the resources and only then think about the future possibilities. It is necessary to think with a long-term perspective and about how to survive with the usage of far fewer resources and minimal damage to nature. All human activity processes should be "green" and sustainable. "Green" contains equality, quality and environmentally friendly processes.

Mainstream economics should be changed by taking a Green Economics approach. From my point of view, Green Economics is to be based on the Human Green Being (HGB) concept which is based on green consumption, green production, education, health and work which interact between each other. The interaction between these four factors and all processes are based on three pivotal values: environmentally friendly action, quality and equality (see Figure 12).

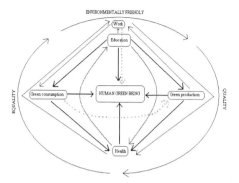

Figure 12: Simplified Human Green Being schema © Kristina Jociute 2010

Every human action, impact upon nature or damage to any of these 3 values has feedback in either the short run or long run. Most relevant feedback occurs when humans neglect the environmentally friendly value. Everything shouldn't be concerned with how to achieve happiness as it is really not precise and is a subjective concept. Everything should be concerned with the human green being, i.e. how to live and act in a "green" way and what influences this "green" being. Humans will then live in the right way as their consumption and production will be "green", i.e. no overconsumption, no overexploitation of resources, being responsible while consuming and producing. Education as well is included in the HGB as it helps to raise the quality of work, and to spread knowledge about Global environmental, social and economic processes and their sustainable relations. The most important factor for any human is their health as upon this depends their quality of life, and their ability to study and work. All these factors are influenced by nature and the ecosystem as humans do not live in a vacuum.

Due to environmentally friendly factor feedback to humans they should change their thinking about consumption, production and finance. In addition, there should exist equality between nature and human, social, incomes and consumption equality. Above all, the most important factor is the quality of all the human action processes.

Conclusions

Economic growth at any price is dangerous for every individual, as well as the whole of society and the entire Planet. The Global Economy has grown notably over past century, i.e. GDP has grown. However relevant issues such as poverty, inequality and negative climate change results caused by the irresponsible action of humans have deepened. The poorest 20% of the population consumed just 1.5 % of the world's private consumption, whereas the richest 20% of the population consumed 76.6 % of the world's private consumption (in 2005).

The number of undernourished people worldwide reached 1.02 billion in 2009. However, per capita daily consumption of calories exceeded the minimum required rate (1800kcal per day).

This data shows over consumerism under which a major part of the world's population consumes more food than it needs, taking those used natural and non-renewable resources from future generations, whilst leaving one part of the population to starve. Irresponsible human activity has also damaged nature and resulted in the over-exploitation of non-renewable resources, a rise in global sea levels, a change in vegetation zones, an increase in disease levels, and a change in ecosystems.

Therefore it is time for humans to stop and think about their green being on Earth. The Human green being concept is based on green consumption, green production, education, health and work under such values as quality, equality and environmentally friendly being. Under this HGB conception negative feedbacks will be avoided, thus helping to preserve the only living planet we have.

A version of this chapter was first published in the Proceedings of the 5th Annual Green Economics Institute Conference at Mansfield College, Oxford University, held in July 2010, published by the Green Economics Institute.

References:

Amin, A.A. (2009). Economic Growth and Human Development with Capabilities Expansion. Available at: http://www-3.unipv.it/deontica/sen/papers/Amin.pdf (last accessed 17/07/2010).

Bergh, J.C.J.M. (2007). Abolishing GDP. Vrije Universiteit Amsterdam, and Tinbergen Institute. Available at http://www.tinbergen.nl/discussionpapers/07019.pdf (last accessed 16/07/2010).

Earth Council Geneva (ECG) (2007). Biodiversity. Available at: http://earthcouncil.com/ecgsite/content/view/44/1/ (last accessed 18/07/2010).

Food and Agriculture Organization of The United Nations (FAO), Statistics Division (2006), Food and Agriculture Statistics Global Outlook. Available at:

http://faostat.fao.org/Portals/_Faostat/documents/pdf/world.pdf (last accessed 17/07/2010).

Food and Agriculture Organization of The United Nations (FAO), (2010). Hunger. Available at:

http://www.fao.org/hunger/hunger-home/en/ (last accessed 17/07/2010).

Halberg, T. And Halberg, Ch. (2007), Average weekly food consumption of families around the world. Avalable at: http://blog.halbergphotographers.com/2007/12/11/average-weekly-food-consumption-of-families-around-the-world/ (last accessed 17/07/2010).

Heinemann, V. and Kennet, M., (2006) „Green Economics: setting the scene. Aims, context, and philosophical underpinning of the distinctive new solutions offered by Green Economics", Int. J. Green Economics, Vol. 1, Nos. ½, pp.68-102.

Heinemann, V. and Kennet, M., (2008). Framework Paper for the Sustainable Development Commission. The Green Economics Institute. Available at: http://www.sd-commission.org.uk/publications/downloads/Miriam_Kennet_thinkpiece.pdf (last accessed 16/07/2010)

Huitt, W. (2007). Maslow's hierarchy of needs. *Educational Psychology Interactive*. Valdosta, GA: Valdosta State University. Available at http://www.edpsycinteractive.org/topics/regsys/maslow.html (last accessed 18/07/2010)

International Labour Organization (ILO), (2010). Social security. Available at: http://www.ilo.org/global/Themes/Social_Security/lang--en/index.htm (last accessed 18/07/2010).

International Labour Organization (ILO) (2008), World of Work Report 2008 - Global income inequality gap is vast and growing. Available at:

http://www.ilo.org/global/About_the_ILO/Media_and_public_information/Press_releases/lang--en/WCMS_099406/index.htm (last accessed 17/07/2010).

International Labour Organization (ILO) (2010), Global Empoyment Trends. Available at: http://www.ilo.org/wcmsp5/groups/public/---ed_emp/---emp_elm/---trends/documents/publication/wcms_120471.pdf (last accessed 18/07/2010).

MacCracken, M.C. (2009), Climate Science in Six Well-Documented Findings. Available at: http://www.climate.org/topics/climate-change/science-in-six-findings.html (last accessed 17/07/2010).

Maital, Sh. (2009), The Man Who Invented GDP. Available at: http://timnovate.wordpress.com/2009/02/22/the-man-who-invented-gdp/ (last accessed 18/07/2010).

Pearce, F. (2009), Overconsumption Dwarfs Population As Main Environmental Threat. Yale Environment 360. Available at:

http://www.organicconsumers.org/articles/article_17573.cfm (last accessed 17/07/2010).

Shah, A. (2001). Effects of Over-Consumption and Increasing Populations. Available at: http://www.globalissues.org/article/216/effects-of-over-consumption-and-increasing-populations (last accessed 17/07/2010).

Shah, A. (2008), Consumption and Consumerism. Available at: http://www.globalissues.org/issue/235/consumption-and-consumerism (last accessed 16/07/2010).

The United Kingdom Environmental Change Network (UKECN) (2000). Climate change. Available at:

http://www.ecn.ac.uk/Education/climate_change.htm (last accessed 18/07/2010)

United Nations Secretary-General BAN Ki-moon, United Nations (2002). Available at:

http://www.un.org/millenniumgoals/bkgd.shtml (last accessed 18/07/2010).

World Bank (2007). Replicate the World Bank's regional aggregation. Available at:

http://iresearch.worldbank.org/PovcalNet/povDuplic.html (last accession 18/07/2010).

7.4 Introducing Green Economics: Renaissance, Reform and Methodology. Green Economics – A Global Movement for Change

By Miriam Kennet

Green Economics has become one of the most contemporary global movements for change. In the age of austerity it has taken over from the round of stimulus packages, as governments all over the world attempt to claw back from the crippling debt and porous infrastructure that has been created by 60 year orgy of post war drunken resource use and exhaustion.

The world economy and the world's ecosystem services are experiencing what can only be described as the aftermath of an enormous hangover of over consumption, waste and over spending on a devastating scale, which has put human civilisation and the economy into the "intensive care" ward. Suddenly, frugality is the name of the game, saving and only spending on essentials is how people are managing their lives and their government budgets in most developed countries. In the UK David Cameron's "Big Society" is a thinly disguised attempt to disband almost every cost of welfare, education, health care and any costs of government and push it back to the private sector and profiteering by large companies in a major ideological shift.

What is so sad is that this huge 60 year party was only attended by people in the first world - and mainly by white middle class men in the west. The rest weren't invited; they were there to provide the waiters, the inputs to the party, the raw materials, resources and staffing! The frills and the entertainment. Now everyone has to pay for this party and to clean up the mess. The conducive climate for human civilisation has been damaged, the plentiful biodiversity like butterflies and bees, not to mention healthy fish stocks have been irreparably depleted and squandered and the seas are polluted and have major dead zones incompatible with life itself. Lamarck warned 200 years ago that man would continue to expand until he had totally damaged the planet and then would destroy himself!

We need as a species to stop and take stock – the party is over, if we don't stop drinking from the fountain of waste and exploitation of nature and eco systems we may well have had our day and be joining the rapid extinction of species.
As the Head of the Environment Agency in Europe has said, there is nothing that says we ourselves are immune from this process! So we need to watch out and do something about it quickly. Hence the age of green economics, not the age of spending on green consumption or

green wash, or even the green stimulus. Green economics has never meant green stimulus. Green economics is about living within our means and paying for what we use as we go, NOT leaving the clean-up for the next generation!

We need to clean up and put our house in order. We often say oikonomics is about managing the estate or managing our household. That household is the earth and all its resources, all of us humans, all living things and all the planet's systems. We have unbalanced the climate, the sea plankton which regulate it, the earth systems have been unleashed, the glaciers are melting, the north pole is navigable suddenly and the seismic character of the earth with volcanoes and earthquakes has been set in motion.

Green economics is the one system which factors all this in. It works by preventing poverty and inequality and does NOT start from a premise of as one intern said to me once "I am here to get rich quick". Green economics is about putting the house in order. In this case it's about clearing up, not before our parents get home and see the stains on the carpet and cigarette burns on the curtains, but about clearing up the house before we hand it on to our children – before they notice what a total mess we have made and start to bitterly resent us for what we have done and the depleted resources we have left for them!

Suddenly we are all faced with the complete loss of the illusion, as it was all an illusion, that modern economics had conquered all and was all powerful to lift the "bottom billon out of poverty" by means of more GDP growth, more expansion, spending in the economy and ever more resource use, especially oil and fossil fuel, using up most of the provisions laid down for 1000s of years and squandered in one or two generations.

The age of plenty is over. If we want a future, it must be the age of green economics which teaches us firstly how to share with each other. The people who never shared in this bonanza are now in some cases better placed to lead us out of the mess.

The USA, with an average carbon footprint of 25 tonnes a person, is in no position to lead the rest of the world, currently bickering with the UK over who caused the worst oil spill in history, finishing off whatever fish stocks were left in the ocean. India and Africa, with very low carbon footprints of less than 2 tonnes each per person, are gaining ground.

What we have found is that while the developed world is arguing over who spilt the wine, in parts of Africa, not only do they not have the wine, but they are actually still using stone-age implements. We found agriculture was being done with wooden tools, wooden ploughs, no anvil, no bronze-age innovations, people without shoes, let alone fashion items, and small children tending the animals in the fields with an average life expectancy of around 30 to 40 years!

The age of plenty passed them by completely, with 65% of them still unable to read and write, high female mortality and a complete failure to implement the Millennium Development Goals. If we call ourselves civilised, we cannot allow this situation. We need to consider what we have done and we need to take action to change it. Over use, hogging and squandering of our resources is no longer fashionable and is no longer a desired outcome of our economics system.

Green Economics Methodology : An Introduction

Green economics has worked hard to create an economics which is now fit and ready to lead the world forward. Our journey now has come a long way. We have been told that we have indeed created a new discipline in economics, Green economics, which is ready to take its place amongst economics theory, discipline and practise.

Green economics is NOT just about the environment, green is about efficiency in economics (Heinemann 2010). I always thought it was about reclaiming economics and provisioning for the needs of everyone and everything on the planet, other species, nature, the planet and its systems. He said it was a progressive discipline, and about ensuring that economics is used for progression, not regression. Green economics is therefore about doing and about SHARING, sharing with each other, the rest of humanity, and about sharing the planet with other species and with the planet's systems. If we don't want to unleash multiple earthquakes and volcanoes we need to maintain a suitable climate and temperature range around 14 degrees. Everything has an impact and every system has feeder input requirements. We have responsibilities to all these systems and to each other.

That time has come. We need to get a grip and manage better. However this year one thing that has become completely clear is that if we thought we had tamed nature and that our economics system was "in charge- and had conquered nature" this was a total fallacy, as nature has shown. Just one volcano in the northern hemisphere was enough to ground all aeroplanes for days on end and to disrupt the economy severely.

The Green Economics concept is as complex as it is timely. It is inclusive in all senses valuing not great wealth or riches, but diversity, sustainability, caring sharing and sensitivity for all of life on earth including our own and those of others.

It is time to end the party, it is time to share, everyone should have access to proper drinking water as a minimum. We should not rest until that job has been done. It is not that difficult to do, we just need to notice. To notice each other, the whole human family and to notice the biodiversity and the little things that bring us happiness. These are going to be the pleasures of the 21st century- NOT the arrival of a new Porsche in the household.

7.5 The Green Economics Response to Economic and Environmental Crises

By Miriam Kennet and Michelle S. Gale de Oliveira

Introduction

As we begin the second decade of the Third Millennium, we are facing a new variety of opportunities and challenges for life on this planet, specifically in terms of the burgeoning economic and environmental crises. Green Economics offers a unique, valuable, and timely response to these issues, and has been recognized the world over as the only full solution to the current dual crises. This chapter offers a guide to Green Economics, focusing on several key areas. It will examine the reasons Green Economics is needed and its value for Italy in particular. Then, it will consider where Green Economics is spreading, and the development and chronology of the discipline. Further, it will look at the features of Green Economics, its strategies, and the cultural background to the discipline, before moving on to address instruments. Finally, it will analyse recent   events and other issues of significance to Green Economics.

Why we need Green Economics

Today, human civilization is in the midst of a new Renaissance. We have arrived at this place out of necessity, and have finally come to the point of questioning our own role in creating the environmental and economic crises that only beginning to wreak havoc on planet earth and its inhabitants. We have reached this place after three hundred years of mass-production, high-consumption, and rejection of traditional respect and value placed on nature. In the last ten years we have seen the earth react to human behavior, and a global economic crisis has ensued, closely linked to the global environmental crisis. Today, the planet is faced with the many effects of climate change, massive biodiversity loss, and the failure of the economy to provision for the "bottom billion" of the world's poor, who have gained no absolute advantage in the rise of the global capitalist economy. For the first time in millions of years, humanity is at a crossroads, one in which we must decide either to continue down the path of mainstream, business-as-usual economics, or to choose a new strategy – one of survival.

"We are living in an age of global transformation – an age of Green Economics"
Ban Ki Moon, United Nations Secretary General, December 2008

Natural capital is a concept which mainstream economics has found hard to accommodate. Current scientific evidence clearly shows that this loss of natural capital is affecting the real and the mainstream economies and will begin to cost up to 20% of the world's GDP unless we act to prevent this economic risk, which in comparison could cost us just 2% of global GDP (Stern at the London School of Economics (2009).

Science advises us that our global climate is changing and that average global temperatures are increasing. Further, this increase in global temperature will be larger than the bounds within which our civilisation has developed over the last 10,000 years (Mithen 1996). In fact, researchers point to evidence that future warming will be up to 10 degrees centigrade in some areas, more than 1990 levels, conditions that have not been experienced on earth since before the time when human beings evolved on the planet. This brings into sharp focus "Economics and Reality," (Lawson 2007), and that there is no economics outside the ecosystem. It extends Lawson's work on critical realism in social theory and economics and adds back the physical real world (Lawson 2007).

Green Economics: A case for study of Italy and its importance

The crisis is global, but it has immediate effects for the people, land, and biodiversity of Italy. The seat of ancient civilization, the home of culture, tradition, and political grandeur, Italy is nonetheless threatened by the affects of climate change, biodiversity loss, and their impacts on the Italian economy and way of life. In Venice, sea-water levels are rising, spelling disaster for the ancient city. In Bolzano, warmer weather has meant less snow in winter and less water in summer, damaging tourism and hydroelectric power. Throughout the peninsula, olive cultivation and vineyards, agricultural staples, are under threat from temperature changes and the tropicalization of vegetation and species. In fact, with the increasing temperatures around the world, species are being forced to migrate at an alarming 5metres per day, and the agricultural eco-system is altering. Italy also faces economic issues such as an aging population and impending pension crisis, the effects of changing tourist trends in the face of climate changes, and the economic affects that rising water levels can have on Italy's sea-borders. In addition to this, Italy struggles with a lack of political will to combat these issues, and never has there been a more important time to address human contributions to the environmental crisis. Such issues point to the urgency in finding a new economic strategy, one which will consider those things which are of real value – not consumerism, but cultural heritage, for example. In all things, Green Economics specifies exactly that mindset that the mainstream avoids: that the good life consists of quality, rather than quantity.

Where Green Economics is spreading

Green Economics emerged as *the* economics story for today, gaining momentum from previous years successes and drawing attention to its valuable contribution to modernity's complex issues. This new discipline has drawn immediate attention from all quarters, featuring in the most unexpected of places. Green Economics was the headline story at the European Business Summit, Brussels, in February 2008, was launched by the UN in December 2008 in Geneva, adopted and promoted by key activists, from top politicians and celebrity figures to policy makers, campaigners, top academics, and major players in the business world. The British government has been training top civil servants in the discipline, and Green Economics has been warmly received by various Western European Governments, Balkans' governments, African governments, for example. Italian business leaders and leading academics in Bolzano, Venice and Rome have been introduced to green economic solutions, and the Green Economics Institute is working with the International Labour Organization in Rome to promote green jobs solutions to the global economic downturn and environmental crisis. The discipline's coming-of-age has dovetailed with the launch of the Green New Deal and The Economics of the Environment and Biodiversity (TEEB).

Greening the Economy has become a particular focus amongst policy-makers, being regarded by many as one of the only ways of tackling both the economic recession and the environmental crises. Today, it has become apparent that we are on collision course between *Ecology* and the *Economy*. Still, the centres of economic thought remain dependent on mainstream economics and unwilling to diversify, even in the face of enormous market failures and economic meltdowns. Oxford University Press states that its economics focuses purely on an econometrics approach to the mainstream, and is uninterested in covering social or environmental issues. Further, the United Kingdom's Royal Economics Society does not feature any progressive economics in its conferences or its journals. However, such a narrow approach is not true of students, policy-makers or the general public, who, hungry for change, embrace the green economics strand of environmental economics.

Development and Chronology

The Green Economics Institute has been at the forefront of the development of Green Economics. Its goals have been 1) to develop a robust academic discipline, 2) provide policy-makers, campaigners, business-people, and the public with the tools and knowledge to reconsider mainstream economic assumptions and goals. The urgency of the Green Economics Project has increased as social and environmental injustices now significantly affect the world economy. Dr. Rajendra Pachauri, the chair of the Intergovernmental Panel on Climate Change, warns that *"the very survival of the human species is at risk"* (Lean, 2005). Public perception of our position in the world is altering, and the fragility of our survival and well-being, as well as our economy and security is becoming much more evident (Pachauri, 2007; Stern, 2006; Raudsepp-Hearne *et al.*, 2005). In order to effectively analyse the mainstream, Green Economics applies an interdisciplinary approach to economics learning, adopting philosophy and new learning from the natural sciences, and employing these in a holistic assessment of the dual economic and environmental crises.

By combining economics with knowledge from the natural sciences, we argue that Green Economics can incorporate a much wider, more practical, multidisciplinary range of knowledge than other schools of economics. It can therefore also provide a significant impetus to the complete reform and modernisation of standard economic conventions and ideas. In this way it brings to economics a very long-term perspective, the full range of human history and pre-history as well as earth history, while strictly adhering to objectivity, sound qualitative and quantitative analysis and a consideration of the widest possible range of values, including survivability, sustainability, a sense of community, a comprehensive appreciation of social and environmental justice between people, and with non human species, the planet and the biosphere.

Table 6: Chronology of Green Economics

Chronology of Green Economics	
Pigou The Economics of Welfare	1920
Ronald Coase: The Problem of Social Cost	1960
Rachel Carson: Silent Spring	1962
The coming of space ship earth: Boulding	1966
Garret Hardin: The Tragedy of the Commons	1968
Georgescu Roegens The Entropy Law and the Economic Process	1971
Small is beautiful :E F Schumacher	1973
The Gaia Hypothesis: James Lovelock	1979
The other economics summitt (TOES)	1984
Our Common Future :Gro Harlem Brundtland	1987
Steady State Economics: Herman Daly	1992
The Green Economy : Michael Jacobs	1991
Wealth Beyond Measure :Paul Ekins	1992
Economics of the 21st Century Conference London Miriam Kennet	1995
Green Economics: Beyond Supply and Demand to Meeting People's Needs :Green Audit : 1st book on Green Economics	1999
Andrew Dobson Green Political Thought	2000
Oekonomie Der Zukunft : Volker Heinemann	2002
The Green Economics Institute Founded	2003
1st Green Economics Institute Conference at Oxford University Miriam Kennet and Volker Heinemann	2005
Professor Jack Reardon Joins the Institute	2006
International Journal of Green Economics double blind peer reviewed academic journal founded by Miriam Kennet Editor	
Dr Jeff Turk PHD Yale and Cern joins the Institute	2006
The Stern Review on the costs of climate change	2007
Green Jobs Initiative ILO	2007
Green Economics Interns College Founded by Sophie Henstridge	2008
Launch of The Green Economy UN Geneva UNEP Miriam Kennet	2008
Professor Graciela Chichilnisky joins our team	2008
Michele Gale Director Joins the Institute	2008

Gower Publishing Green Economics Book series Initiated	2008
The Green New Deal	2008
TEEB Report on biodiversity costs UN	2010
First two books launched in our Series with Gower	2010
Millionth visitor to Green Economics Institute website	July 2010
BBC makes programme about Miriam Kennet and about Green Economics	2011
BBC makes 3 programmes about Green Economics	2011
Award for Green Economics Institute work on gender equality	2011
Reader Series Book Launch	2011
Handbook Series Book Launch	2011
Launch of Green Economics Masters Course Birmingham City University	2011
Earth Summit RIO +20 on Greening the Economy: rethinking growth	2012

Features of Green Economics

Green Economics reclaims economics as long term, holistic and realistic discipline, encompassing the entirety of earth's history, firmly dependent upon and embedded within nature. The discipline both incorporates and celebrates "difference," diversity, equity and inclusiveness within its concepts of society and community.

All the economic processes and systems are designed to work as part of and within the limits of nature rather than to conquer or steward it. Its definition is that economics simply manages the provision for needs, returning to the "Oikonomia" of Xenophon. More specifically, its aims are to provide for the needs of mutual very long term survivability and sustainability for the planet, nature and all of its people as beneficiaries and such its context and scope are innovations. Its philosophy is to manage economics for nature as usual, rather than to manage the environment for business as usual.

By its nature, Green Economics is an interactive process of economics by doing. The means are as important as the ends, and the ends are as important as the means. For example, if an economic decision succeeds in equitably distributing resources but fails to include women or minorities in decision-making, it cannot be considered viable. Green Economics always includes diverse methodologies and practitioners at its core. The mainstream economic mindset illustrates this, seeking to solve women's poverty by producing and recognizing white middle class male economists. In Green Economics, women are empowered in their own economic decision-making and provisioning. Instead of imposing one system on the world, we work with and create the spaces that allow diversity to flourish. This is one of the most challenging lessons of the whole project as it is the opposite of the conditioning of mainstream economics on economists and wider society.

Strategy of Green Economics

Perhaps the most controversial and important of all debates stems from the question of responses to the environmental crisis. Four possible responses are available, namely, regulation, market-solutions, lifestyle changes, and eco-technological solutions. Green Economics offers a timely perspective on each of these.

First, regulation is one of the key political responses to climate change and biodiversity loss, seen for example in the Kyoto Protocol and last years' unsatisfactory attempt to reach international agreement at the Conferences of Parties (COP15) in Copenhagen, Denmark. This option is proving perhaps one of the most difficult measures to implement, however, the necessity of achieving an international, inter-governmental accord is nonetheless a vital element to mitigating climate change and halting biodiversity loss. Green Economics acknowledges that states remain the strongest actors in the international realm, and thus promotes regulation as a key response, but looks to other factors as well.

The second option is the market-based approach, in which controversial options such as carbon credit and pollution credits can be traded across international boundaries, allowing firms to profit from their adjustments and therefore offering a greater impetus to corporate action. The UK government has recommended this carbon trading on the individual level as well, recognizing the potential for carbon credits to be traded like war-time ration cards. Green Economics recognizes that this is also a useful economic opportunity, but warns of the danger of over-simplifying environmental subjects. This mechanism can be seen on an entirely anthropocentric basis, further embedding the concept of nature's purely instrumental value in the social psyche. On this basis, Green Economics is aligned with deep green thought, which recognizes nature's "inherent" and "intrinsic" value rather than simply focusing on its "instrumental" value, or capacity to provide services to the human economy.

Thirdly, the business community has pointed largely to the opportunities of eco-technology, for example, green engineering, procurement, and IT. These seek to provide technological solutions to the systemic crisis, for example through the implementation of renewable energy options and carbon-capture projects. While many of these solutions are useful, mostly viable, and needed, Green Economics cautions that a reliance on "techno-fixes" could easily blind society from the equally urgent need to change practices, choices, and consumption habits.

With this in mind, lifestyle change is promoted as the most important variable in solving the environmental crisis. Lifestyle change means a reorientation toward human impacts on the planet, recognizing that the environment is not a prop in the hands of human actors, but rather we are merely actors cast on the environmental stage. Understanding this, human society will focus on adapting and mitigating climate change through a completely new perspective, one that is both a revelation to our fast-paced, consumption-driven lives but also a fulfilling and meaningful process that will engender greater community bonds and a longer term vision of reality.

Finally, it is useful to reflect on the issue of "green-washing." Those under the Green Economics banner argue against "green" initiatives that have little actual merit, existing for a purpose often contrary to the ideals of social and environmental justice. Some of these "green" policies and programmes hinder or oppose a green outcome, providing only for "business as usual" and exactly the sort of "progress" that has brought us to the global economic and environmental crises. Examples since the economic meltdown include supporting Shell's use of third generation biofuels as the eco-innovation. This represents the more managerial interpretation of Greening the economy, or Corporate Social Responsibility agenda founded in instrumental stakeholder theory. Or, to mitigate climate change, policy might point to carbon storage and sequestration as recommended in the Stern report (2006), but this is unproven technology and regarded as an unreliable techno-fix by some, allowing society to procrastinate and momentarily avoid greater lifestyle changes.

Cultural Perspectives and Background

Among the influences in its development are the enlightenment, post-modernism, limits to growth and the search for sustainability, and eco-feminism. The Enlightenment Project has had a major impact on modern understandings of economics and the role of humanity in the natural world. The Enlightenment also tended to look for logic and reason rather than wisdom in nature, an attitude shown by Bacon (in Thomas 1983): "The human mind which overcomes superstition is to hold sway over a disenchanted nature. What men want to learn from nature is how to use it in order to wholly dominate it and other men. That is the only aim." With this perspective in mind, Green Economics seeks to revise the Enlightenment conceptualization of the environment, rewriting the cornerstone of the last 300 years of economic history, in which the foundation of today's environmental and economic collapse was laid. Green Economics argues that nature has its own intrinsic value, which it extends to animals based on the ethics of Singer *Practical Ethics* (1994) who argued for the rights of all sentient beings. Green Economics extends this to all life forms, and thus seeks to complete the Enlightenment project by reforming economics to "provision for all people everywhere, all other species, the biosphere, systems, and planet."

Learning from environmental and ecological economics, Green Economics places itself under the environmental economics umbrella, and gains much from the Limits to Growth dialogue as well. It recognizes that, as stated by the Sustainable Development Commission in 2005, the amount of resources used and "needed" under the current system is entirely unsustainable, or an equivalent of 5 planets' worth of resources. Green Economics focuses on different models, including the de-growth, lower-growth, lower-carbon and zero-carbon models, with the view that a sustainable system must not only be able to live within its own limits, but also, as Nozick insists, to leave "enough and as good" for future generations.

As part of its inclusionary focus, Green Economics extends decision-making power to those voiceless under the mainstream economic system: women, underdeveloped communities, and the indigenous. It does so recognizing that these "other voices" have been kept silent while the mainstream decided the fate of the environment, society, and economy. Their voices are now understood to be of tremendous value in light of the devastating effect of their exclusion. Thus, Green Economics takes a great deal of learning from feminist economics and eco-feminism, utilising the contributions of green economists such as Marie Mies, and activists such as Vandana Shiva, whose work highlights the disproportionate effect of environmental degradation and economic exclusion on women and the indigenous, while pointing to women and indigenous communities as an untapped source of traditional and holistic learning.

Thus, Green Economics is informed by a variety of attitudes toward nature, both ancient and modern, inclusive of formerly silenced voices, and emboldened by learning from the various waves of green thinking.

Instruments of Green Economics

Issues of significance today

As this chapter has demonstrated, the world is changing rapidly, and the environmental and economic consequences of human behavior can no longer be ignored or regulated under the mainstream system. In recent months, we have seen accelerated climate change lead to increased melting of the arctic ice sheets, a relatively small Icelandic volcano partially air-traffic over the North-Atlantic, the value of the Euro plummet, and threats of a second global economic downturn flood newsstands. Marine dead zones are spreading, not only thanks to increased ocean temperatures and coral bleaching, but also because of the horrendous British Petrol rig disaster, which continues to dump 40,000 gallons of crude oil into the Gulf of Mexico every day. This year began with the disheartening lack of compromise at the Conference of Parties (COP15) in Copenhagen, but the nations had another chance in November at Mexico City's COP16.

Current issues of concern

Biodiversity in crisis, Row over the IPCC, Green Transport, China's Rare Earth metals, Congo and Green IT, Bees and Mobile frequencies, Energy policy and oil, Stern Report, TEEB, Ecosystem Services, Large mammals loss, Chris Thomas' 5m p/day of species migration, Millennium Ecosystem Report, Intrinsic vs. Instrumental values, coral bleaching, marine crisis, albedo effect, PCB & DDT, Pristine Marine Environment has more top predators (ie, in Chagos) Marine Trophic Index declining, Chemical pollution evident in marine biota, bluefin tuna decreasing, natural capital and human capital wordusage, neither are protected but should they therefore be classified in economic terms to further encourage their being seen as economically valuable or should there thusfar lack of protection be a sign that economically costing species is useless and harmful?, MDGs, 153 billion, mainstreaming of biodiversity into economic development.

Issues of particular concern in Italy include:

Developming good practices in olive regions, soil erosion/runoff/use of herbicides, but biodiversity is generally high in olive regions, using the lifecycle approach, Venice as a sign for the times, agricultural problems from species migration and soil erosion, tourism failing from lack of snow. Energy and hydropower failing because of lack of water, tropical vegetation encroaching. The OECD regards vulnerability to environmental and natural risk as an area of particular threat to Italy.

Picture: The Economics of Ecosystem Services and Marine environments. There is serious concern that marine micro organisms which control climate and eco systems are being

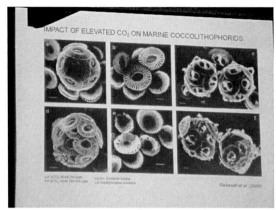

IMPACT OF ELEVATED CO₂ ON MARINE COCCOLITHOPHORIDS

impacted and hurt by elevated CO2. Photo Miriam Kennet from a Green Week EC Brussels June 2010 Presentation on Biodiversity, author unknown.

However, we want to address all its elements so we might select lifestyle changes and if we are worried about less developed countries we might argue that this should involve less consumption in more developed countries and an acceleration of economic growth in the less developed countries or those catching up.

If we want to solve the problems in the Congo then we might notice and try to change developed countries supply chains for mobile phones, which include Congo minerals such as Coltan which are fuelling war, genocide, child soldiers and total disaster on every level, at a rate unequalled since the Second World War. A Green Economics perspective would suggest we might want to rework our supply chains and also consider our consumption patterns.

A previous version of this chapter was first published in Encyclopedia Trecanni (in Italian).

7.6 Tackling Poverty and Climate Change, an opportunity for China

By Sandra Ries and Lu Wei

The two defining challenges of our century are tackling poverty, and climate change. Tackling global poverty and extreme inequality have, in a serious sense, been on the agenda of most governments and development agencies for the last 70 years. What is striking about the development trajectory now is that from a sustainable point of view, the goals for development should in many ways be significantly different to the earlier development models that aimed for industrialization, and economic growth. The western way of living has come to be seen as the epitome of development, and currently we still see countries imitating this image of development. It is now, however, important that action is taken to combat the effects of climate change. This is why green development is so necessary. This chapter outlines the role of China, and its position and possible developing role in tackling poverty and climate change.

Issues of contemporary poverty reduction strategies

Eliminating poverty is an imperative goal that world leaders have committed to tackle. The Millennium Development Goals (MDGs), adopted by world leaders at the UN Millennium Summit, September 2000, reveal the widespread view that deep poverty is immoral, can be prevented, and needs action. The MDGs set out time bound targets with the deadline of 2015, and the goals range from reducing extreme poverty, hunger, disease, promoting gender equality, education and environmental sustainability. In many ways the MDG"s reflect international and national development policy. They emphasize the idea, and acknowledgement, that people over the world are seen as living in a single social space, and in this space, their well being is compared. The MDGs have furthermore provided a basis for a new development consensus during the last decade. In themselves, the MDGs do not constitute a development policy paradigm, but are nevertheless seen as the foundation of a particular approach to development and poverty in the last decade. They are not only the foundation for an international development cooperation approach, but also applied within an analytical and policy description, about how development and poverty reduction should be achieved. The message of this strategy is to advocate the best national strategy for achieving poverty reduction, which is largely achieved by promoting close integration with the global economy, through deep liberalization, and through the harmonization of global standards (Gore, 2008; Bendana, 2004). This contradicts sustainable development. Climate change is already a serious problem in many countries, and predicted by scientists to become ever more threatening if we do not change consumption styles soon. Poverty and climate change are intrinsically linked and part of policy making should recognize that unmanaged climate change would in fact harm the advances in development over the next few decades. In the example of China, we see how damaging economic growth has been for the environment, and the opportunities will be discussed.

China's Performance: MDG 1 (Reducing poverty) & MDG 7 (Environmental Sustainability)

China has been measured as quite a successful country on the United Nations Development Programme (UNDP) MDG assessments, with a high likelihood of MDG 1 being achieved by 2015. According to the UNDP, China has reduced the number of people living in extreme poverty from 85 million in 1990 to 26.1 million by the end of 2004 (UNDP). Due to the different methods of calculation and different standards of estimating the poverty line, there are huge deviations in the number of people who are actual living in extreme poverty. In 2008, Chinese Government readjusted the poverty line again. The new poverty line increased to 1196-yuan-a-year, about $180(Tang, Min 2009 ADB). Based on the new threshold, the number of Chinese living in poverty would be much bigger; about 43 million people were living below the poverty line in the country's rural area in 2007. The number in urban area was more than 22 million. However, the success of reducing poverty has come at the expense of the environment. At the moment, China is the world"s biggest emitter. Between 1994 and 2004 the annual average increment of greenhouse gas emissions was about 4%, whereas the share of CO_2 in total emissions increased from 76% to 83%. At the current rate of emissions, Chinas output is expected to double each decade. If this unit of output is to remain constant, China"s emissions will be around 30-35 billion tonnes in 2030, which is also the worlds global budget for 2030 (UNDP; Stern, 2010).

In the last 30 years China's economic development has been extraordinary. In just 3 decades, growth has averaged more than 9% a year. Despite its enormous growth, China is categorized as a developing country, and is still dealing with problems such as a weak social safety net, corruption, sustaining adequate job growth for its 1.3 billion citizens, and an ever-widening inequality gap, and of course environmental deterioration (OECD: Environmental Performance Review: China). China has experienced a very fast industrialization, and focus on rapid economic growth has resulted in people moving to the urban centres for work. The increase in the urban share of the population in China has led to extremely high levels of pollution. The urban share of the population has recently risen from 17.9% to 44.9%. Industrialization and urbanization have led to an increased quest for natural resources which put pressure on land use, forest management and environment protection. The air pollution created by industrialization has caused many premature deaths per year, and the water pollution is a source of many health problems. Due to climate change and degradation of the eco system, the agriculture, water resources and bio diversity of china are facing severe pressure, which also leads to future risks of food shortages (OECD: Environmental Performance Review China).

China's goal is to build a moderately prosperous society, but the inequality gap is widening, and this is also a problem. The difference in per capita income ratio between urban and rural residents is about 3.3:1, which ranks china as second highest in Asia. According to a survey released by the Chinese Academy of social sciences, China"s richest 10% of the population own 40% of all private assets, while only 2% of total wealth goes to the bottom 10% (Sicular, Ximing,

Gustafsson & Shi, 2007). Traditionally, China has had a very eco-friendly philosophy. According to the ancient Taoist philosophical-religious tradition, human beings are an integral and inseparable part of the natural realm. In this holistic view, development of any kind, could only occur in accordance with nature"s boundaries, and protection. This traditional perception of the environment was however heavily disrupted since China began its industrialization, especially since the reform that took place in 1978.

It is true that China is now the largest greenhouse gas emission country, but the rich or industrial countries had been for a long time by far the largest missioners, and because of the hysteresis in the climate change response, these countries are largely responsible for the majority of the stock of anthropogenic greenhouse gases in the atmosphere. Facing the truth and facts, we are not here to try to come to a verdict about whom should be more culpable, but rather to find the best ways for China to deal with the two issues that for the moment, at least technically, contradict each other: climate change and poverty the same time. As people in developed countries are trying to find ways to solve the economic problem of the Age of Austerity, people in developing countries like China, will have to choose the harder and less cost effective way, the environmentally friendly way, to get out poverty without causing pollution. It is therefore again at least technically, it will take a much longer time for China as well as other developing countries to eliminate poverty, and they will be less likely to achieve the MDG 1 by 2015. The poor who have done least to create the problem, now will be forced to take the same responsibility.

In the 1970s, China experienced a radical transition from a self contained, centrally planned economy, to a more open and market friendly one. The leading motto „Development First – Environment Later", became very characteristic for this period. Several areas and cities situated mostly on the eastern part of the country expanded tremendously since the launch of the so called open door policy originally initiated by Deng Xiaopeng in 1978 (Han, 2006).

So what now?

The   Chinese government is focusing on economic growth, featuring less input, less consumption, fewer emissions while maintaining high levels of efficiency. China is still set on economic growth, but is also increasingly becoming aware of the necessity for sustainable action and is working on decarbonisation. China has much of the world's viable resources of rare earth metals needed for green technology. The Copenhagen Summit December 2009 was the dramatic scene both of China's entry onto the world stage as keeper of the raw materials for powering the " green " technology revolution and also realising its own profound and critical powers to intervene. At Cancun COP 16, Kyoto climate conference, December 2010, China emerged from this intermediate, perhaps shocking phase both to itself and to the outside world and is now considering starting to take a mature position, possibly a lead and to participate fully. It is showing more understanding of and acknowledging its own pivotal role in this climax of human civilisation. China holds many of the key cards and is slowly starting to mature into the role. China is investing heavily in economic resources, research and development as a strategy which relies on technological advancement and innovation as a basis for tackling climate change. In 2008 China set aside 4 trillion Yuan (almost £380 billion) for a stimulus package for climate change mitigation projects. China has also made some progression in the area of renewable energies. China is currently one of the world's main producers of photovoltaic generators, solar water heating technology, and wind power plants (China's Government White Papers: III Strategies and Objectives for Addressing Climate Change; Xing, 2010). China has also begun to take the lead in investment in educational achievement and the knowledge economy which are characteristics of a mature green economy and she has made a very significant start in this respect. However there is still a long way to go, from political promises to real sustainable development. Green is also foundationally characterised by social and environmental justice and equity. There are still development issues concerning the approaches to development, but there may be cause for optimism, as China evolves very rapidly. China could, if it desired, take the lead in green, sustainable development. Low carbon growth opportunities are vast, and China is in a position to compete, and to lead in this sector if it moves fast, considering its natural resources. The challenge is how to organize this transition in accordance with green principles in the round. Stern (2010) has suggested that public policies and public investment are key factors to creating a positive environment for innovation and change. This, for example, could be a policy on coal taxation, which would provide incentives for investment in alternative technologies. If China saw this moment as an opportunity- as investing in green technologies, as promoting their competitiveness in a time of serious environmental change, it would provide incentives for other countries to do the same, and fast.

This chapter started by introducing two defining challenges of our century, overcoming poverty and managing climate change. The MDGs are addressing important factors, but there are problems surrounding the approach taken to tackle the problems. A global development consensus needs to be agreed upon, on the notion of global sustainable development, bringing poverty reduction and climate change together, based on mutual interest, and economic development for the poorest. Where we would see 'global development means used to achieve global development goals', instead of the current „national development means used to achieve global development goals" (Gore, 2008; Richards, 2003). If it were the case that global development means were used to achieve global development goals and also fulfil the guiding concepts of green economics, for simultaneous social and environmental development goals, then China, indeed would be in an impressive situation to take a leading role in combating climate change.

This chapter is based on a paper by Sandra Ries (Denmark) and kindly amended by Professor Wei Lu (China) and a previous version was originally published in the Autumn 2010 edition of the Green Economist. Published by The Green Economics Institute.

References:

Bendana, A. (2004) Good Governance and the MDG's: Contradictory or Complementary? Focus on the Global South October 2004.

China's Government White Papers: III Strategies and Objectives for Addressing Climate Change. http://www.china.org.cn/government/whitepaper/2008-10/29/content_16682609.htm

Gore, C. (2008) The Global Development Cycle, the MDG's, and the Future of Poverty Reduction. Paper read at the 12th EADI General Conference at Geneva.

Han, F. (2006) The Chinese View of Nature: Tourism in China's Scenic and Historic Interest Areas. School of design, Faculty of Built Environment and Engineering, Queensland University of Technology, Queensland.

National Development and Reform Commission: People's Republic of China. China's National Climate Change Programme. http://en.ndrc.gov.cn/newsrelease/P020070604561191006823.pdf

OECD Working Party on Environmental Performance: Environmental Performance Review of China. 1-12 (http://www.oecd.org/dataoecd/58/23/37657409.pdf

Richards, M. (2003) Poverty reduction, Equity and Climate Change: Challenges for Global Governance. . Natural Resource Perspectives 83.

Sicular T, Ximing Y, Gustafsson B, & Shi, L. 2007. The Urban- Rural Income Gap and Inequality in China. . Review of Income and Wealth 53 (1):93-126.

SID- Society for International Development (2008): Climate Justice Briefing. In: Development- Climate Justice and Development, H. 51, (18.12.2009).

Stern, N. (2010) The Road from Copenhagen: Options for China. . Paper read at China Development Forum

UNDP: Human development report 2007/2008: Fighting climate change: human solidarity in a divided world. Human development report office. Occasional paper. 1-21

United Nations Development Programme: MDGs in China: http://www.undp.org.cn/modules.php?op=modload&name=News&file=article&catid=32&sid=6

United Nations Millennium Development Goals. United Nations. http://www.un.org/millenniumgoals/environ.shtml

Xing, Li (2010): The rise of China and the capitalist world order. Farnham, Surrey, England, Burlington, VT: Ashgate Pub. Co (International political economy of new regionalisms series)

7.7 Health and Well Being in a Polluted Environment: A Case Study of Chronic Obstructive Pulmonary Diseases (COPDs) in Selected Cities in England and Wales

By Jeffery Sappor

Background of the study

The United Nations Environment Programme (UNEP – 2011) describes a green economy as "one that results in improved human well-being and social equity, while significantly reducing environmental risks and ecological scarcities". In other words, we can think of a green economy as an economic environment that achieves low carbon and pollutant emissions, while resources are efficiently used to promote societal inclusion and prevent loss of biodiversity and ecosystem services. However population health and the ecosystem are being affected with emission being released into the atmosphere from industry, transportation and waste disposal. This research will assess an association between Chronic Obstructive Pulmonary Diseases (COPDs) and health as a result of environment pollution emitted from transport and waste disposal system (Sunyer et al 1997; Sonia et al 2005) using GIS and remote sensing technology.

I was inspired to take on this research after participating in a forum with the lung suffers society on the topic, "Air Pollution and Lung Diseases in Slough – Windsor". I realised GIS can be used to assess COPDs patients suffering from fumes or gases emissions from tobacco smoking and link cases of COPD infection or spread of pollution using an overlay of wind data. Also, geo spatial analysis can be used to illustrate why pollutants from the fumes are recognized as the most common chronic respiratory diseases worldwide, including the United Kingdom, with an increasing prevalence of morbidity and mortality higher than bowel cancer, breast cancer or prostate cancer (Mckeown 2007; Chauhan and Johnston 2003; US EPA 2011; WHO 20011: 2008). The lung suffers society members present were excited that I want to carry out a research into COPDs using the GIS concept, and are prepared to offer support. The study will examine efforts being undertaken to prevent people getting COPDs, promote population understanding of the risks of having poor lung health, support improvements to the diagnosis of, and care of people with the disease. Having already undertaken a study into HIV/AIDS using the GIS concept and interest in green economics, I will implore similar approach to air pollution and its impact on COPDs.

Concepts of what constitutes a quality life have been a controversial issue since Aristotle's theory to Maslow's hierarchical theory of needs (Nordenfelt 1993). These concepts have enabled a definition described as 'wellbeing' to be introduced by the local government act 2000, which seek to promote a safe economic, social and environmental economy. Wellbeing is also described by the UK Government Whitehall working group in 2006 as "a positive physical, social and mental state, not just the absence of pain, discomfort and incapacitation", which includes good health and attractive environment (Steuer and Marks 2008; DEFRA 2012; UNCSD 2012; Huitt 2007). Thus, attractive environment and combined effect of policies will enable people have reasonable access to social, economic and environmental resources to attain personal goals and participate in society (Welsh Government; Hunter and Killoran 2004).

One of the greatest challenges that will face health systems globally in the twenty-first century will be the increasing burden of non – communicable chronic diseases such as COPDs (WHO 2002). Since the early 1960s, emerging respiratory diseases has been attributed to tobacco smoking. However, significant proportion of fossil fuel emissions by vehicles, industry and energy production has been recognised as potential collaborator to COPDs.

Aim

Arguably two main strands in quantitative spatial techniques and experimental theory will focusing on the possibilities and potentials between air pollution and COPDs

Firstly, papers which outline or analyse fundamental conceptual approach to air pollution from transport, industry and waste disposal will be reviewed from multi-disciplinary basis using GIS techniques. For example, published reports and research only target some of the pollutants such as the particulates (PM_{10} and $PM_{2.5}$), nitrogen oxides, carbon monoxide and sometimes sulphur dioxide. Conversely, ignored pollutants found in smaller quantities become harmful toxins, are detected mainly in patients during hospital visit (the guardian 2012; scientific America 2012; WHO, HELI 2004). The pollutants in small quantities are known to be more toxic and cause severe health problems than the larger emitted pollutants. Although the European law has helped cut down some of these toxins from exhaust fumes and chimneys, other harmful pollutants are still found at dangerous levels in Europe (such as benzene, 1, 3 - butadiene, lead, ozone, ammonia and polycyclic aromatic hydrocarbons). The guardian 2012 environmental report based on a European Environmental Agency (EEA) report indicated that 30% of city-dwellers are exposed to a complex mixture of air pollutants particularly hazardous to health above a yearly EU target level. These pollutants mix together with existing atmospheric elements create new chemical compounds, some of which become toxic. Understanding the 'state' of and key trends influencing air quality in Europe (UK) is a critical first step in dealing with COPDs.

The second part of the research will assess the welfare of COPD patients through assistance received and how policies ensure that the green economic agenda is being accomplished. Influential papers indicate that many, who live with the condition usually over age of 35 can constitute economic burden associated with long-term medical management and disability.

Telehealth solutions, a patient-focused health cost reduction company estimates the direct cost of COPD to the UK healthcare system to be between £810 million and £930 million a year, with certain regions being worse affected than others.

Objectives

The purpose of this study is to explore a multidisciplinary approach in examining collected data in selected cities in England and Wales on people suffering from any chronic obstructive pulmonary disease. GIS would be used to express a visualised data that indicates endemic areas, while a time series analysis will indicate changes over a period. GIS and Remote Sensing will assist to indicate how behavioural changes are distressing the possibility of effectively controlling or reducing air pollution effects on health.

Analyses and interpretation will validate international data from such surveys as well as investigate the subjective phenomenon as described by the patient. The study will also use well-being measurement to examine assistance COPDs patients receive, as appropriate support, to live longer, happier and healthy life. It will also examine policies that are implemented to ensure green economic issues are attained.

Relevance of the study

The study will create a narrative literature that allows for flexible and resourceful presentation of interpretive findings, while demanding adherence to sound interpretive research. With limited resources and budget constrain, escalating health research such as COPDs can cause a drain on the economy. However, this study will demonstrate the use of limited resources available to engineer awareness into controlling increasing COPDs infections.

Different techniques have been used in campaign awareness programmes, including the media (Television, Radio, and newsprints), books, schools, churches, parents/relatives, workshops etc, yet there is increasing reports of COPDs. A geo spatial inclusion to data, allows clear visualisation of relevant information and scope of COPDs, indicating population areas prone to infection from air pollution.

It is also likely to support monitoring activity of reported cases from clinical view, societies, councils, environmental agencies and government institutions such as the United Nations Environment Programme (UNEP) and World Health Organisation (WHO). The WHO vision a 2008-2013 Action Plan themed: "The Global Strategy for the Prevention and Control of Non-Communicable Diseases". Also developed by Ghana as a Medium-Term National Development Policy Framework on the pathway to green economy under the theme: Ghana Shared Growth and Development Agenda 2010-2013.

The UK Department of Health /Medical Directorate/Respiratory constituted a team in February 2010 to advice how "local communities can prevent people from getting COPDs, understand the risks of having poor lung health, secure improvements to the diagnosis and care of people with the disease, and reduce health inequalities". The UK Department of health estimates around 835,000 people *have been diagnosed, h*owever over 3 million undiagnosed people have the disease, with one person dying every 20 minutes from COPDs in England and Wales, about 25,000 people a year (NHS 2012; BLF 2012; NHS and NICE 2010).

Also based on the UNEP-led green economy initiative launched in late 2008, this research will use GIS to achieve aspects of the three main activities: analyse sustainability; provide advisory services on ways to move towards a green economy and to engage a wide range of research, non-governmental and business institutions. The conclusions will add to existing knowledge, support the green revolution and medical interventions by health professionals to improve health issues as a result or air pollution.

It is hoped that the themes revealed in this study will generate additional understanding and insight for future ground-breaking research.

Method

The theoretical literature will review work done by known individuals, groups or organisations through recognised discussions, books, presentations, journals and magazines. The empirical study will process and integrate health data with geographical area data in GIS analytical software (ESRI – ArcGIS, ERDAS Imagine or MapInfo software). Many processes such as overlay analysis, buffer analysis, network inter linkages, data query, statistical analysis, interpolation or extrapolation. Then a multi – disciplinary approach will be implored in perspective to produce maps that will justify the theoretical literature and created maps in relation to COPD cases, especially in regions with incinerators, airports and heavy vehicular traffic environments.

The result will be analysed in terms of the education, data collection, monitoring and evaluation of COPD infections. As used by David B. et al in mapping air pollution, this research will implore the regression method to analyse COPDs and represent the result in a GIS map form.

Data will be obtainable from the lung society, department of health and city councils for the selected areas. Also unstructured interviews will capture detailed patient experiences verbatim. This study will be discussed in line with the economic, socio-cultural as well as environmental impacts on the population.

Recommendations will be based on awareness activities that had been effective and the idea of COPDs as observed during the study. It may track progress budget allocation and local change with emphasis on the Comprehensive Area Assessment reports.

Collaborations

As data is a key instrument in this study, however, the lung society has indicated to provide the research with available data. This research will also be under close observation and collaboration between the Birmingham City University and the Green Economics Institute.

Results and Conclusions

Getting the analysis right is a good starting point but not sufficient for achieving environmentally efficient outcomes. Continued research such as this and other policy interventions are often necessary to complement environmental and health issues.

Interviews will reveal valuable insights from a patient's or family perspective, into the impact of chronic obstructive pulmonary disease on their daily lives. The brief interaction with the lung society at Windsor hospital, participants described feelings of frustration, tired of breathlessness and loss of social activity.

This research will provide valuable insights into the increasing socio-economic impact of air pollution on society; how suffers view the overall impact and subsequent degree of coping with chronic obstructive pulmonary disease from day to day.

Reference:

Anderson, H.R., Spix, C., Medina, S., Schouten, J.P., Castellsague, J., Ross, G., Zmirou, D., Touloumi, G., Wojtyniak, B., Ponka, A., Bacharova, L., Schwartz, J., Katsouyanni, K., 1997, "Air pollution and daily admissions for chronic obstructive pulmonary disease in 6 European cities: results from the APHEA project" from the European Respiratory Journal website: **http://erj.ersjournals.com/content/10/5/1064.full.pdf+html** [accessed October 2012]

British Lung Foundation (BLF), 2012, "Lung Health" from the website: http://www.blf.org.uk/Conditions/Detail/COPD [accessed October 2012]

Chauhan, A. J., Johnston, S. L. (2003), "Air pollution and infection in respiratory illness" obtained from the British Medical Bulletin website: http://bmb.oxfordjournals.org/content/68/1/95.full and accessed October 2012 [accessed October 2012]

David, J.B., Collins, S., Elliot., Fischer, P., Kingham, S., Lebret, E., Pyrl, K., Van Reeuwijk, H., Smallbone, K., Van Der Veen, A., 2001, " Mapping Urban Air Pollution Using GIS Regression – Based Approach" obtained from the International Journal of Geographical Information Science magazine from the Taylor and Francis website: **http://www.tandfonline.com/doi/abs/10.1080/136588197242158** [accessed October 2012]

Defra National Statistics Release, February, 2012, "Emissions of air pollutants in the UK, 1970 to 2010 – Supplementary" from the website of DEFRA (Department for Environment, Food and Rural Affairs): http://www.defra.gov.uk/statistics/files/National-Statistical-Release-AIR-supplementary.pdf [accessed October 2012]

Huitt, W. (2007), "Maslow's hierarchy of needs", an Educational Psychology *Interactive* from Valdosta State University: http://www.edpsycinteractive.org/topics/regsys/maslow.html Retrieved [October 2012]

Hunter, D.J., and Killoran, A., 2004, "Tackling health inequalities: turning policy into practice?" obtained from the NHS Health Development Agency website: http://www.who.int/rpc/meetings/Hunter_Killoran_Report.pdf [accessed October 2012]

McKeown, D., 2007, "Air Pollution Burden of Illness from Traffic in Toronto – Problems and Solutions" obtained from the Public Health website, Toronto Canada: http://www.toronto.ca/health/hphe/pdf/air_pollution_burden.pdf and accessed October 2012

National Health Service (NHS) – National Institute for health and clinical Excellence (NICE), 2010, "CHRONIC OBSTRUCTIVE PULMONARY DISEASE – Management of chronic obstructive pulmonary disease in adults in primary and secondary care (partial update)" This guideline partially updates and replaces NICE clinical guideline 12 obtained from: http://www.nice.org.uk/nicemedia/live/13029/49397/49397.pdf [accessed October 2012]

National Health Service (NHS), 2012, "Chronic obstructive pulmonary disease" from the website: Open University book edited by Nolte, E., McKee, M., 2005, "Caring for people with chronic conditions - A health system perspective", obtained from the World Health Organisation International website: http://www.euro.who.int/__data/assets/pdf_file/0006/96468/E91878.pdf, accessed October 2012

Nordenfelt, L., 1993, "Quality of Life, Health and Happiness" from the website: http://sh.diva-portal.org/smash/get/diva2:17056/FULLTEXT01 [Accessed October 2012]

Scientific American, 2012, "Breathing European air shortens lives -report" from the magazine website: http://www.scientificamerican.com/article.cfm?id=breathing-european-air-shortens-liv and accessed October 2012

Sonia, B. A., Vollmer, W. M., Sullivan, S. D., Weiss, K. B., Lee, T. A., Menezes, A. M. B., Crapo, R. O., Jensen, R. L., and Burney P. G. J., 2005, "The Burden of Obstructive Lung Disease Initiative (BOLD): Rationale and Design" from the informa healthcare website: http://informahealthcare.com/doi/abs/10.1081/COPD-57610, accessed October 2012

Steuer, N. And Marks, N., 2008, "Local wellbeing: Can we Measure It?" from the website: http://www.youngfoundation.org/files/images/YF_wellbeing_measurement_web.pdf [accessed October 2012]

Sunyer, J., Kogevinas, M., Kromhout, H., Antó, J.M., Roca, J., Tobias, A., Vermeulen, R., Payo, F., Maldonado, J.A., Martinez-Moratalla, J., Muniozguren and the Spanish Group of the European Community Respiratory Health, 1997 "Pulmonary Ventilatory Defects and Occupational Exposures in a Population-based Study in Spain" obtained from the American Journal of Respiratory and Critical Care Medicine website: http://ajrccm.atsjournals.org/content/157/2/512.short, accessed September, 2012

The Guardian 2012, "Air Pollution still at Dangerous Levels in Europe" reports from the website: http://www.guardian.co.uk/environment/2012/sep/24/air-pollution-dangerous-levels-europe [accessed October 2012]

United Nations Conference on Sustainable Development (UNCSD Rio+20) and Share the Worlds Resources, 2012, "Happiness and Well-being: Defining a New Economic Paradigm" from the website: http://www.stwr.org/economic-sharing-alternatives/happiness-and-well-being-defining-a-new-economic-paradigm.html and http://www.uncsd2012.org/rio20/content/documents/690Bhutan.pdf [accessed October 2012]

United Nations Environment Programme (UNEP) 2011, "Green Economy - About GEI" from the UNEP website: http://www.unep.org/greeneconomy/AboutGEI/WhatisGEI/tabid/29784/Default.aspx, accessed October 2012

United Nations Environment Programme (UNEP), Advisory Services 2010, "Ghana's Pathway to Green Economy" from the UNEP website: http://www.unep.org/greeneconomy/AboutGEI/WhatisGEI/tabid/29784/Default.aspx, accessed October 2012

United States Environmental Protection Agency, advisory services report 2011, "Ghana's Pathway to a Green Economy" obtained from the US EPA website: http://www.unep.org/greeneconomy/AdvisoryServices/Ghana/tabid/56355/Default.aspx [accessed October 2012]

Welsh Government, 2011, "Environment – Protection and Quality" from the Welsh Government website: http://wales.gov.uk/topics/environmentcountryside/epq/airqualitypollution/?lang=en [accessed October 2012]

WHO 2010, "Global Status Report on non-communicable diseases" obtained from the WHO website: http://www.who.int/nmh/publications/ncd_report_full_en.pdf [accessed October 2012]

WHO, 2004, "Health and Environment Linkages Initiative" obtained from the Health and Environment Linkages initiative (HELI) site: http://www.who.int/heli/en/ and accessed October 2012

Wikipedia 2012, "Third Industrial Revolution" from the website: http://en.wikipedia.org/wiki/The_Third_Industrial_Revolution#First_and_Second_Industrial_Revolutions [accessed October 2012]

World Health Organisation (WHO) 2002, *Innovative Care for Chronic Conditions: Building Blocks for Action" obtained from the* World Health Organization website: http://www.who.int/diabetes/publications/iccc_exec_summary_eng.pdf, accessed october 2012.

World Health Organisation (WHO) 2008, "Outdoor Air Pollution - Children's Health and the Environment" a WHO Training Package for the Health Sector of the World Health Organization, *obtained from the* World Health Organization website: http://www.who.int/ceh/capacity/Outdoor_air_pollution.pdf, accessed october 2012

World Health Organisation (WHO) factsheet (media centre) 2011, "Chronic obstructive pulmonary disease (COPD)" obtained from the World Health Organization website: http://www.who.int/mediacentre/factsheets/fs315/en/index.html, accessed october 2012

One of the local grocery stores in Ghana. Photo taken by Aase Seeberg